D1607324

Management Strategies in Financing Parks and Recreation

John Wiley & Sons, Inc. Series in Recreation
Edited by Tony A. Mobley

Charles K. Brightbill and Tony A. Mobley, Educating for Leisure-Centered Living, 2nd Ed.

Monty L. Christiansen, Park Planning Handbook: Fundamentals of Physical Planning for Parks and Recreations Areas

Michael Chubb and Holly R. Chubb, One Third of Our Time? An Introduction to Recreation Behavior and Resources

Theodore R. Deppe, Management Strategies in Financing Parks and Recreation

Christopher R. Edginton and John G. Williams, Productive Management of Leisure Service Organizations: A Behavioral Approach

Arlin F. Epperson, Private and Commercial Recreation: A Text and Reference

Patricia Farrell and Herberta M. Lundegren, The Process of Recreation Programming: Theory and Technique, 2nd Ed.

Joseph Levy, Play Behavior

Jean Mundy and Linda Odum, Leisure Education: Theory and Practice

Paul. H. Risk, Outdoor Safety and Survival

Lynn S. Rodney and Robert F. Toalson, The Administration of Recreation, Parks, and Leisure Services, 2nd Ed.

Grant W. Sharpe, Interpreting the Environment, 2nd Ed.

Grant W. Sharpe, Charles Odegaard and Wenonah F. Sharpe, Park Management

William F. Theobald, Evaluation of Recreation and Park Programs

Management Strategies in Financing Parks and Recreation

THEODORE R. DEPPE
Indiana University

JOHN WILEY & SONS
New York
Chichester
Brisbane
Toronto
Singapore

Library of Congress Cataloging in Publication Data:

Deppe, Theodore R.
  Management strategies in financing parks and recreation.

  Includes index.
  1. Recreation—United States—Finance. 2. Parks—
United States—Finance. 3. Recreation—United States—
Management. 4. Parks—United States—Management.
5. Recreation—Canada—Finance. 6. Parks—Canada—
Finance. 7. Recreation—Canada—Management. 8. Parks—
Canada—Management. I. Title.

GV182.15.D46 1983   333.78′3′0681   82-21840
ISBN 0-471-09966-X

Printed in the United States of America

10 9 8 7 6 5 4 3 2 1

Preface

Creative management of park and recreation agencies requires a high level of knowledge and professional expertise in the area of finance and budgeting. This is especially true in recent years as administrators are caught in an era of inflation, recession, "stagflation," and fiscal stress. This book discusses the social, economic, and political climate in which public leisure service agencies operate and explores management strategies that can be used by administrators and staff in working with their boards, public officials, legislative bodies, and the general public in gaining financial support for their programs. Although the primary emphasis is on public park and recreation agencies, the information in this text can be used by managers of schools, and voluntary and private agencies offering leisure services.

The study of finance and budgeting can be approached from the perspective either of the legislative body, the finance officer, or chief executive or of the professional practitioner. This book is designed primarily to speak directly to park and recreation administrators and their staff. It recognizes that park and recreation agencies operate within many different climates, requiring various adaptations or approaches to the management strategies discussed. The size and location of the agency's administrative authority (i.e., city, school, county or state), fiscal dependence of the agency, and the social, economic, and political climate of the community will influence the financial status and the budgetary procedures employed.

Management Strategies in Financing Parks and Recreation is the result of a long-term interest and study of financial management in the field of parks and recreation. Professional administrative positions in the field, working under school boards, city managers, and city councils, provided my realistic and practical foundation in dealing with politicians, boards, city administrators, and the general public. Since joining the faculty at Indiana University, my main focus in teaching, research, and service has been in the area of management and administration. For over twenty-five years I have taught a course in business procedures, which deals primarily with finance and budgeting for parks and recreation. One of my main concerns each year since developing this course in 1958 has been to find an appropriate required text. Parks and recreation texts in management and administration, many of which are excellent, often lacked the scope and depth needed in studying finance and budgeting. Therefore I turned to the fields of business and public finance for required or recommended readings. For a number of years I have used *Municipal Finance Administration* published by the Municipal Finance Officers Association. In recent years texts published by the International City Management Association (*Management Policies in Local Government Finance*) and the Municipal Finance Officers Association (*Local Government Finance*) have served as valuable references. These books are excellent publications for public administrators and finance officers; however, they also lack in-depth and professional park and recreation analysis so necessary for students and practitioners in the field. As a result of constant urging by and recommendations of students and professionals in the field, I undertook the preparation of this book.

A double audience will be served by this text: the upper-level undergraduate students and graduate students majoring in parks and recreation, and also professionals serving in various positions in the broad field of parks and recreation. Although its major purpose is to delve in some depth into finance and budgeting functions, this book discusses in a realistic and practical manner management concerns such as organizational structure and climate, politics, planning, policy development, evaluation, and leadership style.

In developing and constantly updating my course and in preparing this volume, I have drawn much from the fields of business, public management, and public finance. A sabbatical leave study provided me with a unique opportunity to visit 27 cities and counties in the United States and Canada to gather first hand information on budgeting practices. This study was responsible for stimulating a two-way interchange with professionals in the field, which has resulted in the "down to earth," realistic approach to budgeting incorporated in this text. I have also included budgetary procedures that are practiced only in some of the more progressive agencies and local units of government. It is hoped that more administrators will explore the adoption of these techniques and strategies in order to improve the management of their organizations.

Heavy administrative and teaching responsibilities in a rapidly growing and dynamic department delayed a strong desire to put my experience, teaching, and research into writing. The encouragement by students, colleagues, professionals, and alumni has motivated me to place a high priority on writing this book. To these individuals, I am indeed grateful.

Acknowledgment must first be given to the graduate students who attended my class over these many years. Their enthusiastic responses, feedback, and suggestions have been a source of inspiration and satisfaction. On entering the field, they have sent back their successes and problems, as well as valuable documentation (budgets, manuals, reports, etc.) of budgetary practices used by their agencies.

In preparing this manuscript, I have used data from many public documents produced by governmental and park and recreation agencies, which have made this text more meaningful and realistic. I am grateful to these public officials and professionals for sharing this information.

Several members of the faculty of the Department of Recreation and Park Administration at Indiana University have provided suggestions, innovations, and materials that have been incorporated in my classes and in this book. I am indebted especially to James Peterson and Daniel Sharpless for their suggetions and critical review of certain sections of the manuscript.

Dr. Tony Mobley, Dean, School of Health, Physical Education and Recreation and Consulting Editor for John Wiley & Sons, has continuously given me encouragement and stimulation, particularly when I seemed to have too little time to devote to the book. I am grateful to Joseph Bannon of the University of Illinois at Urbana-Champaign and to John Christian of the Hennepin County Park Reserve District for their careful review of and comments on the manuscript. Special recognition is given to Marie Jones, departmental secretary, for her valuable assistance and professional expertise in preparing the manuscript and for the additional support that she provides daily to me and other members of the faculty.

Most important, I owe more than I can say to my wife, Alice, for her masterful blend of love, encouragement, stimulation, confidence, prodding, and patience. To her, this book is gratefully dedicated.

Theodore R. Deppe

Contents

Chapter 1

Creative Management

anagement of a leisure service agency in an ever changing, unpredictable society is becoming more difficult. Urban life, compounded by the decay of the urban environment, hurried pace of living, economic uncertainties, racial strife, environmental degradation, unemployment, and inner city poverty has not only developed into an urban crisis but has created many new problems for administering local public agencies. More and more attention is being focused on agency effectiveness, accountability, responsiveness, resistance to change and, above all, problems of fiscal economy and productivity.

Demands for solution to these problems and the need for providing more and better services has increased the government's role, at all levels, to such an extent that local officials are finding it difficult to find sufficient financial resources to meet demands placed on them. Other agencies, both semipublic and private, are also facing similar problems. In reality, most local agencies are losing ground. Many prescriptions offered as cures for these problems have often failed to provide the remedy for making urban life more tolerable and satisfying. As a result, local governments are rapidly facing economic stagnation and fiscal distress.

People faced with the reality of working and living in this changing urban environment are becoming increasingly frustrated with the ability of organizations to solve their problems. As a result, taxpayers are becoming disgruntled with government's delivery of services. For many people the quality of both life and the quality of their living environment are gradually deteriorating. There seems to be growing evidence indicating an alienation and cynicism to-

ward politics and government; it is in this climate that park and recreation professionals must function. They are faced with difficult problems in providing leisure services to their many publics.

The park and recreation profession has a key role to play in easing societal problems and meeting the leisure needs of people residing in urban environments. Two major responsibilities in providing leisure services are evident: First, recreation's overall mission is improving the quality of life for all citizens through the provision of meaningful experiences. Second, the park's goal is directed toward the acquisition, development, and maintenance of parks and other recreation areas and facilities for the enjoyment of recreation opportunities and creation of a better living environment. The extent that leisure service agencies are successful in focusing their attention on these two central missions will determine the acceptance of professional park and recreation services by the American public.

Challenges facing local agencies in providing leisure services are not new. However, obtaining adequate financial resources to underwrite these much needed services is becoming more difficult. Currently this situation calls for management utilizing new and different approaches in addressing agency challenges.

MANAGEMENT CONCERNS

An agency that is aware of the changes taking place in today's urban community, can define citizen needs, and can translate them into programs that are responsive to those needs will be better prepared

1

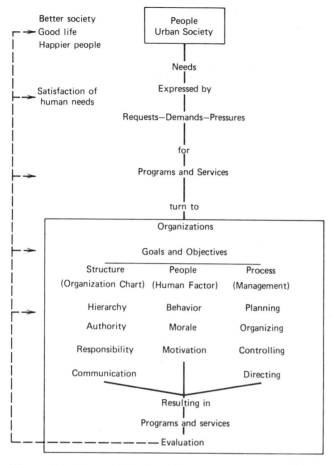

Figure 1.1 Conceptual view of management

to meet the challenges of the 1980s and beyond. A new strategy of management and organization must be clearly understood by administrators and boards of local leisure service agencies. Figure 1.1 illustrates a conceptual view of management concerns of providing leisure services.

The development of an effective management system is based on the understanding of several ingredients. First, recreation and parks is a people business. The leisure service agency that concentrates on individuals living largely in an urban setting is clearly on target. Management strategies and finance and budgeting procedures must be focused on people and their needs. History shows that the growth of public and private organizations has been based on requests, pressures, or demands of citizens seeking programs and services that will satisfy their needs and interests. Generally, individuals or groups look toward existing organizations for help, which in the leisure services field represent private, commercial, semipublic, and public organizations. In the urban setting local agencies primarily contribute to leisure needs, with the state and federal parks and

other facilities providing supplementary support to local organizations.

Each agency has its unique mission and contributions to make. Municipal park and recreation agencies maintain the basic services and facilities for the total community. Churches, voluntary youth agencies, private clubs, and industries provide programs to their membership according to the goals and objectives of their particular organizations. However, most agencies that are concerned with leisure services have similar goals—individual and community improvement. Management strategies of each of these organizations must be based on the premise that only through working together can the overall leisure needs of people be met.

Administrators have the responsibility for properly organizing agencies and providing an effective and responsive management system in which to operate. Most texts in administration and management delve into such topics as goals and objectives, organizational principles and theories, personnel management, and the overall management process. Because this text is primarily concerned with one aspect of the management process—finance and budgeting—other management topics will be discussed only briefly. They do, however, merit full study as these administrative responsibilities influence the budget and financing processes.

Goals and Objectives

It has been stated that the measurement of the effectiveness of an organization should be based on the results accomplished in meeting the agency's goals and objectives. An administrator's responsibility is to work with and through individuals and groups to accomplish these goals and objectives. This, of course, implies that the organization has written objectives that are defined so that they can be measured.

Two questions that the leisure service agency should ask itself are: (1) Does it have written objectives to guide its operation? If the answer is yes, then (2) Does it actually operate so as to meet them? Most agencies have specific goals and objectives that can be found in their administrative or program manuals; however, evidence may suggest that these goals and objectives are not used as a management tool in the planning, operation, and evaluation of the program.

Newer concepts of budgeting such as program performance and zero base are mandating the use of management by objectives (MBO), establishing priorities, and performance measurement as integral parts of the budget process. In the section pertaining to budget development, steps suggested for integrating MBO into the budgeting process will be explored.

Organizational Climate

How an agency is organized and the leadership style of the administrator greatly influence the finance and budgeting procedures of the agency. Also, the organizational climate established by the chief executive and the board is of equal importance. An administrator has the responsibility of organizing an agency so that it will function efficiently and effectively. He/she should be aware of the newer concepts of organization theory as well as know the basic principles of organizing the department. Management of organizations is becoming increasingly more complex. Modern-day administrators should be knowledgeable about what happens to their "organizations in action" and of their employees' impact on the management and operation process of the agencies.

Organization has been defined as *the process of relating persons, facilities, and programs in some logical and systematic way in order to accomplish the goals of the organization.* Most administrators structure their agencies by using the traditional well-known principles of organization. Such a structure is viewed as a pyramid or hierarchy of authority. Authority or power to act or control exists at the top with the boss or chief executive and is distributed downward (delegation) throughout the organization. Each person in the organization is accountable for given responsibilities, which are described in a job description. Employees, in turn, are given authority to perform their responsibilities and ultimately are held responsible for their actions.

Most agencies have formal organizational charts that give a clear picture of the employee's position in the organization, showing to whom the individual is responsible and the direct lines of communication. Although such an approach of forming an agency is important, organizations consist of people who often operate contrary to the generally accepted principles of organization. Thus the leadership style of administrators and the climate that they establish for employees will ultimately determine the success or failure of an organization. As suggested earlier, administrators should be aware of the various theories regarding organizations and implement the approach that best fits both their leadership styles and organizations.

Thompson, in *Organizations in Action,* places the many organizational theories into two fundamental models—rational models and natural systems models.

Rational Model. The rational model includes three well-known approaches to studying organizations: scientific management theory, evolved by Frederick Taylor; administrative management theory, most frequently found in the area of public administration; and the human relations theory, which was the first to recognize humans as social beings having great implications to the organization.

The rational model assumes a closed system with the control of the people within the organization as the main target. Emphasis is on the formal organizational structure and processes, that is, give employees a specific job with sufficient authority and responsibility and the results will be positive and predictable. According to Thompson, "the developers of the several schools using the rational model have been primarily students of performance or efficiency, and only incidently students of organizations."[1] The rational model can be likened to a well-oiled machine. The manager gives the order, you turn the switch on, and everything will run smoothly as planned. Thus the outcome is considered to be predictable.

Natural Systems Model. The natural systems model resulted from the works of Chester Barnard, published in *Functions of the Executive.* Barnard, whose system is described as open in its totality, views the organization in a constant state of interaction with its environment (Figure 1.2). A constant process of exchange and interaction between the organization and individuals and agencies from the outside occurs. The organization interacts with and is dependent on a broader environment—state and federal agencies or individuals—and is also embedded in a local environment. Often organizational problems stem from outside the department rather than from within. Organizations must learn to handle complaints, and problems coming from the "open environment." Interaction with this larger environment occurs at all levels within the organization and not only with the main office or the chief executive.

Barnard also emphasizes the human being and not the efficiency that was the heart of the scientific management theory. He suggests that the organization is comprised of employees, with motives, purposes, and ambitions, who often work in a setting that is overwhelming in complexity. In this complicated setting, individuals are frustrated by their inability to bring about change. Often there exist differences between the workers' and the organization's

[1]James D. Thompson, *Organizations in Action,* McGraw-Hill, New York, 1967, p. 6.

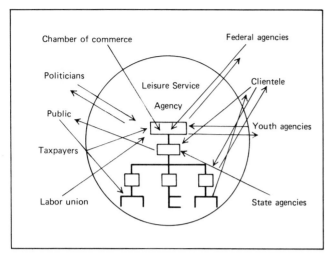

Figure 1.2 Interaction of the leisure service agency with its environment.

motives and goals. The natural systems approach recognizes that organizations are informal and, therefore, informal communication is well practiced, that is, a complete antithesis of the rational model theory, which stresses formal channels of communication and chain of command.

I suggest that the natural systems theory best represents the current conditions in which leisure service agencies operate. Many local executives express that "crisis management" is the name of the game. Almost daily, managers' well-made plans are put aside to solve a problem or "put out a fire." All the problems facing organizations would suggest that the modern-day administrator must possess a different leadership style from those that have operated under the older and more traditional approaches.

Leadership Style

The leadership qualities exhibited by the administrator and the organizational climate that is created contribute greatly to the overall success that an organization achieves. The literature is rich in discussing the various leadership styles practiced by leaders of private and public enterprises. Each administrator is responsible for determining which style will best enable him/her to work with employees in accomplishing the goals and objectives of the agency.

The administrator who manages an agency in an autocratic fashion will find it difficult to function effectively in today's complex organizations. Autocratic leaders have been described as individuals who centralize authority in themselves, often rule through fear, do not have confidence in subordinates, seldom delegate authority to others, and make most of the decisions. Such persons should not be con-

sidered as leaders and certainly do not fit the management approach advocated in this text.

The urban management system of the 1980s must be guided by leaders who understand how organizations work and how people function. To be an effective administrator, today's leader must possess a leadership style that fits with the nature of organizations. Administrators must surround themselves with the most capable staff that can be recruited and then establish a creative climate for them to function. Molding the staff into a well-coordinated team that will operate collectively toward goals will contribute to the success of the agency. The executive's job is to stimulate workers to work toward achieving their greatest potential.

Natural systems administrators must have the ability to make decisions. They must be students of such management concerns as negotiation, bargaining, politics, and problem solving. In order to move organizations forward in accomplishing their missions, effective leaders must also know how to uncover and then utilize the citizens that represent the "power elite" in the community.

It has sometimes been questioned whether organizational structure or employees are more important. The answer lies somewhere between these two extremes. Even the most perfect organizational setup cannot get results if operated by incompetent people. Conversely, even the most skilled and competent personnel cannot get good results if they are placed in a poorly structured agency. However, the leadership style of the executive will make a difference in the financing and budgeting procedures that are promulgated by the local leisure service agency.

Evaluation

One of the weakest links in the management process of local leisure service agencies is that of evaluation. This is happening in an era of increased accountability—growing public concern directed toward a closer scrutiny of governmental performance—when taxpayers are asking what they are actually getting for their money and what are the benefits and accomplishments of governmental programs. The pressure for improved productivity has been especially strong at all levels of government.

The management concerns identified in Figure 1.2 stress the process of evaluation as it relates to several facets of the management process: the organization itself, its structure, employees, and operation; programs and services; goals and objectives; citizen needs; and the impact of citizens and the community.

In emphasizing the internal aspects of an organization, most agencies have established procedures for evaluating their employees. Procedures vary from evaluating employees' personal characteristics (reliability, appearance, personal relationships with others, punctuality, etc.) to that of evaluating performance. Performance evaluation is concerned with the efficiency and effectiveness of employees in accomplishing their jobs and meeting the objectives that have been established jointly by the manager and employees.

It is becoming more common for the efficiency and productivity of the employees and the management process itself to be directed toward all levels of government. Introduced as important elements of performance budgets and the planning programming budget system (PPBS) during the 1960s, each new approach to local government budgeting in recent years has concentrated on the establishment of an effective method of measuring and improving the efficiency and productivity of local governmental units.

The creation of a functional budgeting and reporting system to monitor workload and employee performance has proved less than satisfactory in service-oriented professions. Establishing an effective program evaluation mechanism that includes good measurement indicators of performance has met considerable resistance in many local park and recreation agencies. Also, the park and recreation profession has been slow to take the leadership in establishing performance standards that can be used by executives. Local administrators are often forced to create their own indicators of performance in response to mandates of local public officials. More attention must be directed toward evaluating and measuring performance of organizations.

Program evaluation has long been included in the management process of local leisure service agencies. However, one of the main measurement tools has been the response of the public (attendance) to the programs and services offered. Many professional park and recreation administrators agree that the evaluation of leisure service programs is not comprehensive and is often not too meaningful and that local agencies must improve their tools for determining the effectiveness of programs and services.

Since the initiation of the program approach to budgeting during the mid-1950s, budgets have tended to stress the programs offered and some system for evaluating them. The cost of programs and the preparation of plans, which often includes goals and objectives, have provided local reviewing bodies with basic information that has proved valuable in determining whether programs should be expanded, reduced in scope, or deleted.

The program/performance concept of budgeting developed by Lakewood, Colorado, established an approach to program evaluation that is used by many agencies throughout the country. Lakewood's budget provides for the following four categories of program evaluation inputs that are used for a comprehensive evaluation of programs and municipal services.

Demand. "Is this program necessary? How much service is required?"
Workload. "How much service are we providing? How does that compare to the need for that service?"
Productivity. "Is the program being run efficiently? How much does the program cost?"
Effectiveness. "How well is the program doing? Is it solving the problems it was created to solve?"[2]

Using these program evaluation inputs as an effective management tool is an extremely complex issue causing real problems for park and recreation administrators.

One of the primary management concerns discussed earlier is that of making goals and objectives an integral part of the management process. As previously discussed, some approach to management by objectives must be incorporated into the management and budgeting system of leisure service agencies. The presence of meaningful, measurable, and realistic program goals in an agency's budget document will enable the organization to evaluate better its effectiveness in meeting citizens' needs. Success in which local agencies achieve their goals will ultimately be measured by how well the organization has directed its resources to meet or satisfy the needs of the public. Each agency should carefully consider whether their programs are meeting their objectives. The measurement of the total effectiveness of the leisure service programs is a challenge that the park and recreation profession must meet.

FACTORS INFLUENCING MANAGEMENT

Several factors will influence the financing and budgeting procedures of local leisure service agencies. They should be clearly understood by boards, administrators, and employees of each agency.

Political Aspects

Professionals in public leisure service agencies work in a political environment. Those in semipublic and private agencies will in some way be influenced by governmental agencies that are controlled by elected public officials. These agencies often seek cooperative relationships with governmental units,

[2]Bill Henderson and Randy Young, *Program Performance Budgeting: An Effective Public Management System for Evaluating Municipal Services.* Special Bulletin 1976A, Municipal Finance Officers Association, 1976, p. 4.

use their areas and facilities, or receive funding from the government.

If park and recreation agencies are to compete successfully for their share of the shrinking tax dollar, they must develop the art of working with elected officials who are serving on legislative bodies at all levels of government. Successful administrators are those who are able to "work politics without playing politics." There does not seem to be a magical answer that will effectuate this relationship. Perhaps administrators should use the good logic of common sense, sound judgment, and a clear understanding of the political process.

There are two kinds of leadership in a community that are frequently at odds and often unnecessarily and disastrously counterproductive: (1) political, or in most cases legislative, leadership, which represents the grass-roots participation of the community in government and (2) technical professional leadership.

The elected or appointed members of the legislative body should be viewed as serving as a broker between the community and the governmental unit. The job of these policy-determining bodies is clear and simple. It consists of establishing plans and directions of the political community and approving policies that are guidelines for action; allocating available resources of the community for public purposes; and providing general supervision of the management of the governmental agency it serves. Legislative bodies must understand that effective general supervision represents a fine art of delegation without abdication. Just as the general public has confidence and trust in the person whom they elect to public office, so must the public official have confidence in the local governmental agency and, as such, should not meddle in the operation of the various departments providing services to the community.

The second kind of leadership—technical competence—is the type of leadership that rests on special knowledge, experience, and professional competence that will provide leadership for the management of the department. In this sense, the engineer, the physician, and the parks and recreation manager possess the qualifications for professional or administrative leadership.

When administrators fail in this role, they are charged with incompetence and indifference and a loss of respect from the political community and the public at large results. When policymakers or politicans forget or assume roles that are not part and parcel to their positions, there is meddling, confusion, and disruption within the operating department. It is important to understand that political or legislative leadership and administrative leadership

do not operate in separate vacuums. Therefore park and recreation administrators must be skilled in working in the political arena.

Almost every aspect of financing and budgeting for parks and recreation discussed in this text is conducted within the atmosphere of politics. This is as it should be, since elected public officials have the responsibility for determining and directing public policy that is fundamental to the political process. It is in the political arena that budgets are approved, tax rates are set, programs and services are determined, and approaches for obtaining adequate revenues are decided. Political pressures are sometimes received to hire the party faithful or to initiate a program or service to fulfill a campaign promise. Mandates from higher levels of government create many problems for local authorities for finding sufficient funds. Political decisions at the federal level have major impacts on local communities. Management strategies that will be discussed throughout the text are designed to enable the leisure services manager to work effectively in this political environment.

Public Pressures

Pressures of all kinds are brought against leisure service agencies for securing special privileges, programs, services, and facilities. These may be good or bad, political or nonpolitical, internal or external. For example, citizens in a neighborhood may seek the expansion of summer recreation programs to include their neighborhood, the local garden club may seek area and facilities for family garden plots, or federal officials may demand that recreation facilities be redesigned for the handicapped. Over the years the expansion of programs and services have resulted from individuals and groups requesting new or expanded services. This, of course, is as it should be and the agency must adopt appropriate management strategies to handle these requests.

There are also occasions when a council member at a local governmental level may make demands on an agency to construct a minipark on a vacant lot in his/her district, or a city council member requests expanded use of the swimming pool and the allocation of departmental funds to underwrite the local swim team, primarily because he/she has two sons who are excellent swimmers. Then again there is always the mayor or business executive who wants the agency to hire a son or daughter as recreation leaders.

Unless appropriate planning, hiring procedures, or policies are available, these types of pressures may result in unwise expenditures of public funds or in expanding programs that are not a part of the budget plan or perhaps in adding unnecessary programs.

It is not uncommon for leisure service agencies to spend money for these newly demanded programs that are not in the budget; as a result, other programs suffer. Also, persons are sometimes employed with the full knowledge that they are not qualified for the position.

The aforementioned types of pressures are just a few examples facing local administrators that require an appropriate response from the board or administrator of the agency.

Favored Treatment

Organizational funds are sometimes wasted because higher than necessary prices are paid for supplies, equipment, property, or services. This happens primarily because the business affairs of the agency are not always conducted in a professional manner. Sometimes this occurs because public officials show a degree of indifference when they are spending money in their budgets.

Favored treatment may result from outside pressures, political patronage and, sometimes, from giving business to personal friends. A few examples will help to illustrate the problem. In some communities a merchant may sell athletic supplies to the public school board or leisure service agency without bids and at prices that would be higher than would be requested by other dealers handling the same supplies of equal quality. On occasion the merchant has served as a member of the school board or perhaps on a parks and recreation board. Other examples of specialized treatment are when specifications are drawn up so that certain manufacturers are favored regardless of the quality or fitness of their product or job specifications are developed to fit the person that the agency is interested in employing.

In fairness to the large number of agencies that are operating on a highly professional level, it should be noted that these illustrations do not represent common routine practice everywhere, but such cases occur altogether too frequently, particularly in units of local government that are dominated by political pressures.

Irresponsible Management Practices

There are times when administrators and staff do not use good professional judgment in the operation of their agencies. For example, agency funds are expended with greater freedom and with less discretion than if the responsible authorities were spending their own personal monies. On occasion, agencies may continue to perform functions that are no longer relevant. These programs are justified on the basis that they have been a part of the budget for years. It can also be found that agencies sometimes continue to retain seasonal personnel for additional weeks or months just because funds are in the budget and these workers would have a difficult time finding employment if they were discharged.

A somewhat common practice is for departments to return to the general fund any money that is remaining at the end of the fiscal year. If a balance is achieved, often the legislative body feels that the department does not need the total amount budgeted and suggests a budget reduction for the new fiscal year.

If local government is to become fiscally responsible and its management practices accepted by the public, many of the irresponsible management practices must be abolished.

Legislative Control

Parks and recreation, like all other public functions, are creatures of state government and therefore local cities or counties do not have the inherent right of local self-government in these matters. The right and powers that local goverments do have to operate a park and recreation department are determined by state statutes. Laws established by the state that impact on local government can be classified as mandatory, directory, and permissive legislation. These types of laws include provisions of what local agencies must do, must not do, or may or may not do at their discretion. For instance, the Indiana Park and Recreation Law is an example of permissive legislation that permits local governments to establish park and recreation departments by enacting a local ordinance. On the other hand, state boards of health require local agencies to submit water samples from their swimming pools for approval—a mandate.

State legislatures have, from the time of their inauguration, passed a multitude of laws that influence the park and recreation movement. Some of the laws are obsolete, worthless, or actually harmful. Other laws are highly political and give local politicians power to control local boards and agencies.

Besides legislation that governs the organization and operation of local agencies, there are a myriad of laws that govern the financial and budgeting practices of local agencies. As state enactments dominate the management process of local agencies, it is vitally important that park and recreation managers become knowledgeable about the legislative process and act forcefully and effectively for sound legislation that will govern local agencies in their operation of the program.

Legislative control should enable and enhance the provision of local leisure services rather than restrict or disrupt the operation of these agencies. Throughout the remainder of the text, constant references will be made to legislative control of financing local park and recreation programs.

Decentralization of Control

As previously mentioned, parks and recreation are functions of the state and to some extent there are state agencies, that is, departments of natural resources, state park divisions, state recreation commissions, that exercise some degree of control over local operations. However, most public leisure service programs and services are administered by local authorities.

Americans have traditionally been opposed to the federal government performing services that could be provided by the state government. They usually desire to keep the control close to the people. Likewise they oppose the state government offering services that could be made available by the local government. Finally, people are against the government providing services that can be furnished by private enterprise or the people themselves.

It is of little surprise that over a period of many years, a large number of small political units were created in decentralizing control to local communities, to provide services to those living at the local level. Of interest is the fact that the smaller the division of government (town, township, school district) is, the greater number of officials are involved in the transaction of the business affairs of the unit. These small governing units were often found not to use the best methods of managing the business affairs of their unit. With an increase in the numbers of agencies offering programs, the overlap and duplication of units and functions were inevitable.

In an effort to provide better services and to afford a more professional approach to management, consolidation of school districts and consolidation of governments have gradually taken place throughout the country. Although extreme decentralization resulted in many problems, consolidation of units into larger governmental units has created other concerns. It has been found that bigness alone does not assure efficiency and quality of services. Political scientists predict that the consolidation of local governmental units is a trend that will continue in the years ahead. The merging of local agencies will influence the provision of leisure services in urban areas throughout the country.

Fiscal Dependence

Leisure service agencies have varying degrees of control over their finance and business affairs. This results from their fiscal status—whether an agency has fiscal dependence or independence.

Fiscal independence exists when a board has the legal right to prepare its budget, levy taxes, and expend monies without securing the approval of the mayor, city council, or some other governmental agency. In Illinois, for example, the Illinois Park District Law enables the establishment of a special park district and the board has the power to determine its budget, levy taxes, and spend money without receiving approval from another individual or agency. Public boards have complete fiscal independence. In Kansas, recreation commissions have fiscal independence within certain mill levy limitations.

Fiscal dependence, on the other hand, is when the board or agency cannot levy taxes or spend money without securing approval, in whole or in part, from another individual or governmental agency. In Indiana, for example, the park and recreation board, organized under the Indiana Park and Recreation Law, is required to submit a budget to the mayor, city council, County Tax Review Board, and the State Tax Commission for approval.

The degree of fiscal control varies widely among agencies throughout the country. In some cases the reviewing body must, by law, approve the budget as submitted. Some park and recreation departments must submit their budgets to an outside agency that has the power either to require a reduction in the total amount or actually to eliminate specific items in the budgets.

Leisure service agencies that are designated as human service organizations by the United Way of America fall under the fiscal dependence category if they are funded by the United Way. The Girl Scout executive, for example, must gain approval of the budget from her board. The budget is then presented to a budget review committee and finally to the Board of Directors of the United Way before approval is gained.

Sunshine/Sunset Laws

In recent years the escalating role of government in local affairs has caused an expansion of bureaucracy and level of employment by local government. As a result, an urgent concern was expressed by politicians and citizens for a method to assess the performance and relevance of various segments of government and for more citizen participation in governmental operations. Two types of legislation were passed to solve these problems: sunshine laws and sunset laws.

Sunshine or "open meetings" laws have been enacted at the federal government level and by almost all state and local governments. These laws are designed to open the workings of governmental agencies to the public. Generally, growing distrust of government has come about partly as a result of unnecessary official secrecy of governmental operations. The "open meetings" were initiated to increase citizen participation and confidence in government as well as to improve the responsiveness of governmental units.

In 1974, 48 of 50 states had enacted laws, specific or general, on open meetings. Only Mississippi and West Virginia apparently lack legislation in this area. Thirty states passed sunshine laws during the 1970s. In studying the provisions of the state laws that have been passed, we see that they vary in their attempts to assure maximum openness. For example, Maryland and Rhode Island merely include a statement of public policy in support of openness, whereas 21 states provided for penalties for those who violate the law. In almost every state that passed sunshine laws, open meetings were also required of city councils and county boards.[3]

It is generally acknowledged that the presence of a state open meeting law will not guarantee open government; however, the chances of open government are improved if penalties are given for those who violate the law. Common Cause and Sigma Delta Chi, the Society of Professional Journalists, have actively lobbied for open meetings laws.

Leisure service agencies should welcome the intent of sunshine laws, as citizen involvement is vital to the success of local leisure service programs. These new laws will definitely have an impact on the "behind the close door" sessions that are often a part of the budget review process in local government.

Sunset laws have emerged as one of the most significant public management issues of the late 1970s. As a result of public disenchantment with the growth of public services, increase in taxes, and lack of accountability for services that often were considered obsolete and wasteful, sunset legislation has been enacted in a majority of states.

In 1977 Colorado was the first state to pass a sunset law. This was the result of initiative taken by the Colorado chapter of Common Cause, the originator of the movement. The basic concept of sunset laws is the establishment of a timetable for the review of programs, laws, and agencies. These laws establishing programs and agencies would automatically terminate on certain established dates unless reapproved by a statute of the state legislative body. Supporters of the movement have stated that "Old agencies never die. They don't even fade away."[4]

Many advocates of sunset laws have stressed that the primary purpose of such laws is to make agencies and programs more responsive and accountable and not merely to see how many can be terminated. In testimony before a U.S. Senate subcommittee in 1976, John Gardner, the founding chairman of Common Cause, suggested 10 basic principles that are essential to any workable sunset law.

First: The program or agencies covered under the law should automatically terminate on a certain date, unless affirmatively re-created by law.
Second: Termination should be periodic (e.g., every six or eight years) in order to institutionalize the process of re-evaluation.
Third: Like all significant innovations, introduction of the Sunset mechanism will be a learning process and should be phased in gradually, beginning with those programs to which it seems most applicable.
Fourth: Programs and agencies in the same policy area should be reviewed simultaneously in order to encourage consolidation and responsible pruning.
Fifth: Consideration by the relevant legislative committees must be preceded by competent and thorough preliminary studies.
Sixth: Existing bodies (e.g., the executive agencies, General Accounting Office) should undertake the preliminary evaluation work, but their evaluation capacities must be strengthened.
Seventh: Substantial committee reorganization, including adoption of a system of rotation of committee members, is a prerequisite to effective Sunset oversight.
Eighth: In order to facilitate review, the Sunset proposal should establish general criteria to guide the review and evaluation process.
Ninth: Safeguards must be built into the Sunset mechanism to guard against arbitrary termination and to provide for outstanding agency obligations and displaced personnel.
Tenth: Public participation in the form of public access to information and public hearings is an essential part of the Sunset process.[5]

---

[3]*Government in the Sunshine,* Hearings before the Subcommittee on Reorganization, Research, and International Organizations of the Committee on Government Operations, U.S. Senate, 93rd Congress, May 21 and 22, and October 15, 1974, pp. 298–307.

[4]*Program Evaluation Act of 1977 and Federal Spending Control Act of 1977,* Hearings Before the Committee on Rules and Administration, U.S. Senate, September 28, 1977; April 19 and June 8, 1978, p. 100.
[5]Ibid, p. 101.

The Council of State Governments reported that 33 states have enacted sunset legislation, whereas legislatures in five other states have included sunset clauses in selected programs. Most of the state sunset laws closely follow the 10 principles suggested by Gardner. In four states (Alabama, Louisiana, Oklahoma, and Rhode Island) zero-base budgeting has been installed as one of the mechanisms of their sunset laws. In a way zero-base budgeting, which requires an evaluation of programs and services each year, is similar to the concept of sunset legislation.[6]

The extent that sunset legislation filters down to local governments is not known; however, there appears to be considerable discussion of such legislation in local governments throughout the country.

Dynamics of Change

Change is the byword for today and certainly for tomorrow. This is nothing new as change has always been a part of the American way of life. What is different, however, is the pace of change that is taking place and the prospect that it will accelerate even more dramatically in coming years. To many Americans the changes that have taken place in the past quarter century are almost incomprehensible. However, it is generally acknowledged that we will make more technological progress in the next 25 years than was made in the last 250 years.

The technological progress that has taken us to the moon and has resulted in laser beams and microsurgery has already had its impact on urban life. It is obvious that the radical change predicted for the future will have an increasingly greater impact on urban America, the life styles of people, the demands of citizens for leisure services, and the management process of parks and recreation agencies.

First, technology will have a marked effect on the American work force. Economists foresee that in the not too distant future, only 4 percent of the population will be needed to produce all the goods and materials needed for the entire population. According to the *U.S. News and World Report* (August 10, 1981), spending was estimated to be $244 billion, with $1 out of every $8 earned in this country being spent on leisure activities. In the future, business and industry will need to increase their efforts in producing and marketing leisure service goods, supplies, and services. Public and private service agencies must also be prepared to meet the leisure demands of a very changing population. Just as television has already dramatically changed the home and the family, the computer and other technological advances will create new life-styles, new social and moral values, and a whole new culture.

The advent of the computer is just beginning to make its impact on the management process of leisure service agencies. Technological improvements in the communications field and the implementation of electric data processing are already creating waves. They will, however, completely revolutionalize the management process of organizations in the future. It is in the area of finance, budgeting, accounting, and planning, the primary concerns of this book, where the greatest changes will occur. Tomorrow's managers must possess the skills and knowledge of a computerized technology if they are to have the capacity to plan, coordinate, and control the operation of their agencies. The projected forces of change will demand a retraining of the present work force and the selection of professionally and technically competent personnel.

Leaders in urban government are already suggesting that a by-product of technology important to local government is worker obsolescence. Technological change has so increased in tempo that the demand for a given set of workers' skills no longer lasts as long as a worker's expected productive life. It is currently estimated that the skills of average workers will be rendered obsolete at least three times during their working careers.[7]

It must be recognized that change often causes conflict for people basically object to change out of fear of the unknown. Because they do not realize how change is going to affect them individually, people usually expect the worst. Eric Hoffer has succinctly stated that:

It is my impression that no one really likes the new. We are afraid of it. . . . In the case of drastic change the uneasiness is of course deeper and more lasting. We can never be really prepared for that which is wholly new. We have to adjust ourselves, and every radical adjustment is a crisis in self-esteem.[8]

If change is addressed in an orderly well-planned fashion with all the persons involved in an organization, the outcome will be more positive. The ultimate solution to the dynamics of change is the professionalism of leaders that utilize technology to provide better leisure service to the community.

[6]*The Book of the States, 1980–81* (Vol. 23), The Council of State Governments, Lexington, Ky, pp. 122–124.

[7]James M. Banovetz, *Managing the Modern City,* International City Management Association, Washington, D.C., 1971, p. 24.
[8]Eric Hoffer, *The Ordeal of Change,* Harper & Row, New York, 1967, p. 3.

PROFESSIONAL CHALLENGE

With the growth of the parks and recreation movement during the last quarter century, it is evident that the provision of leisure services is already big business. Local boards of semipublic and public agencies have the responsibility for determining citizen needs and providing direction for the operation of the agencies. In most cases these boards consist of community leaders and professional people who are aware of the fiscal concerns facing their community, and they expect the organization to operate on a businesslike basis.

Local executives are being evaluated constantly on their ability to provide creative and imaginative leadership to their agencies and community. The success that they achieve may well be determined by the organizational climate that they establish for their employees, their leadership style, and their management skills. The art of management is not merely couched in principles and procedures; it is embellished in leaders' concern of human beings and their ability to work with and for people in carrying out the mission of their organizations. Leisure service professionals must have a mastery of the body of knowledge that undergirds their profession. They must understand the nature of their communities and the people they serve; they must be able to provide the leisure experiences that will foster a better quality of life and environment.

Successful leaders also possess skills, temperament, and maturity to operate in systems that are characterized by the natural systems management theories. Although they must have a mastery of management tools, they must be able to operate in an organization that is constantly reacting to the demands of a complex and rapidly changing society and to those employees who are frustrated in their inability to live and work in such a society. An administrator must be knowledgeable about what really happens within the organization itself and be skillful in handling the many interrelationships in the so-called larger environment—city, state, and nation. "Crisis management" is real, and problem solving, decision making, and "putting out fires" are everyday management concerns. In this web of confusion and frustration able executives must concentrate on the important responsibilities that cannot be shirked.

In far too many cases today's administrators freely comment that "they are running just as fast as they can in order not to lose ground." To be an effective manager takes time; however, most managers will readily admit that they are preoccupied with distractions, time-consuming meetings, a myriad of paperwork, reports and never ending deadlines, and unending time-consuming telephone calls. Management journals are full of articles on time management and the executive's dilemma—"finding time to think."

Successful executives seem to have the ability to isolate and concentrate on essential responsibilities, things that they alone must do and ignore those that can be done by subordinates. This necessitates delegation, indicating that executives must have confidence in their employees, who will carry out the functions of the organization.

Some mayors, councils, or community leaders feel that anyone can serve as an administrator for their leisure service agencies. This concept must be challenged and argued on the premise that a good professional will be able to provide the best leisure service programs and facilities to a community. Outstanding professionals are called for who can provide creative and imaginative leadership in the field. According to Kraus and Curtis:

While many recreation executives are capable, respected leaders in their communities and in the profession, only a few emerge as outstanding professionals. The key factor here is their ability to be creative, open and responsive to the crucial challenges of the present day, to develop exciting and innovative programs and concepts, and—above all—to see beyond the traditional, to envision new roles and solutions for recreation and parks.[9]

MANAGEMENT STRATEGIES

In discussing various elements of management, we see that the management model of the future must be viewed as an agency that is constantly reacting to the demands and problems of a complex, changing society. Administrators must be prepared to develop strategies that will enable them to meet the problems and challenges of the 1980s. There are no right answers or perfect solutions to the problems anticipated. Like a military leader, leisure service administrators must plan their strategies and tactics for coping with the uncertainties that lie ahead.

Chapter 2 will explore the symptoms of an "era of limits" that has dominated the national scene and has wedged a gap between the needs and expectations of the public for governmental services and the ability of local officials to find adequate revenues. The problems facing communities have created enormous stresses on public leaders, which require a careful study of local government's revenue raising, spending, and manage-

[9]Richard G. Kraus and Joseph E. Curtis, *Creative Administration in Recreation and Parks*, Mosby, St. Louis, 1982, p. 373.

ment systems. It seems likely that the fiscal stress and economic uncertainty confronting the country is a long-range phenomenon and tomorrow's leaders must be prepared to handle difficult situations with predetermined alternatives and strategies.

In preparing management strategies for the future, administrators should develop tactics for *proacting* to the anticipated changes and issues and for exerting leadership for creating or designing the future, as well as for *reacting* to the future. The reactor attempts to forecast the changes that will be taking place and then responds to the situations as they arise. This is a followers' approach, letting critical issues or events dominate the agency and shape its response and ultimately its future. The leadership approach might be considered as forecasting the changes that might occur and then developing plans or strategies for shaping the future. This is what creative leadership is all about.

The management model for the 1980s and beyond should encompass broader roles and responsibilities for leisure service agencies than most people envision. Strategies should be developed to explore the political and economic problems, constraints, and alternatives and in utilizing new management approaches that might prove successful in wrestling with the financial stress facing urban America. A brief summary of several principles that should guide the management system of leisure service agencies in the years ahead includes:

- All leisure service agencies should work collectively toward meeting the leisure needs of the community.
- Agencies must explore constantly new approaches for obtaining sufficient revenues to finance leisure service programs.
- Involvement of citizens and community groups in the operation of the agency is vital to the success of the organization.

- Agencies should provide the optimum delivery of leisure service programs within the fiscal resources that are available.
- Agencies must develop and utilize the most modern and progressive approaches to budgeting and managment.
- Managers must look for ways of cutting costs and becoming more efficient and productive.
- Agencies will be judged by the quality of services they provide, which might mean doing fewer things, but doing them well.
- Management systems should take advantage of the latest technological developments in the communications field and computer-based information systems.

Subsequent chapters present the trends and problems in financing leisure service agencies and an approach for fiscal management that should enable local administrators of leisure service agencies to develop strategies in handling fiscal and budgeting concerns of their agencies.

Selected References

Drucker, Peter F., *Managing in Turbulent Times,* Harper & Row, New York, 1980, Chapters 2, 4.

Howard, Dennis, R., and John L. Crompton, *Financing, Managing, Marketing Recreation and Park Resources,* Brown, Dubuque, Iowa, 1980, pp. 186–273.

Kraus, Richard G., and Joseph E. Curtis, *Creative Administration in Recreation and Parks,* 3rd Ed., Mosby, St. Louis, 1982, Chapters 2, 3, 5, and 19.

Managing the Modern City, International City Management Association, Washington, D.C., 1971, pp. 3–204.

Managing Municipal Leisure Services, International City Management Association, Washington, D.C., 1980, Chapters 2 and 5.

Rodney, Lynn S., and Robert F. Toalson, *Administration of Recreation, Parks, and Leisure Services,* Wiley, New York, 1981, Chapters 1–6.

Chapter 2

Financing Local Government

Financing local governmental services is becoming one of the most critical issues facing an urban America. Local governments are plagued with a multiplicity of almost unsolvable problems, with a growing concern among the American public about the ability of cities, counties, and special districts to improve or solve these crisis-like conditions.

Numerous studies and reports have been made, from presidential commissions to state and local investigative bodies, regarding the critical conditions confronting local units of government. In almost every report the indication is that the problems facing local government are highlighted by their lack of financial resources to meet current problems. It is quite evident that local units of government are falling short in meeting these challenges.

Most fiscal problems have been growing over the years; however, several events primarily in the 1970s have created an awareness that local governments are facing a financial dilemma. The 1974–1976 recession placed a squeeze on local governmental finances and budgets. New York City's fiscal crisis hit the headlines in 1975, and Proposition 13 in 1978 in California sent shock waves of earthquake dimensions throughout the country. The fiscal plight of urban America quickly came into focus. The decade of the 1970s also found double-digit inflation, an energy crisis, and economic uncertainty, which brought higher prices along with unemployment.

Despite their financial concerns, the ever present problems of urban sprawl, deteriorating environment, noise and air pollution, racial strife, strikes, unemployment, and other social concerns created citizen demands for more services and programs of local governments. With increased services come larger budgets, expanded revenues, and more spending. As taxpayers were being asked to pay more and more for these services, the so-called "taxpayer's revolt" was inevitable.

FACTORS INFLUENCING LOCAL GOVERNMENTAL FINANCE

There are a number of factors that influence local governments' ability to raise sufficient revenue to finance needed programs and services. Some of the major concerns that have led to taxpayer's concern for financing local services are briefly presented. Because these have a major impact on agency budgets, they should be carefully studied by leisure service professionals.

Urban Growth

A brief analysis of urban development in the United States should place into perspective the current urban and fiscal crisis facing American local governmental agencies. Urban growth experienced a tremendous increase in population during the first half of the twentieth century. By 1970 over 67 percent of the population in this country resided in major metropolitan areas. People were attracted to these urban areas because of the Industrial Revolution that created jobs and by the cultural and economic advantages resulting in a better life. Opportunity was a key element.

With the growth in population and the increased density of people in our urban areas came crowded conditions, racial problems, increased crime, noise, pollution, riots, and protests. Opportunity, jobs, and the desire for improved living standards, which made urban communities so attractive during the first fifty years of this century, gradually disappeared and the movement out of central cities to the suburbs took place. The exodus from central cities and the growth of the suburbs had a devastating effect on the central city. With the movement of mostly middle- and upper-class persons out of the central core, cities became a place for blacks, other minorities, and the poor. Slums developed and industrial plants, which were the drawing power for bringing people to the city in earlier decades, gradually deteriorated. Industry also moved to the suburbs to escape the high costs of maintaining local government services. As a result, the assessed valuation of property dropped and the taxing base was drastically reduced, while the costs for welfare, health service, police and fire protection, and other services increased.

In 1970 census figures revealed that for the first time in history, suburbanites outnumbered those residing in the central city. Many of those who moved to suburban communities for better living conditions were still tied to the central city and an era of mobile commuters was initiated. Commuters earned their living in the city; however, they paid taxes in the suburb where they resided. They still demanded improved expressways, public transit, more parking, and other services from the city and were at the same time able to enjoy the culture of the city—its museums, theaters, parks, and other amenities—without paying their fair share. Suburbanites became parasites of the central city.

Fragmentation of Local Government

With the movement of people from central cities, the growth of a vast urbanized complex of cities and towns (megalopolis) took place. The Bureau of Census describes this pattern of urban growth as SMSA (Standard Metropolitan Statistical Areas), which is defined as "a cluster of heavily settled communities that are geographically, socially, and economically related to each other and the central urban core."

As each community sought its own identity and local governing body, the growth of governmental units increased. It soon became apparent that many of the problems and services (i.e., pollution, crime, planning, transportation, etc.) do not restrict themselves to legal boundaries, so special-purpose districts were created. The U.S. Bureau of Census reported that there were 264 SMSAs in 1971 embracing a total of

22,185 local government units—cities, counties, townships, school districts, and special districts. In 1977 it was estimated that SMSAs expanded to 272, with 25,869 local governmental units. The 1980 census report identified 323 SMSAs and revealed that 169.4 million or 75 percent of the U.S. population lived in these areas.

The multiplicity of governing bodies within urban metropolitan regions added to the growing problems. Far too often local governmental units tended to guard their independence and limit their scope to local concerns rather than to explore regional problems. Overlap and duplication of functions were inevitable and competition among governmental units, rather than cooperation, often occurred. Costs of providing services rose dramatically and the competition between agencies for limited financial resources added to the burden of taxpayers.

Growth in Public Services

As urban areas continued to grow and people became more dependent on government for finding solutions to their problems, the demands or pressures on public agencies to provide new or expanded services constantly increased. As a result, it was evident that the following phenomenon was taking place.

Action		Result
Increased demands	=	Increased services
Increased services	=	Increased budgets
Increased budgets	=	Increased revenues
Increased revenues	=	Increased taxes
Increased taxes	=	Increased taxpayer's scrutiny

Growth of governmental services, in good or bad times, can be well documented in all of our government units.

Also, it was during the so-called "rebellious 1960s" that problems facing local governments accelerated. A "think-tank" of business leaders convened by the Indiana Univeristy School of Business concluded that "Mankind was at the Turning Point." In this period, major cities were faced with

- Deterioration of physical environment.
- Disruption of educational institutions.
- Division of society—black and white, young and old, rich and poor, urban and rural.
- Inflation.
- Undesirable urban sprawl.
- Dissatisfaction with work—strikes.
- Disregard for law, order, and authority.
- Rise of the youth culture—which questioned the traditional values of society.

- Criticism of traditional institutions.
- Concern for equal opportunities—women and minorities.[1]

Government at all levels was quick to respond to the demands and problems of the period. The 1960s will be remembered as an era of expanded governmental services and programs, coming at a time when local governments were experiencing increasing difficulties in obtaining adequate financial resources.

Growth in Public Spending

With the demands and growth in programs and services came an increase in local and state spending. According to the Advisory Commission on Intergovernmental Relations (ACIR), local public spending rose from 23 percent of the Growth National Product (GNP) in 1949 to 35 percent in 1975, and declining to 31 percent in 1978.[2] John Shannon, Assistant Director, ACIR, indicated that the dip after 1975 resulted in the economy growing at a faster rate than public sector spending, with indications that spending will move upward again, in spite of Proposition 13 in California.

During the same period (1949–1978), local spending rose from 5 percent of the GNP to over 8 percent. Local government spending (note Figure 2.1) from its own funds remained relatively the same while revenues from the state and federal governments more than doubled.

[1]John F. Mee, *Perspectives for the Future Manager and His Environment,* School of Business, Indiana University, Bloomington, 1975, p. 5.
[2]Remarks by John Shannon, Municipal Finance Officers Association (MFOA), Colloquia on Taxpayer Revolt and Tax Reform, Chicago, September 29, 1978.

Increase in Government Employees

With the increase in local government programs and spending, more people were employed by government. Figure 2.2 shows the rapid rise in the number of local and state employees from slightly under 4 million in 1949 to almost 13.3 million in 1980. During the same period federal employment remained relatively unchanged.

Two factors are responsible for the federal employment picture. First, after 1950 there was a shift in spending from defense to nondefense or domestic spending. Second, the federal government increased its aid to local communities, thus avoiding new federal employment and increasing employment at the local and state levels. In most local and state governments 20 to 40 percent of their employees are funded by the federal government.

In addition to the rise in the number of employees, pay has increased dramatically. With the force of unions and collective bargaining, employees' income more than doubled from 1968–1978.[3] With salaries and wages comprising 60 to 80 percent of the operating budgets of local government agencies, salary increases have been largely responsible for higher spending and budgets.

State and Federal Mandating of Programs

Another trend in recent years has been the increased mandating of programs by state and federal governments. For example, communities are required to add more courts, provide special education programs,

[3]*U.S. News and World Report,* July 17, 1978.

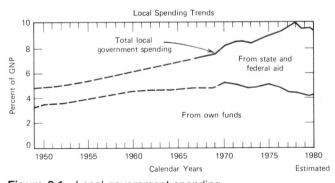

Figure 2.1 Local government spending.
Source. Advisory Commission on Intergovernmental Relations. (ACIR).

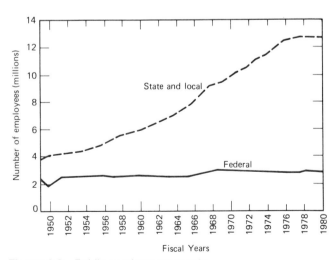

Figure 2.2 Public employment trends
Source. Advisory Commission Intergovernmental Relations (ACIR).

expand programs and facilties for the handicapped, and construct sewerage treatment systems. Although officials at the higher levels of government received credit for these programs or capital improvements, local officials were forced to find part or all of the money to pay for the mandated programs.

With budget limitations confronting local agencies, officials were often forced to reduce existing programs, or eliminate some entirely, in order to have funds for the mandated programs imposed on them.

Inflation

The rapidly escalating costs of conducting services caused by inflation has had a crippling effect on public agencies. Most local governments have not been able to increase their operating budgets high enough to keep pace with double-digit inflation.

During the spring of 1979 the Leisure Research Institute, Department of Recreation and Park Administration, Indiana University, conducted a nationwide study of park and recreation administrators to determine the effect that budget limitations and tax reform movements had on public parks and recreation. Four hundred municipal park and recreation agencies in cities of over 50,000 were randomly selected. A 66 percent response was received. The findings revealed that 44.4 percent of the agencies had increases in their operating budgets; however, only 7.2 percent received sufficient increases to keep pace with the double-digit inflation. Donald Wirth, Director of Parks and Recreation, Evanston, Illinois, commented that "inflation results in general decrease in quality and quantity of services. There will be fewer dollars to do the same job." Inflation combined with cuts in the budget and spending limitation measures has resulted in austerity budgets.

Taxpayer's Distrust in Government

People have never been too trusting of government, especially the federal government. Some feel it is too big, whereas others feel it is too political. Watergate, Agnew, GSA scandals, and Proposition 13 (California) were the clinchers. During the Proposition 13 campaign the surplus accrued at the state level was estimated to be two to two and one half billion dollars. Governor Brown kept the amount secret so even the state legislators did not know the exact amount that was accumulated. Upon passage of Proposition 13, Governor Brown disclosed a five-and-one-half-billion-dollar surplus, which was over twice the amount that had been anticipated, and the bailout of the cities, counties, and school districts took place. During the same period a government agency

in Los Angeles County found one million dollars that was not known to exist. These happenings are just a few examples of why taxpayers distrust government and why people are losing faith in government's ability to solve problems.

Many taxpayers feel that there is waste and inefficiency (fat) in government operations. They feel government should spend less and do more. Most people believe that service levels and programs can be maintained even if taxes are cut. Whether or not these images are correct, they often influence the passage of bond issues, referendums, tax increases, or the acceptance of budget proposals.

State Control over Local Government

Since local units of government receive their powers from the state, numerous restrictions and regulations are levied on them concerning local fiscal governance. Most of their fiscal and budgetary procedures and practices are delegated to them by state statutes. On the positive side, traditionally states have assumed a role of providing oversight and assistance to local government in the overall financial management of local agencies. However, in recent years states have tightened their controls over local taxing and spending powers. With states placing a lid on the communities' ability to raise revenues, local government is faced with a real financial dilemma.

TAX REFORMS—LIMITATIONS (STATE ENACTMENTS)

Although tax revolts are nothing new (Magna Carta, Boston Tea Party, tax limitation bills of the 1930s), Proposition 13 in California heralded a nationwide trend of taxpayers stressing their dissatisfaction with governmental performance and demanding tax relief.

Proposition 13 received national attention and as such sent shock waves of severe intensity throughout the country. John Shannon, Advisory Commission on Intergovernmental Relations, observed that Proposition 13 had a strong influence on other states in passing tax reform bills designed to restrict the spending and taxing powers of the states and those governmental units operating at the local level. He further stated that "if we could measure the shock waves on a scale of 1 to 10: the 1975 New York City crisis might register a Richter-type reading of 5; the 1974–1976 recession about 8; and the passage of Proposition 13 in 1978, almost 10."[4] When you real-

[4]Remarks by John Shannon, MFOA Colloquia, Chicago, September 29, 1978.

ize that 69 percent of the registered voters in California went to the polls (38.5 percent normally) and that Proposition 13 passed by a landslide of 65 to 35 percent, the results of Proposition 13 had a devastating effect in California and certainly provided an impetus for other states.

With the passage of Proposition 13, the following program went into effect, July 1, 1978.

- No property can be taxed at more than 1 percent of estimated 1975–1976 market values.
- No property tax assessment can be increased in any one year by more than 2 percent unless the property is sold, at which time it can be reassessed at market value.
- No local tax can be increased or a new tax imposed without approval of two thirds of the qualified voters.
- No additional state taxes can be imposed unless approved by two thirds of the total membership of both houses of the legislature.

Proposition 13 had a staggering effect on local government in California and changed the local government's reliance on the local property tax, which forced them to rely more heavily on financial assistance from the state and alternative sources of revenue.[5]

The impact of Proposition 13 on other states is not exactly known, however; it is apparent that other states have initiated additional or tighter restrictions on local authorities over their fiscal affairs as a result of Proposition 13.

Restrictions on Local Tax and Spending Powers

Property tax legislation has been in effect since the late nineteenth Century. Over the years, limitations on tax rates, local borrowing, levy limits, and lately, full disclosure laws have been legislated by state governments. The overall objective of this movement has been the reduction of real estate taxes as the principal source of local revenue.

Three approaches to tax and spending powers have been initiated: (1) limits or restrictions on tax rate or tax levy; (2) limits on expenditures; and (3) full disclosure laws.

Rate or Levy Limits. Placing a limit on the local property tax rate is the approach most often used by states. A maximum rate is set that can be applied to

[5]For a more detailed analysis see: *Intergovernmental Perspective*, "The Taxpayers Speak: Proposition 13 and Intergovernmental Relations," Advisory Committee on Intergovernmental Relations, Vol. 4, No. 3, Summer 1978.

the net assessed valuation of the taxing district. If the rate ceiling has been reached, the only way revenue can be increased through this tax is by having an increase in the assessed valuation of the taxing district or by amending state statutes to permit increased levy limitations.

A levy limit establishes the maximum revenue that can be raised by the public agency by using the property tax. Normally, levy limits restrict the growth of revenue to be raised through property taxes to some specified annual increase—that is, equal to the growth in economy of the area or increase in inflation. If the assessed valuation of the taxing district increases drastically, it becomes necessary to reduce the property tax rate so that the levy limit will not be exceeded.

A majority of the states in the United States have used the tax rate limitation as their approach to restricting local taxing power. Since 1970 nine states have opted for the property tax levy limit approach.

If a state places a lid on local taxing powers, it should allow other means for local governments to secure adequate financial resources or provide more state aid to them.

Limits on Spending Powers. The Advisory Committee on Intergovernmental Relations (ACIR) study published in 1977 indicated that only one state, New Jersey, had taken action in controlling local spending, whereas three states (Arizona, Kansas, and Maine) have placed limits on school corporations' spending.

In terms of expenditure limitations, normally a maximum percentage increase is allowed in the annual operating budget. In New Jersey spending by local governments is limited to 5 percent unless voter approval is obtained.

Full Disclosure Laws. Several states have adopted full disclosure laws that are not intended to be limits on property tax rates or limits on spending but which require local officials to provide a warning to taxpayers that their property tax will be raised.

During periods of inflation property values rise rapidly, resulting in higher assessments. In many instances local officials do not lower the property tax rates producing property tax windfalls caused by inflation.

Florida resolved this issue by initiating full disclosure legislation. In brief, each year property is reassessed, generally higher. The tax rate is then reduced so that no additional revenue can be generated. If more money is needed, the city council must place a one-fourth page ad in a local newspaper informing taxpayers that the council proposes to increase their property taxes and that a meeting will be held on a certain time and date. The ad must be surrounded by a thick black border referred to as a death notice. If, after the hearing, the council decides to go ahead and raise the property tax, another ad is placed in the newspaper informing the public of the council's action and the time and date of an additional hearing. At the second hearing another vote is taken and the council can then raise the taxes if it so desires. This procedure gives the local authorities the responsibility of raising taxes and levies and the public is fully informed.

Restrictions on State Tax and Spending Powers

Since 1976 five states (California, Colorado, Michigan, New Jersey, and Tennessee) have passed statutes restricting the growth of state spending. In Tennessee state spending is restricted to the growth in the state's economy. Proposition 13 in California requires approval of two thirds of the members of both houses of the legislature to increase state taxes and revenues. Another attempt to strengthen state accountability has been taken in Colorado. Inflation places taxpayers into higher state income tax brackets. The state of Colorado, in 1978, indexed the personal income tax, preventing unlegislated tax increases based solely on higher incomes. If the practice of placing restrictions on state spending and revenue grows, local government could be affected because it receives substantial revenues from the state.

Reimbursing Local Governments for Mandated Programs

The mandating of programs by state governments is a critical issue faced by most local units of government. California, one of the biggest mandators, provides reimbursement for those programs that cause either added cost or revenue loss to the local government. Local government is allowed to increase their maximum rate to cover this additional cost and responsibility.

In 1978 Tennessee passed legislation that partially reimburses local governments for state mandated programs and fully funds all new state programs for the first year.[6]

---

[6]For a more detailed analysis of trends on state limitations on local taxes and expenditures see *State Limitations on Local Taxes and Expenditures,* Advisory Committee on Intergovernmental Relations, February 1977.

SOURCES OF REVENUE— LOCAL GOVERNMENT

Local units of government receive their revenue from two basic sources—local and external. Over the years a gradual shift in emphasis has taken place. With the movement of population from the central city and the continuing blight of the city, the old and well-established source of revenue, the property tax, has decreased in relative importance, thus growth in funding from the state and federal government has assumed greater significance.

Having no one best means to finance local services, legislators at all levels of government are constantly exploring new approaches for obtaining sufficient revenues to finance local services.

Trends in Financing Local Government Services

Careful analysis of the sources of revenues and the shift in relative importance of these sources points to several significant trends in funding local government. These are briefly presented as follows:

- *Growth of Local Revenue.* The overall growth in governmental services has caused a significant growth in local governmental revenue. Local revenue has grown from 3.7 percent of GNP in 1902; 7.7 percent in 1940; 10.2 percent in 1971–1972; to 10.5 percent in 1979–1980.
- *Decrease in Local Generated Revenue.* Although the amount of locally generated revenue increased significantly over the years ($3.55 billion in 1922; $65 billion in 1972; and $101.3 billion in 1977), the percent of revenue generated from local sources decreased from 91.7 percent in 1922; 62.4 percent in 1972; to 57.2 percent in 1977.
- *Decreasing Reliance on Property Tax.* The property tax is still the major source of local government revenue; however, revenue from this source dropped from almost 75 percent of local revenues in 1922; 61.5 percent in 1942; 48.9 percent in 1957; 39.8 percent in 1971–1972; to 34.0 percent in 1977.
- *Growing Reliance on External Aid.* Local government is growing more dependent on state and federal governments for solving their fiscal concerns. In 1902 only 5 percent of local government revenue came from external sources. By 1972 the state and federal governments provided 37.6 percent of local government revenue. In 1977 external aid rose to 42.8 percent.
- *Increased Emphasis on Miscellaneous Revenues.* In an effort to ease the burden of property taxes and to catch the nonresident or commuter, local government turned to the use of nonproperty-type taxes and user charges.[7]

---

[7]For a detailed treatment of trends and sources of local government revenues see J. R. Aronson, and Eli Schwartz, *Management Policies in Local Government Finance,* International City Management Association, Washington, D.C., 1981, pp. 44–65, 123–210.

Property Tax

The property tax is still the primary source of local government revenue. Although declining percentage wise as a source of local revenue, money from this source still accounts for over one third of the revenue collected by local governments.

The premise behind property taxes is to tax the wealth of a local jurisdiction, which is in the form of real property—land and improvements.

Determining Property Tax Rates. In determining property taxes, local officials use the following formula and steps.

> Property tax requirements ÷ net assessed valuation = tax rate.

Step 1. The first step involves determining the assessed valuation of the jurisdiction or taxing district. The assessor first lists all properties in the jurisdiction and then estimates the current (true) market value of each piece of property—land and buildings—in the jurisdiction. For example, a home that is on the market to be sold for $60,000 would have a market value of $60,000.

The market value of the property is then translated into an assessed value by multiplying the market value by a specific assessment value, which is normally set by state law. The assessment value varies from 30 to 100 percent of the market value. In Indiana, for example, property is assessed at one third of its real value. The home valued at $60,000 would be assessed for $20,000 on the tax rolls. When all property in the taxing district has been assessed and translated into the assessed value, the total assessed valuation of the jurisdiction can be determined.

In all local jurisdictions there are a significant number of properties that are tax exempt and therefore the property owners do not pay taxes. Examples of tax-exempt properties include government property; churches and religious agencies; homestead and mortgage-exempt properties; educational, charitable, and fraternal organizations; and industries that are offered tax-free status as an incentive to locate in the community.

The total assessed valuation of all tax-exempt property is subtracted from the total assessed valuation of the taxing district, which results in the *net assessed valuation* of the district. The net assessed valuation, sometimes referred to as the "property tax base," gives the assessed valuation of the property subject to taxation.

EXAMPLE	
Total assessed valuation of district (one third assessment value computed)	$65,000,000
Tax-exempt property	5,000,000
Net assessed valuation	$60,000,000

Step 2. Before the tax rate can be figured the amount of revenue that must be obtained through property taxes (property tax [levy] requirements) must be calculated. The legislative body must first approve the expenditures for the governmental unit for the fiscal year. From this total all other sources of revenue from nonproperty taxes and fees and charges must be subtracted. The balance left is that money that must be raised by the property tax.

EXAMPLE	
Expenditures—fiscal year	$1,000,000
Estimated revenues	400,000
Property tax levy	$ 600,000

Step 3. Tax rates are generally expressed in terms of mills per dollar or dollars and/or cents per $100 of assessed valuation. Using the formula mentioned and the information determined in Steps 1 and 2, the tax rate (using dollars and/or cents per $100) for the taxing district would be figured as follows.

> $600,000 ÷ $60,000,000 = $0.01 per dollar of assessed valuation
> Tax for each $100 of assessed valuation
> 100 × $0.01 = $1.00 per $100 of assessed valuation (tax rate)

Pros/Cons. Arguments have been made for and against property taxation. It is evident that property taxes are a stable, well-established form of revenue. Also, it is argued that many of the services provided by local government benefit home owners and their property. On the other hand, many home owners feel that they are carrying an unfair financial burden especially when nonresidents and commuters benefit from many of the services financed largely by local citizens. Property taxes are also considered regressive because lower income families pay a greater proportion of their income for property taxes than do those families in higher income brackets.

Special Assessments

Special assessments are often referred to as a tax or service charge that is levied against selected property for an improvement or service that benefits select owners of property. In past years new subdivisions were often developed without including many of the amenities that should have been part of the initial development of the area—curbs, gutters, sidewalks, paved streets, sewers, or park areas.

If residents in a neighborhood would like to make an improvement in their area, they can petition the local governing body to pave their street, provide sewer facilities and services, or to purchase land and develop it into a neighborhood playground. It seems only fair that the cost of such improvements or services, which benefit primarily those in the subdivision, should be financed by those living in the neighborhood and not by property owners residing in different parts of the community. On the other hand, a special assessment might be a compulsory charge against the taxpayers of the area. If, for example, local governmental officials feel that a sidewalk should be constructed for the overall welfare and safety of children in the area, the improvement would be made and charged against property owners.

In recent years new zoning regulations and subdivision controls require developers to include all amenities in their initial plans and development of the subdivision that are essential to the welfare of a neighborhood and community. This approach has lessened the need for use of special assessments to finance such property improvements.

Nonproperty Tax Revenues

In an attempt to take the burden off the property tax, cities, in particular, have attempted to diversify their sources of local revenue by tapping new nonproperty sources of revenue. These other types of taxes along with fees and charges are intended to reach nonresidents who work in the city but choose to live in the suburb or county.

Nonproperty taxes for all units of local government amounted to $17.1 billion in 1978–1979, which was up 11.5 percent over the $15.4 billion figure in 1977–1978. These figures illustrate the attempts being made by local officials to find alternate tax revenues.

Examples of nonproperty tax sources of local generated revenue follow.

Admission Taxes. These are local taxes on admissions of various types of amusement or entertainment—concerts, theaters, professional sports, night clubs, and amusement parks. Such taxes are levied most frequently in central cities in large metropolitan areas. The central city is considered the entertainment center of the area and thus draws large numbers of transients.

Gross Income Tax. This tax is on the gross receipts of all businesses and professional services. It reaches nonresidents who are engaged in a business or profession within the city.

Selected Sales Tax. This is a tax on specific commodities, that is, gasoline, tobacco, liquor, or soft drinks.

User Charges—Fees and Charges. Service charges are made for certain services on the premise that those persons who benefit from the service should pay the cost of providing the service. Charges are made for garbage collection, utilities, and for park and recreation services.

State Aid

Financial aid from the state to local government has grown dramatically during the twentieth century, especially during the past twenty-five years. According to a study conducted by the Advisory Commission on Intergovernmental Relations (ACIR), state aid to local government, measured in current dollars, rose from $52 million in 1902 to $52 billion in 1975. During the same period the proportion of total local revenue received from the state increased from 6.1 to 33.9 percent. In 1976 local units of government received about 35 percent of their revenue from the state.[8]

State governments utilize three possible approaches in providing financial assistance to local jurisdictions: (1) state assumption of financial responsibility (shared taxes); (2) state grants-in-aids; and (3) authorization of local revenue diversification, which permits local government to impose a variety of taxes, fees, and other nonproperty revenues, resulting in a more balanced use of local revenue resources. The last approach gives local government the freedom or right to expand their means of seeking revenue at the local level. Shared taxes and grants-in-aids are the two basic types of intergovernmental transfers of money from the state.

[8]*The States and Intergovernmental Aids,* Advisory Committee on Intergovernmental Relations, February 1977, p. 7.

Shared Taxes. Shared taxes are concerned with the allocation of state-collected locally shared taxes to the local jurisdiction. Locally shared taxes often include income taxes, gasoline taxes, sales taxes, tobacco taxes, motor vehicle taxes, and so forth. Money is generally returned to local government on a per capita basis.

Grants-in-Aids. Grants-in-aids or equalization grants are generally made for specific purposes and are used as a means of redistributing financial resources from the more affluent to the poorer sections of the state. The grant is based on "need" and often a complicated formula is used to determine the amount of funds that are given to local units of government.

State aid to public education has always dominated state funding. The ACIR study revealed that education received 59.9 percent of the states funding of local government in 1975. Counties and cities are next in line receiving 26.3 and 23.4 percent, respectively.[9]

Pass-Through Funds. Formerly, financial assistance to local government from the state, regardless of source, was considered state aid. In studying the impact of state aids on local government, we should consider two important aspects of state aid: (1) those grants originating from and paid by the state government and (2) pass-through grants from the federal government that are given to the state for further distribution to local government.

With the ever increasing role of the federal government in providing assistance to state and local governments, and the inevitable controls and regulations that often result, the need for analyzing the "pass-through" component of state aid was certainly evident. In an effort to obtain information on this problem, the ACIR commissioned the Maxwell School of Citizenship and Public Affairs, Syracuse University, to study the pass-through issue.[10]

The study probed data from state budgets for 1967 and 1972, gathering information on each state payment to local government in an attempt to isolate the federal involvement in each grant. Data were also gathered from U.S. Bureau of Census reports and unpublished documents prepared by the U.S. Department of Health, Education, and Welfare.

The study revealed that the estimated pass-through of federal aid by states totaled $3.6 billion in 1967. In 1972 the amount almost doubled ($7.1 billion), which accounts for 22.6 percent of the fed-

eral aid to states and local government. The pass-through monies were concerned primarily with two functions, welfare and education.

In 1974 a further study was made by the ACIR and the National Association of State Budget Officers (NASBO), which involved gathering data from budget officers from each state. Questionnaires were received from 22 state budget officers. It was found that these states received $14.1 billion in federal grants in 1974. Fifty-nine percent ($8.3 billion) of the money was retained by the state government and 41 percent ($5.8 billion) was passed on to local government.[11]

Results of the ACIR and NASBO studies revealed two additional findings that are worthy of mention.

1. States did not appear to influence local policies and practices. Eighty-three percent of the funds were passed through according to federal requirements.
2. States more frequently attached procedural requirements (accounting, reporting, and auditing) rather than performance requirements to pass-through funds.

ACIR concluded that "it appears that Federal influence on local governments is understated and state influence is overemphasized—in both quantitative and qualitative terms."[12]

Federal Aid

It was not until the early 1930s that local government received direct financial aid from the federal government. Before then federal grants went only to the states. The Depression of the 1930s created an economic crisis that found state and local governments unable to meet welfare and relief needs. The federal government responded with public assistance-type grants. World War II put people back to work in the armed forces and in industry geared to an all-out war production. The emergency grants of the 1930s changed to grants for public works and services.

In the 1960s the crisis of the cities took place and the federal government, once again, stepped in to provide help. Federal grants to local government expanded from $4.8 billion in 1957–1958 to $23.6 billion in 1969–1970.[13] During this period, project or categorical grants were introduced and expanded greatly, from 107 grants in 1962 to over 500 in 1971.[14]

With increased financial aids from the federal gov-

[9]Ibid, p. 11.
[10]Ibid, p. 14.
[11]Ibid, p. 21.
[12]Ibid, p. 23.
[13]Aronson and Schwartz, *Management Policies in Local Government Finance*, p. 204.
[14]Ibid, p. 214.

ernment, coupled with expanded state and local revenues, the growth and complexity of local–federal programs took place. The poverty programs of the Johnson era dominated local government operations during the 1960s. In an effort to alter the growth of the project grants, President Nixon presented to Congress a general revenue sharing program that finally resulted in the passage of the State and Local Government Fiscal Assistance Act of 1972. The primary purpose of General Revenue Sharing (GRS) was to give communities more freedom in spending federal assistance monies. This was a complete change from the categorical grants of the 1960s that subjected local authorities to numerous federal regulations and guidelines, red tape, and required spending for specific purposes, which often did not meet local needs and problems.

It has been estimated that slightly over $50 billion of GRS funds has been returned to state and local governments by September 1980. Local officials strongly backed the renewal of the program in 1976 and many feel that these funds have been critical to the financial survival of local government as public officials were faced with taxpayer's revolts, inflation, and tax reform movements of the late 1970s. The support of the federal government to local units of government has been assuming greater proportions each year, as shown in Table 2.1. Prior to the enactment of general revenue sharing, the federal government provided 13.9 percent of the intergovernmental revenues to local government compared to 86.1 percent from the state. In 1978–1979, the federal government's share rose to 31.0 percent.

One of the major intergovernmental relations issues of the 96th Congress was reauthorization of the general revenue sharing program. Shortly before adjournment of its two-year session, Congress voted to renew the GRS program at a $4.6 billion level over three years. State governments will not be eligible to receive GRS funds during the first year

(FY1981), however, they will be eligible to apply for $2.3 billion authorized for FYs 1982 and 1983.

Summary

The growth of urban America in the twentieth century has created numerous problems that have threatened the quality of life of citizens residing in an urban environment. Local officials are finding it increasingly difficult to obtain adequate funds to solve these human and physical problems. Citizens, concerned about local government's inability to solve these problems and in providing effective programs and services, in spite of increasing taxes, have become vocal and disgruntled, resulting in many taxpayer's revolts throughout America. Tax reform legislation, that is, Proposition 13 (California) and Proposition 2½ (Massachusetts), has greatly influenced local government's ability to finance services expected by the taxpaying public.

Chapter 2 discusses several factors that have influenced the local financial picture. These include urban growth, growth in spending, growth in public services, increase in government employees, state and federal mandating of programs, inflation, taxpayer's distrust in government, and lack of home rule.

Local governments receive their revenue from two basic sources—local and external sources. In recent years the amount of money generated from local sources has decreased, mainly because of efforts to release the burden of local property taxes. Local governments have become more dependent on state and federal government for solving their financial problems. Federal grants to cities and counties expanded from $4.8 billion in 1957–1958 to $23.6 billion in 1969–1970. The categorical grants of the poverty programs that dominated local government operations during the Johnson era were altered greatly by President Nixon with the passage of General Revenue Sharing.

The tax reduction program of the Reagan administration and the budget cuts in 1981 and 1982 have dramatically affected local units of government. Categorical grants of previous administrations were quickly replaced by block grants and reduced funding has created a loud outcry from state and local officials who are forced to provide programs and services with fewer dollars.

Selected References

Advisory Commission on Intergovernmental Relations, *Intergovernmental Perspective:* "The Taxpayer's Speak: Proposition 13 and Intergovernmental Relations," Advi-

Table 2.1 Percentage of Intergovernmental Financial Assistance to Local Government, 1971–1972 to 1978–1979

Year	State %	Federal %	Total %
1971–1972	86.1	13.9	100.0
1972–1973	77.6	22.4	100.0
1976–1977	73.6	26.4	100.0
1978–1979	69.0	31.0	100.0

Source: U.S. Department of Commerce, Bureau of the Census, *Taxes and Intergovernmental Revenue, Counties, Municipalities, and Townships,* 1978–1979.

sory Committee on Intergovernmental Relations, Washington, D.C., Vol. 4, No. 3, Summer 1978.
State Limitations on Local Taxes and Expenditures, ACIR, Washington, D.C., February 1977.
The States and Intergovernmental Aids, ACIR, Washington, D.C., February 1977.
Aronson, J. Richard, and Eli Schwartz, *Management Poli-*

cies in Local Government Finance, International City Management Association, Washington, D.C., 1981, pp. 25–65, 123–210.
Moak, Lennox, and Albert M. Hillhouse, *Concepts and Practices in Local Government Finance,* Municipal Finance Officers Association, Chicago, 1975, pp. 119–166, 201–206.

Chapter 3

Financing Public Parks and Recreation

Problems facing local authorities in financing urban programs and services were discussed in Chapter 2. In spite of increased taxes and expansion of governmental bureaucracy, the quality of life and urban environment have deteriorated and citizens have become vocal and disgruntled about government's inability to solve these problems. Taxpayers' support in the passage of tax reform legislation in a majority of states has crippled local authorities' ability to finance services expected by the taxpaying public. In this climate the park and recreation professionals and their boards must compete for the declining tax dollar. They must be able to draw on the proper mixture of professionalism, good management strategies, and political savvy.

NEED FOR PROVIDING PARKS AND RECREATION

Provision of leisure services is undertaken by voluntary, private, and commercial agencies, as well as is the responsibility of local government. Each organization has its own unique combination to make in the leisure service field. It is essential that all agencies work closely together in providing these services so that more people might benefit, more extensive programs could be offered, and overlap and competition among agencies could be eliminated.

Generally, one of the basic responsibilities of local government is the provision of park and recreation services. Recreation does contribute to the overall health, self-respect, and well-being of individuals. Attractive, well-maintained parks and scenic areas and varied and abundant recreation opportunities add to the quality of life of urban-oriented Americans, as well as the quality of environment in which they live. Public parks and recreation assure that leisure services are made available to all citizens and in all places in urban areas. Unless local government agencies provide these facilities and services, many people will be deprived of such opportunities. An analysis of the growth and development of public parks and recreation during the past three quarters of a century would indicate that leisure services has been accepted as one of the basic or common functions of local government.

PEOPLE WANT RECREATION AND ARE WILLING TO PAY

In an era of inflation, increased unemployment, and other economic uncertainties, agencies providing leisure services have been hard pressed to meet the public's demands for more leisure service with shrinking budgets and rapidly escalating costs. However, the American public needs and wants recreation and is willing to pay for it.

Providers of leisure services find themselves in an era where the leisure industry is booming. Americans' attitude toward recreation was highlighted in an article in *U.S. News and World Report,* entitled "Americans Play, Even with Economy in Spin." The article stressed that:

Recession or not, Americans are reluctant to cut back on their fun—and on the spending they put into it.

Consumers who are pinching pennies on essential items are shelling out hard-earned cash for such amusements as sporting events, vacations, computer games, and roller skating.

It is estimated that 218 billion dollars will be spent on recreation this year, nearly four times the amount spent 15 years ago.[1]

As mentioned in Chapter 1, the amount spent on leisure activities in 1981 rose to 244 billion.

Generally, the provision of governmental services is determined by the expressed needs of people and their willingness to pay. The *National Urban Recreation Study* conducted by the U.S. Department of Interior in 1978 reported that, "People in all urban areas want a well-balanced system of urban recreation opportunities which includes close-to-home neighborhood facilities and programs for all segments of the population."[2] The study further indicated that "local financial resources are not meeting recreation needs."[3]

Although over the years the need for recreation has been accepted by most local governments, the crises confronting urban America are accelerating and local governments are failing to meet these many challenges and problems. It is apparent that park and recreation administrators and their boards must carefully study their communities' fiscal problems and look for both new ways for providing leisure services and new sources of financing their programs.

SOURCES OF REVENUE FOR PUBLIC PARKS AND RECREATION

State constitutions, statutes, and local ordinances allow local park and recreation agencies to receive their revenues from a number of different sources, such as:

- Appropriation from the general fund.
- Special tax levy.
- Special assessment tax.
- Fees and charges.
- Grants from state and federal agencies.
- Other sources of revenue (alternative funding).
- Bonds.

Appropriation from General Fund

One of the most frequently used methods of obtaining money for the agency's annual operating budget is to receive an appropriation from the general fund

of the overall governmental unit. Each fiscal year the agency submits its budget request to the legislative body (city council, county council, or school board) for approval. The agency must compete with other functions of government that also receive their financing from the general fund. The general fund, by far the most common of all funds, incorporates all functions of government that are not financed by a special revenue tax into one fund. A general fund might include functions such as the mayor's office, legal services, police, fire, safety, public works, and parks and recreation. Thus the money needed to finance these functions is determined and a general fund tax is levied on the taxable property of the taxing district.

From the viewpoint of the chief administrative officer and the legislative body the allocation of the financial resources of the local government to various departments or agencies can best be made by collecting money from one tax and then distributing these monies to functions based on the priorities established and community needs.

Special Tax Levy

Some states allow communities and special districts to levy a special tax for park and recreation purposes. Money received from this source is earmarked for parks and recreation and must be spent for this purpose. There are several arguments in favor of this source of financing. Once the special tax has been established, it does provide a dependable source of funding the program. Also, parks and recreation does not compete with other functions in the general fund that may be given higher priority by the legislative body.

On the other hand, once a tax rate is set it often becomes a ceiling. The only way increased funding of the program can be achieved is by increasing assessed valuation of the taxing district, increasing use of nonproperty tax revenues, or raising the tax rate established for parks and recreation. Some states require a vote of the people to increase a tax rate, whereas in others the rate may be raised merely by the approval of the board or the legislative body. In Indiana the Park and Recreation Law gives the common council or the county council the power to approve a specific levy for park and recreation purposes. No limit is set and the approving body has the power to raise or lower the levy.

The Illinois Park District Law permits park districts to levy a tax but limits the amount not to exceed $0.20 per $100 of assessed valuation of the district. In 1980 the Champaign Park District

[1]"Americans Play, Even with Economy in Spin," *U.S. News and World Report,* September 8, 1980, p.52.
[2]U.S. Department of Interior, *National Urban Recreation Study, Executive Report,* U.S. Department of Interior, Washington, D.C., 1978, p. 10.
[3]Ibid, p. 93.

reached its taxing limit and because of inflation and increased demands for more programs and services had to increase its taxing capacity if it were to continue offering quality programs to its citizens. An extensive campaign was initiated to interpret the need for additional financing. A referendum was conducted to increase the tax levy $0.02 per year for the next five years. This meant an increase of $0.10 per $100 of assessed valuation for the district. The referendum was approved by a vote of 1247 to 558 of the citizens of the district.

Special Assessment Taxes

Special assessment taxes, as previously mentioned, provide a means of financing improvements and services that will usually benefit property owners in a particular neighborhood or subdivision. Although special assessments are most often used to finance streets, curbs, sidewalks, sewers, and other such improvements, landowners can use this method of financing park and recreation areas and facilities.

If taxpayers in an area are interested in adding or improving their park and recreation amenities, they would need to seek approval of other taxpayers in the area, however. A petition would be initiated and signatures of a majority of landowners would be secured. The park and recreation agency in the community would be approached and a request made for adding the new or improved programs or services. If the agency and appropriate legislative body approve the request, the cost of the improvement would be financed by adding an increased charge to the property taxes of those benefiting from the program or facility.

Special assessments can be used to finance much needed park and recreation amenities; however, the more well-to-do neighborhoods often are in a better position to gain from this approach. Taxpayers in medium- to high-income areas have the ability to improve their living conditions and amenities, whereas those located in low-income districts often do not have the fiscal resources to better their environment.

By far the best method of financing park and recreation developments is to require developers to include these areas and facilities in their plans and developments. Zoning and subdivision ordinances, for example, should require that these amenities be included in a developer's plans.

Fees and Charges

Leisure service agencies must carefully study their philosophies and beliefs, as well as their past and current practices regarding charging user fees for programs and services. Agencies faced with tighter budgets, rapidly escalating costs, as well as increased demands for more leisure services, must look for new ways of raising revenues. The expanded use of user fees, or offering more programs on a pay-as-you-go basis, is becoming more and more attractive to local officials.

In the early history of the park and recreation movement, public recreation was promoted as a governmental function, one that was basic to the health and well-being of the general public. The provision of park land, facilities, and recreation programs was considered essential to meet the needs of all people. It was generally agreed that all citizens were to assume the financial responsibility for the overall public recreation program, much the same as for public health, welfare, and education. At that time public recreation was given the reponsibility for meeting the needs of the poor and disadvantaged. Recreation was for kids—to keep them off the streets and out of trouble. Recreation was free. The Depression years of the 1930s reinforced these beliefs as well as prolonged them.

As public demands for more parks, swimming pools, golf courses, community centers, camps, and other leisure services grew, the provision of programs for all persons also expanded and the funding of these programs became more difficult. Gradually, agencies initiated fees and charges for certain services and facilities, and for many years there has been general acceptance by the public for paying fees and charges for facilities such as swimming pools, golf course, and zoos and for recreation activities.

There is general agreement among leisure service professionals that the fundamental or basic park and recreation services should be free to the public. Fees should be charged for activities that require skilled or costly leadership, require extensive or special facilities, have limited use, or have high upkeep or operational cost.

For decades public officials and the general public have argued both for and against the use of fees and charges. In the 1980s it appears that the fiscal crisis that emerged in the late 1970s has mandated that local agencies become more self-sufficient.

Proposition 13 in California (1978) created a widespread expansion of new or increased fees and charges to be paid by the general public as well as slowed the growth of spending in cities and counties in that state. A *Los Angeles Times* study of 417 cities and 58 counties in 1978 found that cities recovered almost 30 percent of the total revenue lost as a result of Proposition 13 by establishing or increasing fees and charges.[4] Building and inspection fees, business licenses, and recreation and parks user fees topped the list of new or increased charges levied by cities. The impact of Proposition 13 also had a sizable impact on other municipalities throughout the country.

In the summer of 1979, a nationwide survey was developed by researchers of the Leisure Research Institute, Indiana University, and sent to 250 selected park and recreation administrators to find out how their agencies should respond to a reduction in financial support. Efforts to seek alternative sources of funding and the increased use of fees and charges drew the largest amount of support, with 93 and 91 percent of the administrators favoring these two strategies. When asked to choose one strategy that would be the most effective strategy yet render quality service, the increased use of fees and charges received the top rating.

Martin and Jamieson conducted another PROPS study in the fall of 1979 in an effort to gather additional data concerning the status of user fees for municipal recreation services. The findings of the study indicated that 82 percent of the cities reported increases in user fees in 1979 compared to the previous year. Sixteen percent of the respondents reported considerable increases. A majority of the administrators (57.6 percent) indicated an increase in the number of programs financed by user fees in 1979 as compared to 1978. It was further found that 22 percent of the revenues raised for local budgets were derived from user fees.[5]

In an effort to assist municipal agencies to examine some of their traditional practices and attitudes toward fees and charges, the Heritage Conservation and Recreation Service (HCRS) contracted the Economics Research Associates to study the issues and problems relating to this source of revenue and to develop guides for conducting a feasibility analysis of proposed changes in user fees. A *Fees and Charges Handbook* was prepared to help public agencies become more self-sufficient in providing leisure services.

The handbook revealed two current trends in public sentiment regarding fees and charges.

1. The public is no longer willing to provide public agencies with unlimited tax dollars—this is an era of limits.
2. There is a growing feeling that activities should be supported by those who participate, rather than by the public at large.[6]

The Economics Research Associates, in a study conducted in 1975 of 800 households, concluded that "people are willing to pay for a number of public services—including recreation."[7] It appears that user fees are becoming generally accepted and the old concept that fees represent double taxation is gradually disappearing.

State and Federal Aid

With the local financial resources not keeping pace with the increased demands and rising cost of providing leisure services, local government during the 1960s and 1970s turned to state and federal government for assistance. State governments were slow to respond and it has been found that few states use their own financial resources for local park and recreation programs. Those funds that are directed to local agencies are primarily funds in the form of pass-through grants from the federal government. For example, the Land and Water Conservation Fund Act, passed in 1965, has been one of the principal sources of federal funds that have filtered through the states to local governmental jurisdictions.

The federal government has been the major source of nonlocal revenues used by local government for parks and recreation. The National Urban Recreation Study revealed that $1.2 billion or 35.4 percent of all revenues used by local government for leisure services during the fiscal year 1976 (FY76) came from federal assistance programs. The major programs that provide funds for local park and recreation programs are listed in Figure 3.1.

Three of the federal programs (Land and Water Conservation Fund (LWCF), National Youth Sports Program, and Summer Youth Recreation Program) are committed to provide funds for parks and recreation purposes only. Since 1965 the Land and Water Conservation Fund has been recognized as the major program funding local and state parks and recreation programs. In 1978 the passage of the Urban Park and Recreation Recovery Act added a new program to the already well-established programs. With the budget reductions initiated by the Reagan administration and the "new federalism" program, drastic funding reductions and in some cases complete elimination of programs have resulted. Because the contributions of these programs to local

[4]*Los Angeles Times,* October 1, 1978, Part 1, p. 1.
[5]"Survey Finds Fee Increases Less Drastic Than Expected," *Parks and Recreation,* Vol. 16, p. 8, April 1981.

[6]*Fees and Charges Handbook,* Heritage Conservation and Recreation Service, U.S. Department of Interior, Washington, D.C., March 1979, p. 7.
[7]Ibid, p. 7.

Federal Funds Used for Parks and Recreation by Local Jurisdictions
($ In Millions—Fiscal Year 76)

Federal Program	Total Program Appropriations	Percent of Total Program Dollars Used for Parks and Recreation	Parks and Recreation Use			
			Capital Improvements	Facility Maintenance	Recreation and Cultural Programs	Total Recreation
Land and Water Conservation Fund (FY76) (HCRS)	$127.0	100	$127.0 for land acquisition and facility development	None	None	$127.0
Community Development Block Grant (FY76) (to entitlement cities and urban counties) (HUD)	$1,579.0	8	125.6 for land acquisition and facility development	None	$6.5	132.1
General Revenue Sharing (entitlement period 6 7/1/75–6/30/76) (Treasury)	4,639.8	7	193.8	$122.9 for maintenance and programs		316.7
Comprehensive Employment and Training Act (FY76) (DOL) Titles II & VI (PSE)	3,300.0	12 estimated	None	400 estimated for maintenance and programs		400 estimated
Title III (SPEDY)	595.0	14 estimated	None	200 estimated for maintenance and programs		200 estimated
National Youth Sports Program (FY76) (CSA)	6.0	100	None	None	6.0	6.0
Summer Youth Recreation Program (FY76) (CSA)	17.0	100	None	None	17.0	17.0
Total	$10,263.8		$446.4	$764.4		$1,198.8

Estimated Total Park and Recreation Expenditures by Cities and Counties in Fiscal Year 76—$3379.0 million

Figure 3.1 Federal funding for parks and recreation to local jurisdictions, 1976. *National Urban Recreation Study.* U.S. Department of the Interior.

park and recreation agencies have been significant, a brief description and current status at the time of this writing follows.

Land and Water Conservation Fund (LWCF)

In 1958 the Outdoor Recreation Resources Review Commission (ORRRC) was created and charged with the responsibility of making a comprehensive study of the nation's outdoor recreation needs. The commission submitted its report to the president and Congress in January 1962. One of the major outcomes of the ORRRC report was the expanded role of the federal government in the financing of outdoor recreation at the state and local levels of government. .

The Land and Water Conservation Fund Act passed by Congress in 1965 established a federal fund for the purpose of financing the unmet outdoor recreation needs of the American public. Two main purposes of the fund were to: (1) provide funds to existing federal land managing agencies (National Park Service, U.S. Forest Service, U.S. Fish and Wildlife Service, and the Bureau of Land Management) for the acquisition of additional lands for their systems and (2) forward grant-in-aid funds to the states, and then through them (pass-through grants) to local units of government.

Approximately 40 percent of the total LWCF yearly appropriation was allocated to the federal agencies mentioned, whereas the remaining 60 percent was distributed to the states. The states, in turn, were given the authority both to determine the amounts that were distributed to local governments and the priority order of project funding.

Federal guidelines provided that the federal monies distributed to the states and local governments must be on a 50/50 match basis. Also, the money received must be spent for only land acquisition and facility development purposes. Since the passage of the LWCF in 1965, and through the FY79, over $2.53 billion of matching funds has been appropriated to the states and local governments. As this amount has been matched by state and local monies, a total of over $4.4 billion of outdoor recreation funding has been provided to state and local governments. In FY79 the LWCF assistance to the states totaled $385.6 million.

The U.S. Department of Interior reported that through the fiscal year 1979 over 25,000 acquisition, development, combination, and planning projects have been approved and funded by this program. Approximately 1.93 million acres of new land have been acquired. Fifty-nine percent of LWCF's monies have gone to "close-to-home" locally sponsored park and recreation projects.

Prior to initiation of the Land and Water Conservation Fund, only four states had comprehensive outdoor recreation plans. In order for states to receive LWCF grants, each state was required to have a statewide comprehensive outdoor recreation plan. Through FY79, states have received $24.5 million from the federal government to maintain and update their state plans. Today all states have plans that serve as guides for allocating recreation resources in the state.[8]

Most park and recreation authorities agree that the LWCF has made a substantial impact on outdoor recreation space and facility needs; however, the National Urban Recreation Study did uncover a number of problems that still existed. One of the main concerns expressed by the study was that the LWCF has "done little to eliminate recreation facility deficiencies in the nation's cities."[9] The greatest recreation deficiencies for land and facilities exists in the nation's largest cities. Most of these cities are financially hard pressed and unable to afford the 50 percent match for receiving LWCF money.

In conducting the National Urban Recreation Study, the Heritage Conservation and Recreation Service and National Park Service study team consulted with state and local officials in a sample of the nation's most highly populated urban areas. Several recommendations were offered by local officials, which would make the LWCF more effective in solving local park and recreation problems and deficiencies. These recommendations have been deleted from this text because of the actions of the Reagan administration and Congress. In FY81 the amount appropriated to the states was reduced to $228.75 million, and in FY82 a complete withdrawal of federal funding to state and local agencies resulted. Funding of federal agencies in 1982 was increased to $155.4 million.

General Revenue Sharing (GRS)

The General Revenue Sharing financial assistance program was originally established by the passage of the State and Local Assistance Act of 1972 (PL92-512), which authorized the distribution of $30.2 billion to state and local government over a five-year period. In 1976 an amendment of the act (PL94-488) renewed the program for an additional

[8]*Land and Water Conservation Fund, Annual Report,* U.S. Department of Interior, Washington, D.C., 1979.
[9]*National Urban Recreation Study,* Executive Report, p. 45.

three and three quarter years with an authorization of an additional $25.5 billion.

General revenue sharing funds were viewed as a welcome change by local officials from the categorical grant approach of the 1960s. Many local officials were troubled with the red tape and restrictions that accompanied categorical grants. Also, these grants proved to be ineffective in solving problems confronting communities. On the other hand, revenue sharing was based on the allocation of basically unrestricted money from the federal government to local and state government. Total allocation of GRS funds is divided with one third going to state government and two thirds to local units of government. Funds are available for both capital improvements and operation and maintenance of local programs. However, GRS funds cannot be used to match existing federal programs.

In the original act (1972) communities were given considerable freedom in spending GRS funds. Expenditures were to be kept within the bounds of nine priority categories: public safety, environmental protection, public transportation, health, recreation, libraries, social services, financial administration, and capital expenditures authorized by law. The 1976 renewal act contained two significant changes that were responsible for removing some of the restrictions of the earlier act.

1. Local communities were allowed to use revenue sharing funds to match other federal assistance programs.
2. Local governments were given the freedom to spend funds for any purposes that are legal under existing state and local laws.

Local autonomy and local initiative in the use of GRS funds were the primary goals of the revenue sharing program. Caputo and Cole, in their study of the impact of GRS on American cities, found that GRS has widespread support of local officials. In fact, many local authorities maintain "that GRS funds have been critical for the fiscal survival of their localities."[10]

Caputo and Cole were interested in knowing how recipient units of government spent their revenue sharing monies. Their study revealed that during the four entitlement periods spanning 1973–1976, in cities over 50,000, recreation received between 4.2 and 10.9 percent of revenue sharing funds. In 1976 only law enforcement, fire, and environmental protection received more general revenue sharing funds. Their study also found that suburban areas spent

more of their revenue sharing funds on recreation than central cities did.[11]

In 1975–1976 local jurisdictions (cities, counties, townships, and villages) allocated $316.7 million of their GRS money for recreation purposes, which represented 7 percent of all GRS funds (see Figure 3.1). Cities alone spent $185,424 million on recreation. Because local government is given a virtual "no strings" requirement as to how GRS funds may be spent, it is interesting to note that $193.8 million or 4 percent of the money was allocated to capital improvements, with $122.9 million or 3 percent for maintenance and program purposes.

Although some cities have not given adequate priority to allocate revenue sharing funds for park and recreation functions, the trend for using these funds for operation and maintenance functions has made GRS a vital resource in meeting the critical needs of local recreation programs and park services.

The Comprehensive Employment and Training Act (CETA)

In 1973 Congress passed the Comprehensive Employment and Training Act (CETA). Public Law 93-203 eliminated several manpower and antipoverty programs and substituted an employment and training program operated at the local level by prime sponsors. Thus federal funds or grants were made to prime sponsors (state and local governmental units designated by the U.S. Department of Labor), who were empowered to conduct CETA programs themselves or contract or subcontract with other local government units, semipublic, or private agencies to carry out the program. Persons who qualified for CETA employment were assigned to local and state agencies to perform public service jobs.

Prime sponsors determined who could obtain federal funds and who were responsible for monitoring and evaluating the effectiveness of local agencies in carrying out the objectives of the program. The primary purpose of CETA was to hire economically disadvantaged and unemployed persons for public service jobs in communities of high unemployment. Other purposes of CETA were the training of youth and adults whose skills were inadequate or obsolete and the provision of personnel services such as job search, counseling, and job placement.

Like many other federal assistance programs, the CETA program came under heavy attack with charges of corruption, misuse of funds, and waste of funds. Local agencies expressed concern about the

[10]David A. Caputo and Richard L. Cole, "General Revenue Sharing: Its Impact on American Cities," *Governmental Finance*, November 1977, p. 25.

[11]Ibid, p. 25.

lack of funding continuity, delays in funding approval, and cumbersome and costly administrative procedures that tended to hamper the effectiveness of the program. Despite these problems, CETA made an impact on local governmental units.

Of all federal assistance programs, CETA made the greatest impact on local park and recreation programs. With over 75 percent of local park and recreation budgets designated for salaries and wages, CETA funds played an important role in financing program and maintenance costs. In 1976 approximately 50 percent of all federal dollars designed for local recreation programs came from CETA funds.

In most park and recreation agencies, especially in large cities, it is estimated that approximately one third of their staff was funded by CETA programs. Since most CETA workers were unskilled and lacked training for higher level jobs, it is understandable that 80 percent of CETA employees filled unskilled maintenance and clerical positions. Only 20 percent were placed in professional positions.

In gathering data for the National Urban Recreation Study, the Heritage Conservation and Recreation Service (HCRS) commissioned Kirchner Associates to study the impact of the CETA program on parks and recreation in 17 urban areas. In the report published in 1977 some of the major problems experienced by local recreation agencies with the CETA program were as follows:

CETA employees lack training and are not qualified for positions. They require more training than new non-CETA employees.

CETA employees need greater supervision on the job than do non-CETA employees.

There is a lack of CETA funds available for training and/or supervision of CETA employees.

There are no CETA funds for materials or equipment.

The unpredictability and lack of continuity of CETA funds makes planning and organizing programs difficult.

CETA employees cannot work during the evening and/or weekends, when recreation facilities experience the greatest use.

CETA employees have high absenteeism, low morale, and bad attitude. They are less productive than regular employees.[12]

In spite of the problems identified, the Kirchner Associates study reported a "significant and growing reliance on CETA to fund park and recreation per-

sonnel." Local recreation agencies requested and received a good number of their staff from CETA programs. The greatest use of CETA employees was found in large, fiscally troubled cities.

With the fiscal crisis facing urban parks and recreation, the use of CETA funds allowed many park and recreation agencies to maintain recreation services that otherwise might have been cut. Since CETA employees were responsible for maintaining existing program and service functions, it was generally recognized that agency operations would be severely reduced if CETA funds were to be discontinued or cut back. Also, maintenance of areas and facilities, especially in large cities, would be greatly affected.

In a study conducted by Beeler in 1980 of the effects of CETA on park and recreation agencies in the Great Lakes Region, it was found that park and recreation departments employed CETA staff in unskilled positions (95.9 percent), assigned them primarily to park related services (77.1 percent), and delegated them to maintenance of existing departmental programs and services (85.0 percent).[13]

The CETA program was one of the first programs to be severely reduced as a result of the Reagan administration and the budget cuts approved by Congress for 1982. As many local parks and recreation departments relied heavily upon CETA funds for operating basic services, the reduction of this source of federal funds will have a major impact on local programs and services.

Community Development Block Grant Program (CDBG)

In an effort to allow cities and counties to establish their own priorities for tackling urban problems, Congress, in 1974, approved the Community Development Block Grant program. The Community Development Block Grant (CDBG) consolidated seven categorical grants, which included HUD's Open Space program, a program that encouraged open space acquisition in urban areas.

The law provided funding of $8.3 billion to be distributed by HUD to communities over a three-year period, ending in the fiscal year 1977. Recent legislation provided an additional $10.95 billion for another three-year period. Local units of government entitled to CDBG funds include central cities of metropolitan areas, suburban cities of 50,000 or

[12]L. Bell, *CETA and Urban Park and Recreation, National Urban Recreation Study,* Technical Report No. 8, Washington, D.C., 1977, pp. 194–196.

[13]Cheryl S. Beeler, *Effects of Three Comprehensive Employment and Training Act Programs on Selected Functions of Municipal Parks and/or Recreation Departments,* unpublished doctoral thesis, Indiana University, 1980.

more, and urban counties with population of at least 200,000. In addition, smaller cities are eligible for discretionary grants.

The primary intent of the CDBG program is to assist local government in dealing with the problems of urban blight and in providing programs that benefit low and moderate income groups. Studies made of the CDBG program indicate that the larger, economically depressed urban areas have tended to give a low priority to park and recreation programs and services. The National Urban Recreation Study revealed that in 1976 $1579 million were distributed to entitlement cities and counties. Eight percent or $132.1 million were spent on parks and recreation. Although CDBG funds can be used for recreation programs as well as for acquisition, construction, and rehabilitation of recreation facilities, over 95 percent ($125.6 million) of CDBG funds spent on recreation during 1976 was used for land acquisition and facility development. The remaining 5 percent ($6.5 million) was allocated to recreation and cultural programs (see Figure 3.1).

In a special study made by the Brookings Institution on *Community Development Block Grants and Urban Recreation,* several major findings on the impact of CDBG on local parks and recreation are highlighted in the *National Urban Recreation Study.* In the study of 61 cities, it was found that:

Seventy-nine percent of the jurisdictions spent a portion of their CDBG funds on recreation.

A higher percentage of the core cities allocated a share of their CDBG funds to parks and recreation (28 out of 30) than did satellite cities (8 out of 12) or urban counties (7 out of 11).

Although localities are spending more for parks and recreation under the CDBG program than they did under the previous categorical grant Open Space Program, they are spending proportionately less to preserve open space.

One-fifth of the jurisdictions used CDBG funds as a match for other Federal recreation funds, primarily from the Land and Water Conservation Fund.[14]

One of the major limitations of the CDBG program has been that these funds cannot be used for maintenance of park and recreation facilities and grounds. If the CDBG program is to meet local park and recreation needs and problems, the constraints on using such funds for operation and maintenance should be removed.

[14]U.S. Department of Interior, *National Urban Recreation Study, Executive Report,* pp. 100, 102.

Urban Park and Recreation Recovery Program (UPRRP)

In 1978 the 95th Congress passed the Urban Park and Recreation Recovery Act in recognition of the severe deficiencies that were found to exist in urban recreation in the United States. The Heritage Conservation and Recreation Service was given the responsibility of directing a five-year program that sought to rehabilitate recreation and park facilities that had fallen into disuse or disrepair. The program was intended to complement other existing federal programs and seek to encourage innovations in recreation programming, as well as to stimulate and support local commitments to recreation system recovery and maintenance.

Congress authorized $150 million a year for the first four years of the program and $125 million for the fifth year. Three types of matching grants were available for urban recreation system recovery.

Rehabilitation grants were matching capital grants (70 percent federal—30 percent local) to local governments that must be used for rebuilding, remodeling, expanding, or developing existing outdoor or indoor recreation areas and facilities.

Innovation grants were matching grants (70 percent federal—30 percent local) to local governments that were to be used to cover the cost of personnel, facilities, equipment, supplies, or services designed to demonstrate innovative and cost-effective ways to enhance park and recreation opportunities at the neighborhood level. These funds were not to be utilized for routine operation and maintenance activities.

Recovery action programs grants were a 50/50 matching grant that could be used for resource and needs assessment, coordination, citizen involvement, and planning and program development activities to encourage public definition of goals.

Matching grants were to be used to acquire land for the local recreation system. Eligibility for receiving assistance of UPRRP funds was based on need, economic and physical distress, and the relative quality and condition of the urban park and recreation system. UPRRP, like CETA, has felt the impact of Congress and the Reagan administration's budget reduction. Congress reduced the funding of UPRRP to $20 million in FY81, $7.6 million in 1982, and has recommended no funding to the program for 1983.

Other Sources of Revenues

The primary sources of financing programs and facilities already discussed in this chapter provide most of the funds for operating park and recreation programs. However, most agencies have been successful in supplementing these traditional approaches by generating other sources of revenue. In times of financial stress and limits, local authorities must look for additional sources of funding, invoke the most cost-effective management procedures, and look for new ways to provide leisure services to the public.

Local authorities are often so accustomed to the traditional approaches of financing their programs that they are sometimes hesitant in searching for new sources of revenue or in changing current operating procedures. It is quite easy to argue that alternative funding is either not politically feasible, takes too much time and effort, or may be too hard to collect or that the public will not buy other methods of finance since they are overtaxed already.

There appears to be no simple solution to the problem. No single best source of funds is best for every community. Administrators should not wait to be forced to find new funding. It seems imperative that they should take the initiative in discovering new sources of funding if local agencies are to continue to provide services demanded by the public.

In California, as a result of Proposition 13, leisure service agencies were forced to turn to other sources of funding, as well as expand the use of user charges, as already mentioned. Richard Trudeau, General Manager, East Bay Regional Park District, has emerged as one of the leading spokespersons for alternative funding and special fund-raising strategies. He has traveled extensively throughout the country speaking on "successful fund-raising strategies."

Workshops, seminars, and state and national professional conferences have concentrated on the importance of generating additional funding for parks and recreation. Some of the ideas that have been successful are old and well-accepted methods of raising funds or managing a department. Others are new and not generally used by agencies throughout the country. The following management strategies have succeeded in helping local agencies to obtain additional funds for the program.

Initiate Efficient Management Policies and Procedures. Administrators and staff should carefully examine operating procedures to determine whether their agency is making the most efficient use of its staff and equipment. The internal economics that result can be either money producers or money savers. A few of many successful ideas follow.

• Establish a cash management program. One of the objectives of such a program is to increase the depart-

ment's nontax revenues by making short-term investments of idle cash.
• Consider leasing equipment rather than purchasing it.
• Use private contractors if they can do a job as good or better and at less cost.
• Lease concessions to private vendors if the service to the public is the same or better than that provided by the agency and more profit is made by this contractural agreement.

Encourage Corporate Giving. Over the years there have been numerous instances in which business and industry contributed to local park and recreation programs. Two recent examples, representative of many approaches to public–private cooperative ventures, are the "Adopt-a-Park program" and "The 5 Percent Club approach."

As a result of Proposition 13, a unique partnership between the Kaiser Aluminum and Chemical Corporation and the East Bay Regional Park District in California has resulted in Kaiser adopting the 88-acre Roberts Regional Recreation Area. As one responsibility of the "Adopt-a-Park Program" initiated by the district, Kaiser agreed to work closely with the park district, for a period of years, in maintaining the Roberts Regional Recreation Area. The commitment totals approximately $100,000 over a three-year period. According to Richard Trudeau, General Manager, East Bay Regional Park District, the idea for this new corporate cooperative venture came from The 5 Percent Club approach that was launched by the Minneapolis Chamber of Commerce in 1977. Based on an Internal Revenue Service rule that permits up to a 5 percent write-off for corporate gifts given to charitable, educational, and community services, The 5 Percent Club was formed. In 1977 30 corporate members of the club gave $16 million to local agencies in the Minneapolis–St. Paul Metropolitan Area. Park and recreation agencies were just one of many agencies that received funds from this source. Besides receiving tax write-offs for their gifts, Kaiser Aluminum and The 5 Percent Club members can take pride in their accomplishments, also getting excellent community visibility as they help to solve community problems.[15]

Seek Grant Support from Foundations/Philanthropic Associations. Foundations and other philanthropic organizations are excellent sources of financial assistance to local agencies in acquiring land, preserving natural and historical resources, or initiating innovative programs. Because foundations vary as to type and purpose, it is important

[15]"Business Asked to Adopt a Park" *Contra Corta Times*, California, February 18, 1979.

that the purpose for which the agency is seeking grant support matches the interest and purposes of the foundation.

There are several types of foundations, including general purpose, special purpose, company or corporate, family and community. Competition for receiving grants is often intense and parks and recreation must compete with causes such as education, welfare, health, sciences, humanities, and religion in receiving funding. In order to be successful in gaining foundation support, proposals must be prepared and presented in a highly professional manner.

Although the proportion of money given to parks and recreation is relatively small, the impact of foundation gifts to many local programs has been significant. For example, the widely acclaimed-Mott Foundation has had a long history of funding community education programs in the Flint Public Schools in Flint, Michigan. In recent years the foundation has given generously to the Genessee County Parks and Recreation Commission for park acquisitions and developments. In 1978 the commission received $1.2 million for the development of Crossroads Village located in the Genessee Recreation Area.

Another example of philanthrophy at its best is the James Whitcomb Riley Memorial Association, established in 1921 to perpetuate the memory of Indiana's beloved poet laureate. Through the years the association has sought gifts and bequests from individuals, philanthropic organizations, foundations, and businesses for the support of three major projects: the James Whitcomb Riley Hospital for Children at the Indiana University Medical Center, Indianapolis, one of the nation's leading pediatric centers; Riley's Lockerbie Street Home in Indianapolis, the mansion where James Whitcomb Riley once lived, which is operated as a public museum; and Camp Riley, one of the finest camps for handicapped children in the country, which is located at Bradford Woods, Indiana University's Outdoor Education and Camping Center. During the past twenty-six years the Riley Memorial Association has invested more than $3 million in the development of Camp Riley and other major facilities at Bradford Woods.

Establish a Local Parks and Recreation Foundation. A parks and recreation foundation provides a vehicle for receiving gifts and endowments from individuals and organizations that are interested in assisting an agency in purchasing land and facilities or in conducting specific programs and services. Generally, citizens, businesses, or foundations often frown on giving money to local government but are often more receptive to giving land or money to community leaders who have joined together in a foundation for the overall benefit of the community. A local foundation is a logical medium for gaining valuable financial assistance.

The Hennepin County Park Reserve District serving the greater Twin Cities Metropolitan Area, Minnesota, has benefited greatly from the Metropolitan Park Foundation, which was established in 1967. The intent of the foundation is to utilize gifts of lands, money, and other property and/or proceeds and income to carry out the basic purposes of the Hennepin County Park Reserve District.

In St. Louis, Missouri, the St. Louis Regional Open Space Foundation was established to assist the city and county in acquiring land for parks and recreation.

As one of its continuing efforts to assist communities to "stretch their limited dollars for maximum effectiveness and public benefit," The Heritage Conservation and Recreation Service has published a handbook on foundations. This publication provides excellent information on how to establish a local parks and recreation foundation.[16]

Increase Involvement of Citizens and Neighborhood Groups. Perhaps the highest form of recreation known is the involvement of citizens and community groups in the organization and promotion of their leisure activities. The effective utilization of people in the operation of an agency serves as a catalyst in gaining support for the agency's programs and services, as well as resulting in expanded program opportunities and wider participation.

The "Partnership for People" program established by the Department of Parks and Recreation, Portsmouth, Virginia, has resulted in an amazing success story. The program is built around citizens recreation and parks forums that are established in 13 neighborhoods in the city. The citizen forums have made effective use of the city's greatest resource—its citizens. These forums consist of representatives of athletic leagues, civic clubs, community groups, PTA's, churches and individuals interested in recreation. According to James Greiner, Director, Parks and Recreation Department, the following results were achieved in approximately one year.

- A 352 percent increase in the number of programs offered in the city.
- Athletic teams increased by 51 percent.

[16]*Foundations: A Handbook,* Heritage Conservation and Recreation Service, U.S. Department of Interior, Washington, D.C., 1979.

- The city recreation equipment budget was reduced by more than 80 percent.
- Seventy-one projects, totaling $100,000, were built using matching city and community funds.
- Current midyear statistics indicate that the forums will raise more than $100,000 to supplement the city recreation budget this year, with previously existing organizations such as civic leagues, athletic associations, and service clubs chipping in an additional $200,000.
- More than 1,000 citizens are involved in the forums as members, officers, and committee members.
- Approximately 235,000 volunteer hours were donated to recreation services in one year, an average of more than two hours for every person living in the city.
- Monies were made available to each of the 13 communities to upgrade existing facilities. Groups of citizens toured locations, held public hearings, and, with staff advice, selected those which most needed improvement. The money was allocated to each community according to the population of that community. More than 200 projects have been selected and initiated during the two years since the program began.[17]

Greiner concludes his *Case Report* with the following assessment of his program.

The results of these efforts is that the city cost per participant for recreation services has been cut in half over the past three years. This result is music to the ears of the tax-paying public, and it shows its appreciation by supporting the department and commission on budget requests. In 1977, citizens groups convinced the city council to reassign a quarter of a million dollars from curbs and gutters to recreation improvements.[18]

The department received the National Gold Medal for Excellence in Parks and Recreation Management from the National Recreation and Park Association in recognition for this outstanding program.

Adopt a Membership Program for the Department. Local authorities should consider the benefits of introducing a membership program for their park and recreation agency. Many leisure service agencies, public, semipublic, and private use memberships as one of their main means of financial support. Although local park and recreation agencies have used membership fees for many of their programs, that is, community centers, senior citizen clubs, hobby clubs, and so on, the establishment of a membership program for the overall agency has been utilized in relatively few cities.

Following the passage of Proposition 13, the East Bay Regional Park District established a membership program under the catchy title of "Have You Hugged a Tree Today?" Citizens were invited to become a tree-hugger or active member of the department. Membership fees varied from a student fee of $15; individual member, $25; family membership, $50; to an endowing member that pays $1000. According to Richard Trudeau, General Manager, the membership program was undertaken for two reasons. "one—as an immediate source of revenue which over the years would show constant growth, and second—as a family constituency which could be relied upon for support when we would go to the voters for a tax override."[19] The district offers a number of benefits to its members: free entry into their parks, waiver of parking fees at various recreation areas, invitations to special events and activities, and the receipt of a calendar of coming events. In addition, family members receive a waiver of camping fees and are given reservation privileges to Del Valle Regional Parks. After two years, membership in the district totaled 1157 active members, resulting in a revenue of $67,179 for that period.

Prepare a Gift Catalog for Seeking Gifts and Donations. An increasing number of agencies have found gift catalogs to be extremely valuable in stimulating gifts and donations from citizens and organizations in their communities. A gift catalog is merely an attractive brochure that lists a wide variety of needed equipment, facilities, and programs that might be sponsored by individuals and organizations in the community. For each of the items listed a price tag is attached so that a potential donor may choose from the extensive shopping list. Items vary in cost from $15 to $25 for a shrub, to $10,000 or more for a picnic shelter in a park. Gift catalogs are widely distributed throughout the community in an effort to solicit giving.

In Champaign, Illinois, the park district has reaped dividends from its attractive gift catalog. Robert Toalson, Director, reported gifts and donations of $73,165 for 1979, which were motivated largely by the gift catalog published by the district.

FINANCING CAPITAL IMPROVEMENTS (BONDS)

The need for financing large and costly capital improvements may require local officials to borrow money so that major improvements can be initiated and the loan can be paid back over a period of years. Borrowing money, normally by selling bonds, means

---

[17]James Greiner, "A 'Proposition 13' That Works for Recreation," *Parks and Recreation* Vol. 14, pp. 29–30, 57, June 1979.
[18]Ibid, p. 57.

[19]Richard Trudeau, speech on "Successful Fund Raising Strategies," National Recreation and Park Association, 1980 Congress, Phoenix, Arizona, October 21, 1980.

that the local government (borrower) incurs a debt when it obtains money to finance the needed capital improvement. This source of funding should be considered a supplement to taxation and not an actual revenue because it creates an equivalent liability that must be repaid from future taxes or revenues.

Usually, funding the acquisition of land or the construction of a major facility—swimming pool, community center, stadium, and so forth—is beyond a community's current financial resources and therefore should not be incorporated in an agency's annual operating budget. Thus an indebtedness is created by borrowing money, and the agency agrees to pay the principal and interest back to the investor at regular intervals over a period of years. The basic concept behind funding capital improvements by bonds is that by spreading the cost of the improvement over a period of years, those individuals, including future generations, who benefit from the facility will provide the funds to repay the debt.

Although smaller capital projects can be financed by current property taxes and special assessments, most capital improvements are financed by bonds. Local authorities have the power to borrow funds for large and costly improvements that have long utility and which are not of a frequently recurring type. A well-planned and interpreted capital improvement plan should be made and integrated with the agency's and local governments' comprehensive master plans, in order to be successful in gaining approval for the bond issue or to receive marketing of the bonds.

As previously mentioned, a number of federal assistance programs provide grants for capital improvements for parks and recreation. In the case of Land and Water Conservation Funds, the local agency has been responsible for providing matching funds. In order to be successful in receiving federal grants, the agency must have an approved plan for its land and facility needs. A capital improvement program that accurately reflects the total priority capital needs of the community is essential for receiving approval for bonding of capital projects, as well as for receiving federal grants.

Types of Bonds

There are two ways of classifying bonds: (1) according to the method of retirement and (2) according to sources of revenue for repaying the local government debt. The two basic types of bonds classified according to their method of retirement are term bonds and serial bonds.

Term Bonds. In the case of term bonds, the entire amount of the bond (principal) is paid at the maturity of the bond. This requires the government body to establish a sinking fund where money is deposited regularly in the fund. The funds collected in the fund are invested to obtain interest earnings. The annual payments and the interest earned should be sufficient to pay off the debt at maturity.

Sinking fund bonds have lost favor among finance experts because of many complications involved in sinking fund administration. Often city administrators or legislative bodies defer payments into the fund or use funds for other purposes. Because of this possible mismanagement of sinking funds, in a majority of states sinking fund bonds are no longer legal or are not recommended for use.

Serial Bonds. Serial bonds provide for regular payments, usually annually, of principal and interest for the life or duration of the bond issue. These types of bonds have become quite popular over the years with local units of government because they avoid the complexities of sinking fund operations. Although there are a number of variations in installment payment patterns available, local authorities most often chose one of the following: straight serials or serial annuity bonds.

Straight Serial Bonds. This type of bond requires the borrower to make equal annual payments of principal until the maturity date of the bond. As the principal is gradually reduced, the interest, which is paid on the remaining balance, gradually decreases each year. This means that the annual debt payment on the bond decreases each year. Having payments higher during the early years of the bond issue has some advantages. For example, when a golf course or swimming pool is new, normally operational and maintenance costs are lower and the drawing power of a new facility is generally high. Often as the facility grows older, the cost of maintenance rises while sometimes the drawing power of the facility lessens.

An additional argument in favor of straight serials can be made on the basis that as the principal is gradually paid off, it will lower the amount of the governmental unit's overall debt. As the overall debt decreases, the government would become eligible for additional borrowing of money for other improvement purposes.

Serial Annuity Bonds. Serial annuities provide for equal debt payments each year for the life of the bond issue. In this type of bond, principal and interest payments are figured so that the payment to the investor each year is approximately equal to those of other years.

Those favoring this type of bond issue argue that the government agency avoid a peak level of debt payments in the early years, as in the case of straight serials, which allows self-liquidating enterprises time to establish an adequate earning power of the new facility.

Serial annuities provide for a more equitable and manageable distribution of payments, which makes it easier on budget makers in planning their yearly budget. Taxpayers are familiar with these types of bonds as they are used in financing a home or paying off a loan on an automobile.

The second manner of classifying is according to sources of revenue used to repay the debt assumed by the borrowing agency. The two approaches most often used by local park and recreation agencies are general obligation bonds and revenue bonds.

General Obligation Bonds. Over the years perhaps the most widely used approach to financing capital improvements has been the use of general obligation bonds. As most projects were believed to benefit the entire community, it was felt that the payment for such developments should be financed by all persons in the community. In this manner the burden for the retirement of the local debt is spread among all taxpayers of the jurisdiction by levying a tax on their taxable property. In using the taxable property of the governmental body as security for the repayment of the debt, local authorities have been successful in gaining support from investment firms to invest their money in financing capital projects. Local governments have received good marks by investors for the repayment of their debts by the use of general obligation bonds. This, of course, results in giving the agency a good credit rating, an important aspect in marketing its bonds.

Recently, community agencies have looked for other methods of financing capital projects. The use of revenue bonds has become more accepted in the past several years.

Revenue Bonds. A revenue bond is an obligation of the borrowing agency to repay the principal and interest to the investor for the financing of a revenue-producing enterprise or facility. Revenues to repay the bond issue must come solely from the revenue of the enterprise. Not all recreation facilities can meet this requirement; however, increasing number of park and recreation agencies have been successful in financing facilities such as golf courses, artificial skating rinks, tennis centers, marinas, and swimming pools by the use of revenue bonds.

For years fees and charges have been used to finance the operation of these facilities. Although many of these functions were self-supporting and even made a profit, it was felt that they did not have the revenue-producing potential to underwrite the operating cost and to pay off the debt. In recent years more and more agencies have taken steps in making selected recreation facilities completely self-sufficient. This has enabled them to finance new and much needed facilities by the use of revenue bonds. It should be cautioned, however, that before a facility should be considered as appropriate for revenue bond financing, a feasibility study should be made to determine whether the facility has revenue-producing potential to pay for the cost of operation and to pay off the debt.

Summary

It is obvious that the fiscal problems facing municipalities and local government have had an impact on funding of leisure service agencies. Although appropriated funds from the general fund and special tax levies for park and recreation are still the primary sources of revenues for parks and recreation, local agencies have had to look to new sources of obtaining sufficient funds. Federal financial assistance programs (revenue sharing, CETA, Land and Water Conservation Funds, Community Development Block Grants, and the Urban Park and Recreation Recovery Program) have provided much needed funds for acquisition of land, capital improvements, and in the case of CETA, employment of personnel. Agencies have been forced to increase their use of fees and charges in order to make programs more self-sufficient. The stress has been on more effective operating procedures and the search for alternative sources of revenue.

The tax reduction program of the Reagan administration and the budget cuts initiated for 1982 have already dramatically affected local governments. The categorical grant programs of the previous administration have been gradually replaced by block grants giving local government more autonomy as to how federal money may be spent. In July 1981, Congress consolidated 57 categorical social services grant programs into nine block grants. Public service jobs (CETA) were virtually eliminated.

Many of the other programs that provided funding for parks and recreation received reduced funding in the administration's attempt to slash the federal budget. Federal funding for the Land and Water Conservation Fund for state and local governments in FY82 was eliminated, whereas appropriation to federal agencies increased to $155.4 million. Congress endorsed the administration's recommendations for reductions in funding the Urban Park and Recreation Recovery Program (UPRRP) to $20 million in FY81, $7.6 million in FY82, and elimination of the program in 1983. Because parks and recreation departments were forced to rely heavily on federal funding, and especially the CETA programs for survival, local officials will have to look to other sources of revenues in the future.

Selected References

Heritage Conservation and Recreation Service, *Fees and Charges Handbook,* U.S. Department of Interior, Washington, D.C., March 1979.

Howard, Dennis R., and John L. Crompton, *Financing, Managing and Marketing Recreation and Park Resources,* Brown, Dubuque, Iowa, 1980, pp. 7–160.

U.S. Department of Interior, *National Urban Recreation Study, Executive Report*, U.S. Department of Interior, Washington, D.C., 1978.

Chapter 4

Trends and Types of Budgets

Each year during budget preparation administrators face one of their most important tasks—obtaining sufficient funds to implement their programs for the coming year. In a way, they might look at the acceptance of their budget requests as a "vote of confidence" from their reviewing officials and legislative bodies. Agencies also have the opportunity to evaluate operational procedures and to assess the relative importance of programs and services. Budget preparation might also be viewed differently—their budget requests reflecting the programs and services offered by an agency and the operation of the agency itself are in a spotlight of public scrutiny.

During the 1980s public officials are confronting a loss of confidence of the general public regarding governmental operations, an uncertainty about the quantity and quality of services being offered, and a concern with the rising taxes levied by all levels of goverment. The picture is quite clear. Over a period of years a tremendous increase in programs, services, and spending has taken place. It has also occurred in our schools, churches, and semipublic agencies, resulting in a cause and effect relationship. We find that

Increased demands	=	Increased programs
Increased programs	=	Increased budgets
Increased budgets	=	Increased revenues
Increased revenues	=	Increased taxes
Increased taxes	=	Increased taxpayer scrutiny

Whenever taxpayers' pocketbooks are hit, nerves become tense and government, at all levels, faces opposition and often increased taxpayers' scrutiny. Tax limitation bills appear on the ballot in many states and a distrust in organizations and government ensues. Local governments are not able to find enough money to solve their problems and public officials are forced to look for new ways to finance their programs. Trends and problems in finance were covered in greater detail in Chapters 2 and 3. Under such conditions it is imperative that administrators of public and semipublic programs be prepared to sell, interpret, and justify their budget requests.

As parks and recreation are only one phase of total governmental services, administrators must recognize that they are in competition for their share of the tax dollar. The success they achieve is determined by how well they do their jobs and how well they sell their services; themselves as professionals; and the cause of parks and recreation. They should ask themselves whether they are presenting an intelligent, informative budget instead of a maze of meaningless figures. Do they receive charges of padded budgets? Is the public baffled and suspicious of their operations?

Budgets can be an excellent method of demonstrating an agency's approach to meeting the leisure needs of citizens. Preparing, presenting, and administering an effective budget requires professional expertise and the use of the most modern management tools. It has been said that a good administrator can no longer be regarded as a soothsayer, who budgets first and prays afterward. He/she cannot afford to operate on the premise "if you can't convince them, confuse them," or "what they don't know won't hurt them."

This chapter will discuss a philosophy of budgeting, trends in types of budgeting, the current types of budgets in operation, and finally, how budgets can be used as an effective management tool.

BUDGETING—A PHILOSOPHY AND DEFINITION

Apparently there is a wide gap between theory and practice regarding a fundamental concept as to what is good budgetary practice. In the field of local government conceptual confusion seems to grip professional and political leadership. Since the 1950s several new program–goal-oriented approaches have been introduced with varying degrees of success. The traditional "line item" concept still dominates local practice because of bureaucratic inertia and resistance to newer concepts. A large percentage of local governments still use the itemized expenditure and incremental approach to budgeting, whereas others are experimenting with newer approaches in an attempt to solve their financial and management problems.

Developing a definition and philosophy of budgets under such diverse circumstances is somewhat dangerous; however, a sound philosophy is basic to success in good budgeting. Legislative officials, governmental administrators, finance officers, accountants, and department heads all have different vantage points from which to consider what is good budgetary practice and what a budget should do. Park and recreation professionals must be good students of the various theories and approaches that are a part of an evolutionary process in the reform movement of budgetary practice in order to operate effectively in whatever approach is mandated by their governmental officials. Also, it is important that all management personnel develop personal philosophies to budgeting that will enhance their professional leadership skills.

Just as approaches to budgeting have changed over the years, definitions are also bound to change. Rather than giving a long list of definitions, I present one here that best describes my philosophy and approach to budgeting.

> A budget is a plan for financing and conducting a program or service for a given period of time—usually a year.

Perhaps a brief dicussion of three key words in the definition will provide the reader with a clearer understanding of the philosophy of budgeting advocated in this text.

Program. The definition suggests that budgeting has advanced from the traditional concept of line item budgeting to a focus on the programs and services provided by an agency. Attention is shifted from the cost items in the budget (object of expenditure) to programs (what is accomplished) offered to meet the needs of the community and the objectives of an agency.

Plan. Budgeting and planning are inseparable. In preparing a program-type budget, program planning and work plans are an integral part of budget development. The plan for performing the program provides an important interpretive tool for budget presentation as well as a management tool for carrying out the program and evaluating its success.

Finance The cost items (objects) in the budget are identified with the cost of performing programs or services whereas the revenues that are received by fees and charges for each program are identified.

Numerous articles and books have been written on budget theory and the many approaches that have been taken to budgeting. One of the newest and most refreshing books on the subject is Edward Lehan's *Simplified Governmental Budgeting,* in which he defines budgeting as a thought process and suggests that a budget is a purposeful distribution of scarce resources. Lehan states:

If rationing is . . . the essential principle of a budget, then our thought process, our judgments about the quality of a budget, in whole or in part, must deal with the relationship of resources to purposes . . . and the comparative worth of purposes . . . [1]

Implicit in Lehan's philosophy is that "budget procedures and documents should focus attention on what is to be sought or done, rather than on what is to be bought." This concept is an important element in my preceding definition. In seeking an answer to the question, "What is good budgeting?" Lehan presents three criteria that can be used for evaluation of the type of budget that he identifies.

The Unit Cost Criterion. Unit costs provide the best means of relating resources (expenditures and revenues) to purposes (defined as goals or work loads). Therefore, budgets and budgetary thinking based on cost center accounting and unit cost calculations tend to ration resources most carefully, producing relatively low unit costs, an important criterion of "good budgeting."

The Investment Criterion. It is an inherently difficult, but not impossible, task to determine the comparative worth of the various purposes supported by a public budget. To ac-

[1]Edward A. Lehan, *Simplified Governmental Budgeting,* Municipal Finance Officers Association, Chicago, 1981, p. 5.

complish it requires the development and maintenance of a suitable data base and a planning and analytical capacity. The relative worth of a "program" depends on how its "rate of return" compares with the rates of return which are, or can be earned by other programs.

. . .

The Literary Criterion. Because a budget represents an understanding between actors in the governmental drama on what is to be done, sought or bought, the format, style and content of budgetary documentation should meet literary, rather than public relations or accounting criteria, for example. High information content, clarity and conciseness are the prized virtues. In addition to accuracy in all computations and honesty in all statements, budget documentation should reflect, as much as possible, the underlying thought process.[2]

In summary, the definition I recommended and the suggestions advanced by Lehan on "What is good budgeting?" provide the foundations for the budget procedures and strategies developed in this text.

TRENDS AND APPROACHES TO BUDGETING

The development of budgeting in the United States and Canada is primarily a twentieth-century innovation. Moak and Killian reveal that:

an historical date in the development of Municipal budgeting is 1899 when the National Municipal League drafted a model municipal corporation act. One of the prominent features of this model was a proposed budget system under the direct supervision of the mayor.[3]

It was not until 1906 that New York City, under the auspices of the newly established Bureau of Municipal Research, organized a budgeting system that was designed around using an object of expenditure system for budgeting and accounting control. This began the so-called "traditional object of expenditure" type of budget which is still used by cities today. The idea of establishing a budget system spread rapidly to other cities, especially large ones, and by the mid-1920s most cities had adopted budgetary methods. The leadership, given the movement by the Municipal Finance Officers Association and the rapid growth of the city manager system of local government, greatly stimulated the spread of budgeting among cities. In the years that followed, budget reform movements were influenced by budget practices used in business and industry and by various mandates by state and federal governments. For ex-

ample, the performance budget was introduced by the Hoover Commission (1949); President Johnson promoted the Planning Program Budgeting System (PPBS); and Jimmy Carter was responsible for installing the Zero Base Budget (ZBB), previously used in private enterprise (Texas Instruments, Inc.), into the state of Georgia and, upon becoming President, into the federal government.

In examining various approaches to budgeting, we see a blending of elements from one approach to another. Each new approach initiated often retains some of the features from the older and more traditional approaches and adds new strategies that are deemed important to meet the challenges confronting organizations and society. A brief discussion of the various approaches to budgeting follows.

Lump Sum Budgeting

Prior to the beginning of the twentieth century, lump sum budgeting was practiced in most cities and states that had initiated budgetary practices. For each of the departments in the city or state a lump sum of money was appropriated and no attempt was made to analyze how the money was to be spent. This gave departments freedom to use the money in any way they deemed necessary.

The lump sum approach to budgeting, as one might well expect, was susceptible to corruption, suspicion, and misuse of funds, and community leaders and reformers of that era became active in promoting a more meaningful, efficient approach to budgeting. As a result, the line item or object of expenditure type of budget evolved and was put into practice.

Object of Expenditure (Line Item) Budgeting

The line item budget, initiated in the early 1900s, was an attempt to correct many of the "ills" of lump sum budgeting and to ensure stronger controls over governmental spending. This new approach stressed "how the money is spent" (object of expenditure), as well as the cost for each object.

In the early stages of line item budgeting, emphasis was placed on specific cost items such as the director's salary, janitor's wages, office supplies, maintenance supplies, heat, water, and so on. Expenditures for these items were listed on a line-by-line basis, thus the term "line item" was originated. It was soon realized that such a long and detailed list of cost items restricted the operation of an organization and complicated budgetary and accounting procedures.

---

[2]Ibid, p. 5.

[3]Lennox L. Moak, and Kathryn W. Killian, *Operating Budget Manual,* Municipal Finance Officers Association, Chicago, Ill., 1963, p. 6.

Local governments soon adopted the "line category" approach to budgeting. Objects of expenditures were grouped into general categories and standardized expenditure classification systems were adopted by most local governments and states. Examples of line categories included services-personal, services-contractual, supplies, materials, current charges, current obligations, properties, and debt payments. This approach tended to simplify the budget process and proved to be the basis for the accounting of expenditures made by governmental units.

Object of expenditure budgets do identify what public funds are being spent for. The legislative body can control how much can be spent for salaries, repairs, equipment, and supplies. However, such management concerns as what these expenditures are used for, what work is performed, what types of programs and services are being offered, and the goals and objectives of an agency are normally missing. Attention is directed to internal concerns—the personnel, materials, supplies, and equipment needed to run an agency or to the various departments within an agency. The external needs and impact, as well as what the agency is accomplishing, is often lost in the maze of expenditure costs.

The traditional object of expenditure budget has been a part of the budgeting scene for almost three-quarters of a century. This approach is still used in a large number of cities today. In all the newer types and approaches to budgets that have been introduced, object of expenditure budgeting and accounting are still included. Standing alone, a line item budget should be considered an outmoded budget and management tool.

Program Budgets

Promoted in the early 1930s, program budgeting was only adopted by a few cities until the 1950s. Program budgeting provides legislative bodies with a method of allocating financial resources for programs and services proposed by an agency. Emphasis is thereby placed on community needs and an agency's approach in meeting these needs. Where object of expenditure budgets identified only the overall agency, program budgets emphasize the programs and services offered by the agency. It is here that the park, golf course, swimming pool, senior citizen's center, and so forth are identified and the cost for each of these programs is developed.

In preparing the program budget, we suggest five steps.

1. Determine the program (plan).
2. Determine the work needed to perform the program.
3. Choose the personnel, materials, supplies, and equipment needed to do the work (objects).
4. Estimate expenditures.
5. Estimate revenues.

Program budgeting, by concentrating on programs and services, gives legislative officials and the general public a detailed plan of the scope of services that will be offered and the work needed to perform these programs. Emphasizing the ends rather than the means gives the public a better idea of the kinds of programs their dollars are supporting. It is only after the objectives have been established, the programs identified, and the work plan is developed that the object of expenditures and costs are determined. In this context, cost items and expenditures estimates have real significance because they are tied to the necessary work to carry out the program.

The program budget added many new dimensions to the budget process over the traditional object of expenditure approach. Most other kinds of budgets developed in later years continue to use the program budget concept.

Performance Budgets

As a result of the Hoover Commission Studies, reported in 1949, the performance budget was created and promoted at all levels of government. Although many adaptations and versions of this approach developed, it was generally recognized as an expansion of the program budget with the addition of work measurement (unit costs). In performance budgets emphasis is placed on the relationship of *input* of resources and *output* of work/service.

In order to implement performance budgeting, one should use a cost accounting system. A reporting system must also be developed to record cost items (personnel, supplies, equipment, and overhead) needed to perform work (input). From the data collected, the cost of performing units of work can be determined—that is, cost per acre of mowing park land, cost per mile of operating a vehicle, or cost per camper day for campers in a resident camp program. With more precise management tools, administrators can better analyze work measurement and with the application of standards they can evaluate the need for and the efficiency of the work being performed.

Like any departure from the generally accepted past practices, many difficulties were experienced in implementing this new approach. Added administrative time and cost made some executives negative toward performance budgeting. The development of meaningful units of measurement, especially in the area of recreation services, also proved to be a dilemma. And finally, the lack of cost-effective, professional standards in the field of parks and recreation made the cost per unit often meaningless.

Although the performance budget was not widely received in this country, the generally accepted principle of good management (identifying programs and work to be performed, evaluating the work done, and making the organization accountable for its operation) have survived and been incorporated in newer concepts of budgeting.

Planning, Programming, Budgeting System (PPBS) Budgets

The Planning, Programming, Budgeting System (PPBS) was first initiated at the federal level when Robert McNamara introduced this system in the Department of Defense in the early 1960s. Because of its success in that department, President Johnson, in 1965, mandated that all federal agencies adopt PPBS. It was not long before the concepts of PPBS spread to state and local units of government.

This new approach to budgeting continued many of the features of line item, program, and performance budgets. Basic components of PPBS include the following.

1. Identifies overall systemwide goals and objectives and relates programs and services to these goals.
2. Places emphasis on long-range planning where the costs and scope of programs and services are projected over a period of time—generally five years.
3. Requires a systematic analysis of alternatives, as well as an evaluation of programs to determine those programs that best meet objectives.

PPBS budgeting has been a much debated approach; however, it has been tried in a number of school systems and cities throughout the country. It has given local authorities an increased awareness of the importance of good planning in the budget process. The main case made for PPBS is that legislative officials are given specific data with which to make decisions on present as well as on long-range goals and objectives of the system.

Currently there are not too many local governments operating on a PPBS; however, the concept of goals and objectives, long-range planning, and evaluation are incorporated in most of the newer approaches to budgeting.

Program Performance Budgeting (Combination)

Since the advent of the program, performance, and PPBS budgeting systems, several other approaches to budgeting have been initiated. Most of these have incorporated selected features from the previously mentioned approaches. In Lakewood, Colorado, city officials felt that the current political and economic environment called for a change in their previous approach to budgeting. Thus the program performance budget was developed.

According to Henderson and Young,[4] although Lakewood had used management by objectives (MBO) and a program budget in the past, "a carefully balanced integration of management by objectives (MBO), Program *and* Performance budgeting, as well as line-item accounting was required to develop a management system" that was developed for Lakewood. Utilizing the "best features" from the other approaches, we have the basic features of the new program performance budget, as follows.

1. *Identify goals and objectives* that are explicit, realistic, and quantifiable and are subject to performance measurement.
2. *Develop program cost centers and evaluation* that stress specific programs and measurable objectives that can be measured by measurement indicators.
3. *Establish a program evaluation mechanism* that will give a comprehensive evaluation of the program.

Indicators utilized were:[5]

Demand. "Is the program necessary? How much service is required?"
Workload. "How much service are we providing? How does that compare to the need for that service?"
Productivity. "Is the program being run efficiently? How much does the program cost?"
Effectiveness. "How well is the program doing? Is it solving the problems it was created to solve?"

4. *Utilize line item accounting* for each of the programs developed.

Although Lakewood's approach has only existed for a short time, it has been recognized by finance and budget experts as a model for good progressive budgeting.

Zero-Base Budgets (ZBB)

Zero-base budgets (ZBB) were developed by Peter Phyrr and first used by private industry by Texas Instruments, Inc. Jimmy Carter, who introduced ZBB to the state of Georgia when he was governor, mandated the use of ZBB for the federal government when he became president.

---

[4]Bill Henderson and Randy Young, *Program Performance Budgeting: An Effective Public Management System for Evaluating Municipal Services,* Municipal Finance Officers Association, Special Bulletin, February 25, 1976, pp. 2–3.
[5]Ibid, p. 4.

Zero-base budgeting is a radical departure from the traditional budgeting systems utilized by governments in the United States. For years it has been assumed that current programs and services are needed (taken for granted) and only incremental increases should be justified. Existing programs are rarely cut substantially or eliminated even if the programs are no longer needed or are obsolete. It has been said that "unnecessary programs never die; they don't even fade away."

Under the ZBB system a comprehensive evaluation and justification of all programs, old and new, takes place and each department builds its budget from the ground up each year—or starts from zero. ZBB should be looked on as a management planning tool that provides both a systematic approach to evaluate all programs and services and a way for reallocating tight fiscal resources for the highest priority programs.

The steps in developing a zero-base budget are the following.

1. Prepare several alternative budgets (decision packages) for each program or activity. Usually a decision package contains:
   (a) A description of the program or service provided.
   (b) A description of the program or service in relation to goals and objectives.
   (c) Measures of performance.
   (d) Benefits expected from the program.
   (e) Levels of service provided—these normally include:
       (1) *Minimum.* Reduce level below the previous fiscal year.
       (2) *Base.* Represents a continuance of current service levels.
       (3) *Increase.* Resources required to meet increased workload or improvement or expansion of the function.
   (f) Consequences of not funding the alternativess recommended.
   (g) Cost data for funding alternatives.
2. Rank in priority each decision package (alternative) against other alternatives for current and new programs.
3. Allocate resources—approvement of programs/alternatives based on available resources.

There have been mixed reactions to zero-base budgeting by critics of public administration, finance, and professionals representing various functions of government. Only time will tell its success and future.

KEY ELEMENTS OF MODERN BUDGETS

The different types of budgets previously discussed indicate the various approaches that can be selected or mandated throughout the country. Regardless of the approach used, there tend to be variations or local adaptations of the type of budget being used.

An evaluation of budgets reveal certain key elements or budget practices that seem to stand out in spite of the kind of budget utilized. Park and recreation administrators should carefully study these key elements and be prepared to cope with the trends that follow. Only a brief listing and explanation of these are given, as a more detailed discussion of each is included in Chapter 5.

1. *Emphasis on programs/services* is basic to all budgets except the line item budget. In ZBB, program identification and planning are incorporated in the decision package.
2. *Programs should meet objectives* is more and more emphasized. Also, programs should meet community needs.
3. *Determining priorities–ranking of programs* is mandated by public officials because local governments lack financial resources to fund programs and solve all community needs. As local governments cannot do everything, programs are often ranked as to priority.
4. *Preparing alternatives* has been receiving more and more attention. This gives politicians (decision makers) choices.
5. *Efficiency-productivity* is demanded because the general public believes that governmental agencies can "do more for less or for the same money."
6. *Accountability* is often stressed with increased pressure placed on public officials to "make things happen according to the budget plan" or to accomplish the objectives stressed in the budget. No longer is it good enough just to stay within the budget appropriated.
7. *Evaluation* of the effectiveness of the program and the overall operation of an agency are receiving more attention as a management budget strategy.
8. *Computer technology* is becoming more essential in newer concepts of budgeting that demand detailed data for accounting and management purposes.
9. *Eliminate obsolete programs* is basic to ZBB and is stressed by sunset laws adopted by a number of local governments and states.

HUD'S FINANACIAL NEEDS ASSESSMENT STUDY

Realizing that local governments have significant problems in financial management, the Office of Policy Development and Research of the Department of Housing and Urban Development (HUD) was instructed to assist local governments in improving their financial management practices. The first step undertaken in early 1978 was to identify the specific problems confronting local governments and to discover what solutions they were taking in solving their problems. In an effort to get maximum involvement of local and state finance experts, a comprehensive needs assessment of local governments' financial management needs was undertaken. Nine national organizations were asked to assist in the project.

Municipal Finance Officers Association
National League of Cities
U.S. Conference of Mayors
International City Management Association
National Association of Counties
The Urban Consortium
Joint Center for Political Studies
Council of State Community Affairs Agencies
National Association of Housing and Redevelopment Officials

In conjunction with HUD, these nine organizations held a total of 49 workshops between February and June 1978, involving more than 850 participants from state and local governments. Eighty-five problems were identified and later these were combined into 41 major problems. A national conference was held in Washington, D.C. on June 8–9, by coincidence only two days after the passage of Proposition 13. Forty-one local government officials were invited. As a result of the conference, 21 major priority problems were agreed upon. Several of the problems related to budgeting were identified in HUD's report.

1. Finance officers often prepared budgets and reports in ways most convenient for their accounting procedures rather than for management and policy uses.
2. There is an inability to tie (together) performance measurement and evaluation, budgeting, and accounting (in order) to hold agencies accountable in terms of services provided.
3. There is a need for capital improvement programming which accurately reflects the total priority capital needs of communities and the impact on operating budgets.
4. Reliable indicators are not used or available for evaluating the performance and impact of local government services and activities.
5. There is a need to increase the ability of the public sector management to utilize more fully the financial management tools available, i.e., long range planning, computer.[6]

With the needs assessment program completed, HUD has initiated a comprehensive Local Govern-

[6]*Local Government Financial Management Capacity Sharing Program Plan,* Office of Policy Development and Research, U.S. Department of Housing and Urban Development, Draft Report, Washington, D.C., July 1978, 54 pp.

ment Financial Management Capacity Sharing Program. One of the first phases of the program was holding three financial management conferences during 1979 for local and state officials and technical assistance providers. These conferences stressed three issues identified by local government officials as their top financial needs: revenue and expenditure forecasting; integration of budgeting, accounting, and auditing and the use of performance measures; and state and federal oversight of and assistance to local government financial management.

At the Detroit conference, held in conjunction with the Annual Conference of the Municipal Finance Officers Association, Donna Shalala, HUD's Assistant Secretary of Policy Development and Research, announced that HUD had awarded a $1.2 million grant to the National Council on Governmental Accounting to finance a three-year research project designed to develop a conceptual framework and revised standards for governmental accounting and financial reporting.

Conferences and workshops are only two of many thrusts of HUD's program. Individuals and organizations, both public and private, have been commissioned to prepare publications and training materials in an effort to provide up-to-date resource materials for local officials. Many excellent publications have already been produced and distributed. A financial management resources center, operated by the Municipal Finance Officers Association (MFOA), provides a national contact point for technical support.

HUD's main objective is to assist local public officials so that they might improve their financial management practices. The need for improvement, as determined by the initial needs assessment study, is great. The ultimate success of HUD's program will be determined by how well local communities meet the financial challenges of the 1980s.

BUDGETS—A MANAGEMENT TOOL

Budgeting should be used by park and recreation administrators as a management tool and not just as a fiscal plan for obtaining funds for the coming year. Regardless of the kind of budget mandated by the local government agency or state, the program budget should be considered as the minimal approach to budget planning. With the addition of MBO and performance measurement indicators, the management tool becomes much stronger and meaningful. Several strategies for using budgets as a management tool are discussed here briefly.

Focus Attention on Programs and Services

Park and recreation professionals should be more interested in emphasizing programs and services and what is happening to people than in concentrating on object of expenditure costs. The budget should therefore highlight external affairs, problems within the community, and the needs of people rather than the internal affairs of an agency.

If parks and recreation's main objective is to improve lives and create a better living environment, the budget must project an agency's plans and commitments to the stated mission so that legislative officials and citizens may evaluate carefully an agency's projected plans. The endorsement of this philosophy is essential.

Determination of Scope of Programs/Services

The proposed budget presents the agency's financial plan for providing programs and services for the new fiscal year. The budget should identify the program plan, the work anticipated, and the cost items needed to accomplish the work and program. Some budgets require that alternatives be given so that the reviewing body is given a choice as to what it is willing to finance for the next year. This technique often forces public officials to make unpopular decisions in regard to allocating resources (money) for certain programs.

When the legislative body approves the budget, a department or agency is given the "green light" to perform the programs incorporated in the budget. Thus the approval of the budget determines the scope or extent of the programs and services that can be offered.

Handling Public Pressures for Additional Programs

On receiving approval of the budget request, an agency should be held accountable to perform the programs and services that were approved. A well-planned budget provides an excellent program plan for the weeks and months ahead. Thus the management of an agency should be geared to operate efficiently and effectively in performing the functions designed to meet the projected goals and objectives. This approach is essential if the MBO approach to management is being used.

Organizations must be alert and receptive to change and the needs and interests of the general public. Budget plans are not set in cement and may

be adjusted or altered if the situation merits it. Major changes in the budget plan should be presented to the agency's legislative board for approval.

Because the agency operates during the fiscal year, public and/or political pressures are often brought on the administrator and board for new and/or expanded services. These requests should not always be considered negative as public pressures do indicate the public's interest in the agency's programs and services. Each request should be carefully studied to determine the merit of the program and the costs for adding the new or expanded services. If the new program can be self-supporting or if additional funds can be obtained from the local governmental administration or from private sources, the new or expanded services can be offered. If additional funding is not possible, the request will have to be denied or deferred until next year. Finding money within the approved budget to initiate the new program might indicate that the agency has a padded budget and that it has no plan to follow. Picking up new services, without additional funding or revision of the present budget plan, also tends to water down existing programs and overloads existing staff. If this practice is followed to any considerable degree, the quality of the programs will suffer. And if money is found to handle one request, it will be difficult to respond to other demands that are sure to come. The strategy mentioned provides a more rational basis for decision making and handling public pressures.

Presentation of Budget

A well-planned budget, first of all, should be a good interpretive document. Citizens and reviewing officials should be able to see exactly what programs are going to be provided and the work plan recommended. Also, expenditure items and costs have meaning as they are related to the work and the program. Sufficient supporting data should be available to justify requests. The professionalism exhibited in the budget document should help to alleviate the charge of padded budgets and meaningless data.

In an era of tight money, inflation, and ever increasing problems facing communities, the climate of budget hearings is often one of cutting the budget, services, and/or the tax rate. When park and recreation administrators are confronted with having a budget request cut, they must respond by asking what part of the program should be deleted or reduced. It is self-evident that cutting dollars and expenditure items (personnel, supplies, equipment) has to reduce work plans and ultimately the program itself. If an agency is able to translate the impact of budget reductions into the changes that would ensure in programs and services, public officials and the general public might logically conclude that the budget has sufficient fat to stand a little tightening. When an agency is forced to continue to operate existing programs at the same level as the past year in spite of a cut in funding, the quality of the program is bound to suffer and ultimately the public will become disenchanted with the operation of the agency.

Efficient Management

Once a well-planned program-type budget has been approved, there is little guesswork on the part of the administrative, supervisory, or program staff as to what program will be conducted, how much money will be spent, who is to be hired, and what to pay employees. These answers should be a part of the budget plan. The mandate from the administrator to the staff should be "conduct your programs and your work according to *your* plan."

The real challenge of efficient management is to determine the most economical ways to operate programs and to perform work. Efficiency and productivity are basic elements of good management. In an era of rising costs due to inflation, energy crisis, and competition for the shrinking tax dollar, administrators must use the most up-to-date budget procedures and management techniques. All employees in the agency must become involved. A creative working climate and good communication between employees at all levels are keys for evaluating and improving departmental programs and operations. This climate can be enhanced by involving employees in the establishment of goals and objectives and in the development of the budget for their division or program. Incentives can be given to employees for innovative ideas that improve the productivity and efficiency of the organization. Operating the agency in a more efficient manner is good business and imperative if the organization is to be accountable to the public for the responsible use of limited tax dollars.

Accountability

In using the traditional object of expenditure budget approach, the agency is primarily accountable for its spending program (object) and for maintaining good business procedures. Administrators are also accountable for their total budget dollars with the primary mandate—"don't overspend your budget."

With newer, more progressive approaches to budgeting, the agency is tested in its ability to make things happen in accordance to the plan identified in the budget. In presenting the program, program performance, or zero-base budgets to reviewing bodies, administrators present the goals and objectives, programs, and work plans that they intend to accomplish. Once budgets are approved, agencies are held accountable for reaching the goals and objectives, conducting the programs, and accomplishing the work.

Evaluation

One of the greatest weaknesses in the management process is that of evaluation. Too often goals and objectives are not identified, and if mentioned, they tend to be too philosophical and vague. Under these circumstances, measuring the success of programs is generally tied into the numbers (attendance) game.

In newer approaches to budgeting, the trend is to incorporate MBO as an integral part of the budget process. When meaningful goals and objectives are set, programs identified, performance objectives established, evaluation of the efficiency and effectiveness of the programs can be achieved. If these steps are taken, a realistic, meaningful evaluation system can be put into operation.

LIMITATIONS IN THE BUDGET PROCESS

Regardless of the kind of a budget used, budget planners have certain limitations in the budget process that must be understood. Several of the major limitations that impact on the budget process are now briefly discussed.

Budget Plans Are Based on Estimates

Generally, budgets are primarily forecasts or predictions regarding future agency operations and programs. To the extent that these "guesstimates" are based on good factual data and sound reasoning, the proposed budget is a reliable and useful tool. Forecasting, however, is not an exact science and the estimates projected in the budget sometimes are inaccurate. For example, weather can affect the operation of golf courses, ice skating rinks, outdoor athletic programs, and swimming pool operations. Weather records often prove valuable in developing programming estimates. However, abnormal weather conditions, that is, the most snowfall a community has had in years, the blizzard of 1978, or an extreme lack of rain during the summer, can play havoc on the anticipated spending or in the receipts gained. Under such conditions a revision of the estimate or possible revision of the plan might be needed and can be explained.

Response to Budget Plans and Programs Are Questionable

Recreation programming calls for involvement of citizens in the planning process and assessment of their needs and interests. Careful planning is essential and usually produces good results. However, the programs and services offered by leisure service organizations are subject to varying responses by the people involved. Because programs are voluntary, it is possible that the response to some activities may be overwhelming, whereas other programs fail to draw sufficient numbers and must be cancelled. It is not uncommon that program plans and budgets need to be revised during the fiscal year because of how citizens in the community respond to them.

Impact of Political, Economic, and Social Forces on Budget Process

Since institutions do not operate in a vacuum, the services they provide must be responsive to such forces as strikes, racial riots, inflation, energy (oil) crisis, and drastic changes in the political process in Washington. The election of Ronald Reagan as president has been a major force in changing the expectations of funding from the federal government. The growth in inflation, discussed in Chapter 2, has had a crippling affect on local government. Most of the concerns mentioned are out of the realm of local agencies' ability to react; however, they do influence local budgets and operations.

Successful Budgeting Requires Good Management

Management of an organization, as considered in Chapter 1, is subject to elements such as organization climate, leadership style, legislative direction and control, and the degree of involvement of employees in the planning and operation of the agency. Because management is a human undertaking and carried on by people who are subject to a wide variety of influences and motivational concerns, good budgetary procedures result from a team-oriented aproach to management. If staff members are not an integral part of planning and budget preparation, they will not be motivated to carry out the programs and work plans developed in the budget. Whether an agency is effective in meeting its goals and objectives is subject to the management conditions found in the organization and the willingness of employees to budget plans and estimates.

Budgeting in a Changing Society

Budget planners must be prepared to cope with the rapidly changing society. In planning a budget for a year or more in the future, organizational personnel must project what the conditions will be and what changes will influence their operation. It is difficult enough to keep pace with current problems and conditions to say nothing of what the conditions will be next year when the budget goes into effect.

ESSENTIALS FOR SUCCESSFUL BUDGETING

Before turning to Chapter 5, "Budgetary Procedures," a brief discussion of several essential ingredients for good budgeting should prove to be meaningful for the budget maker.

Sound Organizational Climate-Leadership

It is axiomatic that a properly organized department or agency will pay dividends in the overall budgetary process. Creative management takes place in an organizational climate that is discussed in Chapter 1. This kind of climate is fostered by administrators who understand the nature of organizations and are willing to establish a team approach to the management of their organizations.

Organizational climate and leadership style have already been discussed in Chapter 1; however, it is worth noting again that they made a big difference in whether an organization will be successful in meeting its objectives. They make a world of difference in the type of budgeting procedures that are fostered by the department.

Adequate Accounting System

To a considerable extent, program planning and budget estimates must be guided by past experience, and, perhaps, one of the best resources for gathering data on past operations is through accounting records. The type and detail of the accounting system maintained by the central finance officer or by the agency itself will greatly influence the information available for budgetary preparation and administration.

The gradual shift in emphasis from line item budgeting to some of the newer approaches of budgeting calls for a change in the attitude of park and recreation administrators as they approach the budget process, and also for new types of information from the accounting system. According to Lehan, governmental accounting divisions, often understaffed and lacking technology, are finding it difficult to cope with the demands associated with output-oriented budgeting procedures. His concern about this situation is expressed as follows.

Adequate accounting and auditing support for output-oriented budgeting has been a critical issue too long ignored or brushed aside as inconsequential, hindering those governments seeking to improve their resource allocation procedures.

This major unresolved issue only recently received the attention it deserves. Evidence of concern about this issue surfaced in the 1980 revision of *Governmental Accounting, Auditing, and Financial Reporting* (GAAFR). The book stresses the centrality of budgetary accounts in governmental accounting and reporting and emphasized the importance of activity classifications, a characteristic of the performance budgeting approach. Further, GAAFR deemphasizes the use of line-item classification control.[7]

The program approach to budgeting, discussed in this book, does not call for the in-depth accounting system demanded for performance budgeting or for the enterprise fund operations that requires cost analysis data. It does call for more information that is maintained by many governmental units utilizing the line item budgeting approach.

Involvement of Staff in Budgeting Procedures

In the discussion of limitations in the budget process the problem of motivating employees to carry out the programs and work programs incorporated in the budget was considered a possible limitation. After all, if workers are not motivated to carry out their programs and to live within the approved budget, their actions, or lack of such, could prove to be a hindrance in the budget process. Therefore if the motivation of employees is essential for an agency's achievement of goals, it is evident that program leaders should be involved in the planning and implementation of the budget.

Program supervisors and leaders, operating on the firing line, are in the best position to inerpret needs, plan programs, determine work programs, estimate costs, and evaluate program effectiveness. If employees have a share in planning "their" programs, they will be motivated in carrying out their plans and in meeting program goals. If administrators and their administrative staff assume the task of program planning and budget development, leaders will have little incentive in executing "top management's" plans, cost estimates, or goals and objectives. Most writers on the subject of management, MBO, and motivation of personnel reveal that the lack of in-

volvement of employees in the budgeting process leads to negative work force performance.

Budgeting Is a Year-Round Continuous Process

If a budget is a "plan for financing and conducting a program or service," certainly one of the essential ingredients of good budgeting is the comprehensive planning of these programs or services and good planning takes time. Often, budget makers cram budget planning into tight deadlines of the budget preparation period. Under these constraints and time pressures it is understandable why budget makers tend to "do it like last year" and simply make a few adjustments to the budget mandated by format and basic instructions handed down from top management.

It is during the actual operation of a program that problems arise, shortages in equipment or supplies are found, reaction to programs are received, and adjustments must be made. If maintenance problems surface during the year that cannot or need not be corrected in the current operating budget, estimates should be obtained when these problems occur so that they will be available for budget planning purposes later on. Notes should be made and information collected on new and innovative program ideas, fads, or equipment that are suggested to or by program leaders while their program is in operation.

Evaluation of programs should be conducted on a weekly, monthly, or seasonal basis. Many agencies make comprehensive evaluations of seasonal activities, that is, summer day camp program, at the completion of the program utilizing seasonal workers and supervisory personnel in the evaluation process. If administrative direction and stimulation are given encouraging year-round planning and evaluation by program leaders involved in the process, final budgetary planning can be made more easily during the intense preparation period that confronts budget planners each year.

PERSPECTIVES IN BUDGETARY PROCEDURES

In studying the total budgetary process (preparation, presentation and adoption, and administration) there are four major publics that are involved: agency personnel, chief executive, legislators, and citizens. Each of these publics has a unique role to play and duties and responsibilities to perform. Lehan, in his latest work devotes a chapter to the budget-making perspectives of each of these four groups. A brief summation of the respective roles of these groups follows.

[7]Lehan, *Simplified Governmental Budgeting*, p. 11.

The Program Leader's Perspective

A budget is a sort of contract between political authorities and program personnel, reflecting work plans (designed, it is hoped, to pursue public goals). Given this contractual nature of budgeting the budget maker's principal task (and highest duty) is to illuminate the relationships between public goals, work plans and associated expenditures and revenues. In budgeting, there is no substitute for a well thought-out, properly presented program.[8]

The Chief Executive's Perspective

From their vantage point as leader of the jurisdiction's administrative forces, chief executives are expected to use budget procedures to:

1. set service levels;
2. establish fiscal policy;
3. supervise administrative work.[9]

The Legislator's Perspective

A legislator's budgetmaking role is primarily responsive. It is rare to find budget proposals developed *de novo* by legislators or legislative committees.... In almost all representative governments, budget proposals are submitted to legislatures by the leaders of administrative formations. Because budgetary initiatives lie with administrative agencies, there is a tendency among legislators to feel inadequate, somewhat less than properly prepared to pursue the triple goals of legislative budget procedure, that is:

1. setting service levels;
2. adoption of fiscal policy;
3. general review of administrative performance.[10]

The Citizen's Perspective

In democratic societies, laws distinguish between citizens who are officials and citizens who are not, setting rather strict rules for official conduct, while reserving a relatively wide sphere of speech and action to nonofficial citizens.

Short of bribing officials, citizens are free to propose and press measures which will effect the collection and disbursement of public funds. They are free to petition, demonstrate, agitate, sue, advertise, speak, write, publish and vote. In some jurisdictions, citizens have access to initiative and referendum procedures, permitting direct influence on taxes and expenditures.[11]

This text focuses on the program leader's persepective—the park and recreation administrator and staff. Because program leaders must work with and through these various publics in the budget process, management strategies are suggested for the many relationships that administrators and staff have with this individual and groups. Also, I recommend that budget makers in the field of parks and recreation examine carefully Lehan's latest works for his excellent treatment of the perspectives of these four groups.

Summary

Chapter 4 discusses the various types of budgets that have been or are currently being used by local governments—line item, program, program/performance, performance, PPBS, and zero-base. The newer approaches tend to focus on the program or service performed and in most instances on meeting program goals. Emphasis also is placed on performance evaluation, establishment of alternatives, ranking and priorities, efficiency and productivity, and accountability.

Accounting officers, operating in central finance offices or at the departmental level, have been challenged to establish accounting systems to provide data for the newer concepts of budgeting. Data processing is becoming more essential in integrating budgeting with the accounting and reporting functions.

The technology presently exists but park and recreation administrators have been slow in accepting these new innovations. It is essential that new concepts of budgetary procedures and processes are incorporated in professional education curricula if future administrators are to be prepared to implement these concepts in the field.

This text addresses the park and recreation administrator's role in working with their staff, chief executives, legislators, and citizens. Park and recreation professionals must develop expertise in using budgeting as a management tool if they are to be successful in gaining approval for their budget requests and in planning, operating, and evaluating programs and services.

Selected References

Aronson, J. Richard, and Eli Schwartz, *Management Policies in Local Government Finance,* International City Management Association, Washington, D.C., 1981, Chapter 5.

Henderson, Bill, and Randy Young, *Program Performance Budgeting: An Effective Public Management System for Evaluating Municipal Services,* MFOA, Special Bulletin, February 25, 1976, 10 pp.

Lehan, Edward A., *Simplified Governmental Budgeting,* Municipal Finance Officers Association, Chicago, 1981, 86 pp.

Local Government Financial Management Capacity Sharing Program Plan, Office of Policy Development and Research, U.S. Department of Housing and Urban Development, Draft Report, July 1978, 54 pp.

[8]Ibid, p. 39.
[9]Ibid, p. 61.
[10]Ibid, p. 69.
[11]Ibid, p. 75.

Chapter 5

Budget Preparation

Chapter 4 discussed the trends in budgeting, the various approaches to budgeting utilized throughout the country, and several key elements of budgets that are currently used by public or semi-public organizations. Despite the type of budget endorsed by the local jurisdiction or state, or the mandates or guidelines presented by the legislative body, it is important that park and recreation administrators adhere to good management principles and operate their organization in an efficient, professional manner. Ultimately, the professionalism of an agency will be judged in this light.

The budgetary process can be broken down into three major phases—preparation, presentation and adoption, and implementation. The approach that the administrator takes depends on several factors: state statutes regulating the process; the type of local govenmental authority (mayor, city manager, or commission); the size of the governmental jurisdiction and its respective departments; the political environment in which park and recreation personnel work; and whether the park and recreation function operates as an agency directly responsive to the chief executive or under a separate board or commission.

Budget making is a lengthly process and involves the legislative and the administrative components of the overall city or county system. The legislative body has responsibility for determining the nature and scope of the budgetary process while local administrators establish specific guidelines, approaches, and deadlines for the budgeting process as well as give direction to their management teams.

An overall climate that is established by the legislative body and city or county administrator greatly influences each agency's approach to budget preparation and the type and caliber of the budget document.

CLIMATE INFLUENCING PROCEDURES

Local governmental agencies vary as to the types of budgets and procedures that are followed in budget preparation. Guidance is generally forthcoming to agency heads as to the procedures to follow in preparing their agency budgets. The governance of the agencies' approach to budget preparation is normally prescribed by state statutes, city charters or ordinances, and local governmental chief executives.

State Statutes

Most states have passed laws that govern or influence the preparation of local governmental budgets. Some states exercise direct control over the type of budgets that should be developed and the budgetary procedures that must be followed by local government. In other states the laws are quite general and permissive in nature. States do have the sovereign right to permit local government to perform local functions, such as parks and recreation. According to the legal doctrine known as the Dillon's Rule, "no local government may organize, perform any function, tax its citizens, or receive and spend money without the consent of the state."[1]

[1]John E. Peterson, C. Wayne Stallings, and Catherine L. Spain, *States Roles in Local Government Financial Management: A Comparative Analysis,* Government Finance Research Center, Municipal Finance Officers Association, Washington, D.C., 1979, p. 1.

Realizing that states do vary as to their roles in local governments' financial management, the Government Finance Research Center, a research arm of the Municipal Finance Officers Association (MFOA), was commissioned by the U.S. Department of Housing and Urban Development's Office of Policy Development and Research (HUD) to study the role of the state as "a regulator, supervisor, and provider of technical assistance in local government financial management."[2] The study directed its efforts toward the state's impact on seven specific areas of local financial management: accounting, auditing, and financial reporting; budgeting; debt management; pensions; cash management; property tax assessment; and revenue.

The MFOA study explored the ways that states were involved in the financial management of local jurisdictions. The methods employed by states in exercising controls over local financial management varies geatly; however, two general approaches seem to be evident: (1) to assist local governments to strengthen their financial management functions and (2) to force or regulate local agencies to follow specific financial management practices and policies. In assisting local governments most states provide training and technical assistance programs, general oversight and suggestions, and guidelines that concentrate on strengthening fiscal procedures and practices rather than on imposing tight regulations on local financial practices.

Because many local governments lack fiscal integrity and financial solvency, and often perform ineffective management practices, states have played a dominant role in the financial affairs of local government, imposing regulations for the purposes of maintaining fiscal control and financial solvency and mandating certain levels of performance of the financial management of local government. Several examples of approaches to regulate local financial management practices include the following.

- Limit the amount of debt that local governments may incur.
- Mandate budgeting, accounting, and financial reporting procedures and forms.
- Place limits on tax rates, thus limiting the revenue capabilities of local government.
- Require approval of bond issues by state government before local agencies put bond issues up for a referendum or for sale.
- Mandate local government to perform certain functions without giving them financial assistance to finance these functions.
- Place limits on local agencies' discretion to borrow money through short-or long-term debt limits.

[2]Ibid, p. ix.

States not only get highly involved in legislation directed toward financial management but park and recreation legislation passed by the state includes many provisions that impact on park and recreation finance and budgeting functions.

City Charters or Ordinances

City charters or budget ordinances prescribe the procedures and format for financial management of local units of government. It is the responsibility of the local legislative body to establish budget policies, format, and guidelines that provide the focus for the chief executive, budget officers, and various agency personnel for the financial management of the city, county, or special districts.

Local ordinances must be developed in careful adherence to state legislation already mentioned. In addition, local authorities should give guidance and direction for their agencies or departments. For example, the city council in Memphis, Tennessee, approved a budgetary process for their municipality that is referred to as "multiple-decision budgeting." A comprehensive budget manual was developed to spell out the concept and the procedures for this approach of budgeting. In Lakewood, Colorado, the program performance budget was adopted by the city council and departments in Lakewood prepare their budgets based on this approach to budgeting.

Chief Executives Instructions and Control

Chief executives have the responsibility for providing direction and assigning responsibility for the local governments' budgetary procedures. In smaller jurisdictions chief executives often serve as the budget director and usually work closely with their department heads in developing the budget. In larger jurisdictions centralized finance divisions and budget bureaus perform major responsibilities in the budgeting process. Centralized finance divisions, which consolidate all financial functions into one division, are becoming quite common in larger local governments. Functions such as budgeting, accounting, assessment, treasury, and purchasing are all incorporated under a single authority, who is accountable to the chief executive.

In larger jurisdictions a budget bureau is organized separately from the centralized finance bureau and the budget officer is directly responsible to the chief executive. The amount and type of authority assigned to the budget division plays an instrumental role in each department head's approach to budget preparation. In one large midwestern city, for example, the budget office has responsibility for preparing the basic budget for all departments. According to the memorandum from the city budget officer to all department and division heads, the procedure mentioned "will relieve the operating agencies of the time consuming job of preparing the basic budget." Also, the memorandum continues, "normal agency activities will be disrupted less if this can be successfully accomplished." In this case it is questionable whether the budget office is assuming too much of the budget development job that rightfully belongs to the agency heads and their staff.

Budget officers play a key and important role in the budget process; organizing and developing budget materials, that is, budget calendar and worksheets and budget forms, and also coordinating budget meetings. Often they assume greater responsibilities in performing significant policy guidance functions and in making recommendations for budget action to the chief executive and the legislative body. Finally, budget officers assume responsibility for budget implementation. It is essential that park and recreation executives establish good working relationships with their budget divisions and seek assistance from their budget officials.

Most mayors, city managers, finance, and budget officials give guidance to their department heads as they develop their budget plans and proposals. Budget calendars and budget instructions or budget manuals are issued to various agency or department heads so that the budget requests from such departments or agencies will be uniform, complete, and finished according to the deadlines set.

Budget Calendars.   Proper setting of deadlines for each step in the budget process is vital if sufficient time is to be allocated for preparation of a quality budget. If park and recreation administrators are unaware of budget time schedules, it is possible that a hurried "do it like last year" job will result. Usually, a "hurried" budget will serve as a meaningless management tool.

Budget calendars are usually established around state and local laws that prescribe deadlines when agency budgets must be presented to the legislative body for adoption and to the general public in the form of public notices and hearings. Every effort should be made by administrative and legislative officials to see that the budget is adopted before the first day of the new fiscal year. It is most unfortunate that a number of local agencies find themselves well into the new fiscal year (four or five months) before their budget is finally approved and a tax rate set.

The size of the local government, as well as legal requirements, will determine the length of time needed for the total budget preparation and adoption procedure. Large governments, for example, may spend from four to eight months, whereas smaller units of government generally need less time, from two to four months, in budget preparation and gaining approval. Examples of typical budget calendars for large and small local governments are presented in Figure 5.1.

The period from July 16 to September 1 (large cities) and August 16 to October 1 (small cities) shown in the budget calendar in Figure 5.1, is the time in which park and recreation administrators and their staff must prepare budget estimates. It would seem highly desirable that departmental deadlines should be established so that the time allotted is carefully utilized.

Budget Instruction Manuals.   Instructions from the chief executive or budget officer regarding the preparation of the budget varies from local government to local government. In smaller governments these instructions may be verbal in nature. The chief executive merely instructs department heads as to the fiscal situation facing the community and the procedures to follow in budget preparation.

Often instructions are in the form of a written memorandum from the chief executive with detailed instructions and forms enclosed. The memorandum may give the financial outlook of the city, county or special district for the coming year and vital information such as expected salary adjustments and approaches to expanding or reducing programs.

Budget manuals are sometimes issued to agency personnel. Most commonly found in city manager cities, these manuals present in a most comprehensive manner the procedures to follow, the approach and detail in which the budget should be developed, and the forms to be used. Often the chief executive will issue a memorandum and other materials to supplement the information in the manual.

BUDGET PREPARATION

The administrator and staff who complain about the time that must be spent in preparing the agency's budget are unaware of the importance of one of their prime responsibilities. This is the time to reevaluate programs and services and overall agency operations and to prepare new plans for the year ahead. Budget preparation is one of the cardinal responsibilities of executives and their staff. Much of the success of an agency might well be attributed to the administra-

Budget Calendar

January 1—Beginning of fiscal year

When		Who	Action
Large Jurisdiction	**Small Jurisdiction**		
July 15	August 15	Chief Administrator	Distributes budget instructions and forms
July 16– September 1	August 16– October 1	Department Heads	Prepare department budget and submit to Chief Executive
September 2– October 15	October 2– November 4	Budget Officer and/or Chief Administrator	Conducts hearings on Departmental Budget
October 16– November 1	November 5– November 15	Budget Officer and/or Chief Administrator	Prepare budget document
November 2	November 16	Chief Administrator	Submits budget to legislative body
November 3– November 23	November 17– November 23	Legislative body	Legislative consideration of budget and public hearings
November 30	November 30	Legislative body	Budget adoption by enactment of appropriation and revenue ordinance
January 1	January 1		Budget goes into effect

Figure 5.1 Example of budget calendars for large and small local governments.

tor's skill in guiding the preparation of the budget request. Certainly a budget is no better than the effort put into its formulation. Park and recreation executives must delegate some of the budget preparation responsibilities to other staff if the resulting budget is to serve as a meaningful management tool.

In preparing the budget plan, one should consider the following steps: (1) determining the program, (2) determining the work needed to accomplish the program, (3) determining personnel, supplies, and equipment needed to do the work, (4) estimating expenditures, and (5) estimating the receipts that will be taken in by each program.

Step 1. Determining the Program

If a budget is to be considered as a financial plan for conducting specific programs and services, attention should first be given to the leisure service opportunities that will be offered by the agency in the coming year. Despite the type of budget used, program identification is basic to budget development. Citizens request park and recreation services. Politicians may make promises of services they would provide if elected. Once elected to office, they often tend to

stress their pet programs in order to fulfill their campaign promises.

Placing the emphasis on programs and services will tend to take the spotlight off how money is spent and will direct attention to the agency's plans for providing activities that are designed to meet the leisure needs of citizens. Because programs are not ends in themselves, the budget planner must first prepare goals and objectives for the agency and then create plans for accomplishing them.

Goals and Objectives. The establishment of goals and objectives is a step that is often missing in preparing budgets; however, it is essential to the effective operation and evaluation of an organization. Simply stated, management by objectives (MBO), or some adaptation of this concept, changes the organization's management approach from an "activity-oriented approach" to a "results-oriented approach." John Mee, Professor Emeritus, School of Business, Indiana University, and a leader in the business management field, presents the concept of MBO quite succinctly when he says, "write your annual report ahead of time and make it come true."

It is up to budget planners to decide just what it is

that they desire to accomplish. After this, they determine the method (program) to accomplish their objectives. The establishment of goals and objectives not only pinpoints the direction the agency plans to take in meeting community needs, it will also serve as a standard by which performance can be evaluated and accountability can be assessed. Before the budget planner can focus on program objectives, overall local governmental goals must be established to provide overall direction to the operating divisions within each agency.

Citywide Goals and Objectives. Local governmental goals, essentially the mandates and priorities of the chief executive and the legislative body, serve as guidelines for divisional or departmental budget preparation. Unless these goals are clearly stated, divisional or departmental goals may be at odds with the overall goals of the local jurisdiction. Several local governments have been successful in gaining citizen participation in their development of goals and objectives. Two brief case studies are presented as follows.

In Lakewood, Colorado, the mayor and city council have recognized the importance of encouraging citizen participation in the budget process. Because past practices of public hearings and requests for advice from various civic groups had received minimal response, the mayor and council requested the city administrator to conduct a citizen's opinion survey to determine the needs and wants of Lakewood citizens and to assess the performance of various programs. The information was given to the mayor and council to assist them in establishing the goals for the proposed budget request and to determine resource allocation recommendations.

Plainfield, New Jersey, has also received nationwide recognition for its approach of gaining citizen involvement in the city's budget process. The city's approach to "budgeting by objectives" involves two key ingredients—a Citizen's Budget Advisory Committee and a citywide citizen's survey. According to Burton Conway, Deputy Administrator, "Plainfield's citizen participation mechanisms are designed specifically to complement rather than take the place of our budget decision making responsibilities."[3]

Guidance or direction from the legislative body is vital to the budget development process. A realistic picture of local governments financial status and the political direction and policy of the elected officials give departments or divisions direction as they prepare their goals and objectives.

Community needs and problems facing local governments are many; however, with citizen input they are more easily identified. Formulating goals that will address these concerns often results in an extensive list, which is normally beyond the monies available to support them. It is up to the governing body to establish priorities as to what community goals should be pursued and the amount of funding that should be allowed in the proposed budget.

As an example of citywide goals that would influence the parks and recreation department budget planner, city officials might mandate one or all of the following goals for the department's swimming program.[4]

LOCAL GOVERNMENT GOALS—
SWIMMING PROGRAM

Increase revenues from swimming pool

Expand swimming opportunities for the handicapped

Provide more free swimming for poor residents

Expand learn-to-swim opportunities for youth

Any one or more of these goals would give the agency direction as it prepares its swimming budget.

Agency Goals and Objectives. With central goals established, the agency must determine its direction, priorities, and responses to legislative mandates. In too many local governments, park and recreation agencies have not established meaningful goals and objectives. In some instances goals and objectives can be found in an administrative or program manual but are often too philosophical and unrealistic, and the agency is not operated in response to the objectives developed. If it can be agreed that the measurement of the effectiveness of an organization should be based on the results accomplished in meeting agency goals and objectives, then the development of measurable goals and objectives is essential to good management.

More and more, agencies are called on to establish realistic, meaningful, and measurable goals and to set up a mechanism to see that they are met. This should not be considered as a mandate or distasteful chore; it should be considered a professional responsibility and a challenge to operate the department in a highly effective manner.

An agency's response to the overall local govern-

---

[3]Personal letter from Burton Conway, April 4, 1978.

[4]The swimming program will be used, in illustrating various steps in budget development, whenever possible, as in the example.

ment's goals suggested for the swimming program might include the following.

AGENCY GOALS—SWIMMING PROGRAM

Increase fees and charges—season tickets/lesson registration

Increase fees for out-of-town participants

Initiate learn to swim classes—handicapped

Expand hours of free swimming—poor residents

Expand classes for intermediate and advanced swimmers

Performance Objectives. After broad agency goals have been set, performance objectives should be established. Experience has shown that it is in this phase of goal setting that many attempts for making MBO a realistic management tool has failed. According to Henderson and Young, Lakewood, Colorado "has used MBO in past years, more or less, as a management tool for identifying broad organizational goals and objectives to be achieved in each forthcoming program year. Major weaknesses, however, had been the absence of meaningful, measurable, and realistic program goals in the budget."[5] The success of Lakewood's program performance budget is based on program goals and performance objectives that are explicit, realistic, and quantifiable. Literature on MBO seems to agree that program objectives should state exactly what will be attained, must be able to measure whether the objective has been attained, and should focus on the results that must be achieved.

Examples of performance objectives that relate to areawide and agency goals for the swimming program might include:

**PERFORMANCE OBJECTIVES—
SWIMMING PROGRAM**

Increase revenue by 10 percent

Initiate swimming lessons for 50 handicapped youth

Draw 3500 children from low-income families for free swimming sessions (Saturday mornings)

Offer four additional classes for intermediate and advanced swimmers—100 new registrations

---

[5]Bill Henderson and Randy Young, *Program Performance Budgeting: An Effective Public Management System for Evaluating Municipal Services,* Municipal Finance Officers Association, Special Bulletin, February 25, 1976, p. 3.

The preparation of measurable performance objectives is one of the most difficult tasks in MBO. If this step is done well, the final step in determining performance measurement will be much easier to accomplish.

Performance Measurement. In order to measure all aspects of the program or activity, performance measures (yardsticks) are needed. The four yardsticks most often used are as follows.

1. *Demand (need)* indicates the scope of the problem and the need to provide programs and services.

DEMAND INDICATORS—SWIMMING PROGRAM

	Actual 1983	Projected 1984
Estimated handicapped youth	—	350
Estimated children—low income	—	1,000
Estimated daily admissions (fee)	35,000	32,000
Estimated daily admissions (free)	—	3,500
Estimated lesson registration	2,800	2,900

---

2. *Workload (Response)* relates to the agency's response to the need or demand. It represents the amount of work provided to accomplish the program.

WORKLOAD INDICATORS—SWIMMING PROGRAM

	Projected 1983	Revised 1983	Projected 1984
Daily admissions (fee)	35,000	34,500	32,000
Daily admissions (free)	—	—	3,500
Lessons registration	2,900	2,800	2,900
Classes—planned	150	150	154
—offered	150	150	154

With the opening of the pool on Saturday mornings for free swimming, a drop in paid daily admissions would need to be projected.

3. *Productivity (Cost)* relates to the relationship between the agency's resources used (input) and the results obtained (output). The agency is charged with producing the desired program with the minimum of effort and expense.

Measures of cost effectiveness are often indicated by the ratio of input to output—dollars per unit or time per unit.

PRODUCTIVITY INDICATORS—
SWIMMING PROGRAM

	Projected 1983	Revised 1983	Projected 1984
Cost per participant—lessons and admissions	$2.29	$2.25	$2.20
Revenue per participant—lessons and admissions	1.75	1.75	1.50

A program can be organized and operated efficiently but might still not accomplish the objectives. This is why effectiveness measurement is important.

4. *Effectiveness (Impact)* focuses on results or how well programs accomplish their intended purposes or meet the needs of society. The development of good performance indicators to measure effectiveness provides a difficult challenge to park and recreation professionals.

EFFECTIVENESS INDICATORS—SWIMMING
PROGRAM

	Projected 1983	Revised 1983	Projected 1984
Percent of actual registration estimated registration	100%	97%	98%
Percent of handicapped youth passing beginning swimming tests	—	—	60%

Leisure service agencies have as their primary objectives the provision of leisure opportunities and the development of land and facilities for parks and conservation purposes. Measuring quality of life and quality environment involves subjective factors and therefore cannot be readily evaluated in terms of the agency's effectiveness in providing these services. This is why public opinion and citizens' response to service offerings are often used as performance indicators.

The park and recreation profession has not directed sufficient attention to the development of performance standards that can be used in measuring the performance of work or programs. As a result, finance officers and other governmental officials have been responsible for establishing these measurement devices for park and recreation agencies. All agency personnel are responsible for the development of performance measures and standards, however, program supervisors and facility managers are often in a better position to suggest meaningful indicators.

One of the priority problems identified by HUD in its study of local government financial management needs was that there is an inability to tie together performance measurement and evaluation, budgeting, and accounting in order to hold agencies accountable in terms of services provided. With the focus now on evaluating governmental services and holding units of government accountable for their actions, the development of an integrated financial management system that includes goals and objectives, program identification, and performance measurement seems imperative.

Figure 5.2 is an illustration from the Lakewood, Colorado, 1981 city budget showing how performance objectives and measurement indicators are presented for the swimming budget for that city. The performance objective suggesting that seasonal recreation programs should be made self-supporting through user fees resulted from a mandate from the city hall of increasing user fees wherever possible and appropriate.

Program Planning Developing goals and objectives and performance measurement goes hand in hand with program planning. Once the programs are identified, that is, golfing, basketball, camping, swimming, and so on, detailed plans for each of these programs should be developed. This approach to budget development makes program planning a necessity, not just a desirable idea.

Program planning is a year-round process and should not be relegated only to the intensive budget preparation period. If left to this limited time period, the pressures of budget deadlines tend to short change good fiscal planning,

Putting good planning into practice, the staff should carefully evaluate each agency program, many of which are seasonal or part time in nature, immediately following the termination of the program. A summer camp or supervised playground program, for example, should be evaluated periodically during its operation and final evaluation made at the end of the season. For agency functions that operate all year long, a continuous evaluation should take place so that the program planner is ready to finalize his/her budget plans during the budget planning period.

If the evaluation process is done in an objective, comprehensive manner, recommendations for possi-

LEISURE | RECREATION

PROGRAM   SWIMMING

PROGRAM DESCRIPTION   To provide swim lessons and open swim for the safety and enjoyment of Lakewood citizens.

PERFORMANCE OBJECTIVES

1. Provide a comprehensive aquatics program to include, but not be limited to, swim team, open swimming, adult swimming, family swimming, and "learn to swim" schedule.
2. Make the seasonal recreation programs self-supporting through user fees.

INDICATORS OF PERFORMANCE

MEASUREMENT	OBJECTIVE	1979 ACTUAL	1980 PROJECTED	1980 REVISED	1981 PROJECTED
DEMAND					
Lesson Registration (Estimated)	1	3,000	3,000	2,500	2,500
Daily Admissions (Estimated)	1	35,500	35,500	35,500	35,500
WORKLOAD					
Daily Admissions (Actual)	1	2,167	3,000	2,500	2,500
Lesson Registration (Actual)	1	29,964	35,500	35,200	35,500
Classes and Activities Planned	1	173	175	175	175
Classes and Activities Offered	1	175	175	175	175
PRODUCTIVITY					
Average Cost per Participant for Lessons	2	N/A	N/A	11.02	11.12
Average Cost per Participant for Admissions	2	N/A	N/A	1.35	1.35
EFFECTIVENESS					
Average Revenue per Participant for Lessons	2	N/A	N/A	10.60	10.60
Average Revenue per Participant for Admissions	2	N/A	N/A	1.19	1.19
% Actual Registrations of Estimated Registrations	1,2	72%	100%	100%	100%
% Classes or Activities with Minimum to 99% Enrollment	1,2	25%	13%	13%	13%
% Classes or Activities with 100% Enrollment	1,2	61%	87%	87%	87%

ANALYSIS

Despite the proposed completion of the approved Morse Park Pool renovation, annual daily admissions in the swimming program are expected to remain stable in 1981 since this facility is at its practical operating capacity. The indoor pool addition to the Green Mountain Recreation Center is not expected to be in use until January of 1982.

The swimming program is near self-supporting (95%). Fee for swimming activities are kept competitive with other public swimming facilities.

RESOURCES

		1979 ACTUAL	1980 BUDGET	1980 REVISED	1981 BUDGET
CATEGORY:	PERSONNEL	$ 52,426	$ 66,647	$ 66,477	$ 66,315
	OPERATING/MAINTENANCE SUPPLIES	4,888	6,261	5,310	5,879
	CHARGES & SERVICES	3,440	6,910	6,060	5,770
	CAPITAL OUTLAY	452	660	496	---
	TOTAL	$ 61,206	$ 80,478	$ 78,343	$ 77,964
FUNDS:	GENERAL	$ 61,206	$ 80,478	$ 78,343	$ 77,964
	TOTAL	$ 61,206	$ 80,478	$ 78,343	$ 77,964

Figure 5.2   Performance Objectives and Indicators of Performance, Lakewood, Colorado.

ble changes or revisions in program, staff, maintenance work, supplies, and equipment should be completed and available when budget time comes around.

Programs should not remain static. Frequently, the budget request representing next year's recommended program is merely a rubber stamp of the current program and budget. It is highly conceivable that some programs might remain somewhat the same, year after year. It is also possible that other programs may need to be changed, curtailed, or even eliminated. New programs might be recommended to be added to meet the changing needs of the community. Program planning should be based on past experiences, staff evaluations, and long-range plans.

For each program provided by an agency, plans for what is to be done, how, when, and for whom should be developed. Factors such as the scope of the program, anticipated participation, clientele served, recommended policies, and other organizational concerns need to be analyzed. In determining a program plan for a swimming program, one should consider some of the types of detail that are listed as follows.

PROGRAM PLANNING DETAIL—
SWIMMING PROGRAM

Hours of operation
Length of season (May 25–Sept. 6) - 15 weeks
Days of operation—open daily - 105 days
Open swimming
 73 days @ 8 hours per day - 584 hours
 29 days (Wednesday/Friday)
 @ 6 hours per day - 174 hours
 Holidays (3) @ 12 hours per day - 36 hours
 ⎯⎯
 Total 794 hours
Family nights (Wednesdays)
 15 @ 2 hours per night - 30 hours
Teenage nights (Friday)
 14 @ 2 hours per night - 28 hours
Free swimming (low income) Saturdays 10 days @ 3 hours per day - 30 hours
Estimated attendance
 Open swimming (fee) - 32,000
 Open swimming (free) - 3,500
 Peak loads—July–August - 3,000/week
 May–June–September - 1,000/week
Subactivities
 Swimming lessons
 Swim team Detailed program
 planning for
 Family nights each subactivity
 should take
 Teenage nights place
 Special events

Often a narrative statement describing the program in descriptive terms is requested. The statement precedes the expenditures needed to perform the program, thus providing a basis for studying the validity of the request. An illustration of a program statement or description for the swimming program that has been planned follows.

PROGRAM: SWIMMING PROGRAM

Program Description

The Lincoln swimming pool will be open from May 25 to September 6, a total of 105 days of operation. Pool is open daily, 1 P.M. to 9 P.M. for open swimming. Family nights on Wednesday and teenage nights on Fridays. Activities include swim lessons, swim team, expanded instruction for handicapped youth, and free swimming for low-income youth.

Good program planning takes time; its rewards can be rich in the approval of existing and new programs that can be provided to the public and in providing a well-managed program.

Step 2. Determining Work Programs

After the program plan has been decided on (Step 1), the work involved in performing each program should be emphasized next. Work programs might be described as a breakdown of the component parts or jobs needed to accomplish the program. They are concerned with organization, management, facilities, equipment, and work methods.

For example, the budget planner in preparing the budget for the swimming program needs to consider how the program will be administered, what supervision is needed, the preseason work necessary to open the pool, daily maintenance, capital improvements that should be initiated, and the job of closing the pool at the end of the season. A further breakdown of each of these basic jobs should also be made. Daily maintenance, for instance, might be additionally broken down into such work programs as maintenance of locker rooms, parking lot, mowing of lawn, and cleaning of the pool and deck areas. Work programs pinpoint the work to be done. All work that needs to be accomplished should be planned in detail.

Budget planners have a responsibility not merely to see that certain work is completed but also to find out why certain jobs are performed the way they are and how they can be done better, or whether some of the work can be abolished, accomplished by another method, or done by private contract. Administrators should always be alert to search for new techniques for accomplishing work programs. This job should not be relegated to chief executives only. All members of their staff should be involved, for it is on the firing line that actual improvements in work methods can be found and ways of increasing efficiency (which reduces costs) can be discovered.

A number of local governments have followed private enterprise in establishing an employee suggestion contest that has proved to be of real value for municipal employees. On several occasions park and recreation personnel have won cash awards for their suggestions in competition with other public employees. In one city, for example, the goals established for employee ideas were that the suggestion

Would save money, time, and/or labor in present operations.

Would accomplish more for the same cost, time and/or labor.

Would improve the safety and welfare of employees on the job.

Would improve the cities' relations with its citizens.

The first two goals relate directly to more efficient work procedures and methods. As good managers, park and recreation personnel should invoke the best work techniques possible. This practice will gain the respect of public officials and the public alike, as well as save money that can be put to other uses. Efficient operation is just as much a part of good budgeting procedures as estimating work programs and expenses.

Park and recreation agencies have been successful in reducing costs by the installation of improved work methods, better personnel utilization, and mechanization of operation. One director of a large metropolitan agency indicated that a redesign of a park area in which sidewalks were moved to the curb eliminated a large share of the edging cost in one of the parks. Other examples given by park and recreation leaders are summarized as follows.

- Radios in supervisor's cars.
- Mechanization of park maintenance operation (chain saws, chippers, stump cutters, sky buckets, litter lifts, etc.)
- Rent certain equipment instead of purchasing.
- Contract work to be done instead of doing it ourselves.
- Use of flowers, shrubs, and trees that need minimum of maintenance.
- Decentralization of maintenance operation.
- Establishment of traveling maintenance crews.

Detailed and well-planned work programs are of tremendous value to administrators in budget pre-

sentation and in the management of their departments. In developing a budget for the swimming program, one must accomplish the following examples of work in carrying out the program plan identified in Step 1.

WORK PROGRAMS—SWIMMING PROGRAM

Administration	- Planning; hiring, training, and supervising personnel; public relations; purchasing; and so on
Supervision	- Locker rooms, pool, grounds
Instruction	- Learn to swim and life saving classes
Coaching	- Swim team
Maintenance	- Preseason, daily, and post season Building and locker rooms, pool, concession area, parking lot, grounds
Capital improvements	- Construction of new concession area

Step 3. Determining Personnel, Supplies, and Equipment

Once program and work plans have been determined (Steps 1 and 2), the next concern of the budget planner is to estimate what it takes to accomplish the work. All cost items that are considered necessary should be carefully itemized. The more experience administrators and their staff have and the more complete the records are, the better the estimates will be. There are many approaches that can be used in estimating cost items.

- Budget worksheets can be submitted to the staff to find out their particular needs.
- Conferences with staff members concerning their requests should be scheduled. It is in the field where the work is accomplished. Staff member's recommendations as to the type and amount of labor, supplies, and equipment needed should be carefully considered.
- A file of current catalogs can prove to be valuable in developing lists of supplies and equipment.
- A check on past purchase requisitions often proves to be of value.
- An analysis of cost records is one of the best ways of finding out exactly what it takes to accomplish work programs.
- The collection of information is a year-round process. To facilitate this, a folder should be kept for each program. As needs are pointed out during the year, notes should be made and filed in the folder. Also, as problems arise or new work programs are deemed necessary, estimates

should be gathered immediately. This information will then be available when budget preparation time arrives.

As work programs change, so do the needs to perform them. A careful evaluation of each work function should produce realistic estimates.

Step 4. Estimating Expenditures

The next step in the budget planning process is to place the dollar figure on the cost items figured in Step 3. Utilizing last year's cost estimates and merely adding a certain percentage increase is not good logic or good planning.

Cost estimates can be broadly classified under two major categories: personal services and nonpersonal services (supplies, materials, and equipment). As salaries, wages, and fringe benefits make up close to 75 percent of most agencys' budgets, the figuring of costs for personnel employed by the agency is of utmost importance.

Salaries and Wages. Good personnel administration is based on a personnel classification plan where positions are classified (by level) by the nature of work performed, the degree of difficulty, and the responsibility of the job. Once the job is classified, the salary or wage can be determined. The principle of equal pay for equal work should prevail.

In estimating the cost of salaries and wages for new employees, one determines the amount by the position classification system as represented by a salary schedule adopted by the local jurisdiction, state agency, or federal government (civil service). In the case of personnel already employed, the adjustment of current budget costs should be made taking into account inflation, productivity (merit), and changes in duties and responsibilities of the job.

Salary adjustments are normally determined by the legislative body. There are a number of approaches used in figuring salary–wage increases.

1. Salary schedules.
   (a) Step increases based on merit.
   (b) Raising of the minimum entry level salary and adjusting salaries accordingly.
2. Across the board raise.
   (a) All employees receive the same raise, that is, 10 percent.
   (b) A 10 percent raise in salaries is approved; however, money is distributed according to merit.
3. Cost of living adjustment.
4. Inequity adjustments based on affirmative action reviews.

There are a number of factors that influence salary and wage budgeting in local jurisdictions throughout the country. These include:

1. Labor unions—collective bargaining.
2. Affirmative action programs.
3. Political climate—legislative body sets raise.
4. Local conditions—cost of living.
5. Inflation—economic situation.
6. Federal guidelines—minimum wage law.
7. Fringe benefits.
8. Regulatory agencies.

Fringe benefits are on the rise in most local governments. Costs for programs such as retirement, health insurance, life insurance, time-off benefits (vacations, holidays, and sick leaves), and workers' compensation make up a substantial part of the budget. The fringe benefit package is often determined by the budget or finance department and computed as a fixed percent of the worker's salary.

In preparing budget detail for cost estimates in salaries and wages, the following data are often deemed necessary: employee position, workload, unit cost per work unit, and total salary. Examples for swimming pool personnel follows.

```
PERSONAL SERVICES—SWIMMING PROGRAM

Pool manager—16 weeks @ $200/wk.          $ 3,200
Attendants/cashier—3 @ $150/wk × 16 wks     7,200
Senior life guard—16 wks @ $175             2,800
Life guards—8 @ $150/wk × 16 wks           19,200
Engineer—16 wks × 10 hrs/wk @ $8.00/hr      1,280
Head swim coach—16 wks @ $175/wk            2,800
Swimming/diving coaches—3 @ $150/wk × 16 wks 7,200
```

Nonpersonal Services. In preparing cost estimates for all other expenses, one recognizes that inflation, change in workload data, and subsequent changes in cost items will greatly influence these estimates. Copying or merely adding a certain percentage increase to last year's budget is not sufficient.

Guidance is often forthcoming from the central administration instructing an agency on how to estimate costs of supplies and equipment. Often a certain recommended percent increase (i.e., 6 percent) is imposed on an agency as a partial counter to inflation. Other approaches used for estimating expenditure costs are:

1. Bids and estimates.
2. Cost accounting data.
3. Record of past purchases—adjusted for inflation.
4. File of current catalogs.
5. Price indexes that are often included in budget manuals or prepared by outside firms.

A widely accepted principle in budgeting is—*be liberal in estimating expenditures*. Cost items generally cost more than anticipated. This does not mean padding the budget. It does recognize that things often cost more than planned.

Step 5. Estimating Receipts

Increased pressures are levied on administrators to make their programs and services more self-supporting. It was noted in Chapter 3 that many of the traditional concepts and practices regarding fees and charges are replaced as agencies are required to stress user-supported services. Budget planners are faced with mandates from their legislative bodies to increase current fees and charges and to institute first-time fees for activities that traditionally have been free to the public. It is evident that the 1980s will force park and recreation professionals to rethink their philosophies and past practices regarding fees and charges and the forecasting of receipts will become a more important part of the budget planning process. The agency's response to the mandating of revenue-producing programs should be couched with the effect that increased charges will have on the overall program and the discrimination that it might have on the low-economic citizens in the community.

The estimating of revenues is based closely on the program plan, that is, goals and objectives, scope of program, changes in programming taking place, and the changing conditions occuring in the community and society. A well-prepared budget should document the sources and amounts of revenue derived from each of the programs that have revenue-producing ability.

The agency that operates the program is normally asked to make accurate revenue estimates. Likewise, persons in charge of the swimming, golfing, or athletic leagues are in the best position to make accurate estimates. Forecasters find themselves in one of two positions. (1) Revenue has been previously received from the program, (2) Revenue is a new, first-time practice. In the first instance the person has previous revenue data with which to guide his/her estimates. When charging revenues for a new activity or for the first time for the program, the planner must seek information from other agencies or local governments, from consultants, or just make a good guess.

The task for forecasting is considered more of an art than an exact science. To the extent that the forecast is made on good reliable information and facts, the estimate should provide a valuable guide for the budget process and the operation of the program. The person's experience and good judgment also pays dividends.

Forecasters should be careful not to fall into the rut of using last year's receipts in making this year's predictions. Estimates are often influenced by unpredictable factors such as weather, inflation, social–economic concerns, public's response to programs, and even fads that influence people's leisure participation.

In many local governments the central budget office requests the agency to submit their revenue estimates on a form requesting figures on revenues received over a three- to five-year period. This is helpful for viewing discernible trends and in providing a foundation of data on which to build next year's estimate. Also listed on the form are the sources of revenue that are expected. Figure 5.3 presents the possible sources of revenues and estimates for the Lincoln swimming pool.

The data found in Figure 5.3 reveal that a significant drop in receipts took place in 1982. In checking the records that were kept, one finds that the pool suffered one of the coldest months of June and August in the history of the city and also that the pool was closed twelve days because of inclement weather. The 1983 estimate was influenced by a decrease in the cost of family memberships (city mandate), which not only projected an increase in the number of families purchasing season tickets but projected a decrease in adult and child season tickets and also general admissions. In 1984 the forecast was influenced by the city mandate and departmental goals and objectives (free swimming on Saturdays and increased fees and charges). (See page 56.) One of the performance objectives set by the department was to increase revenues by 10 percent.

Budgeting is a continuous year-round process. Budget planners in addition to having the responsibility for estimating next year's revenues, must analyze current trends and operations and be prepared to estimate the revenues anticipated for the remainder of the current year. Because the swimming pool is in operation during this budget planning period, the budget planner should not only analyze the receipts taken in to date (6/30/83) but should study the current social–economic indicators and present response to the program and then should estimate the receipts for the remainder of the period. If the pool is having a successful year and the receipts to date are higher than anticipated, the budget maker is in a position of changing the estimate upward. If, however, conditions are unfavorable and receipts are lower than anticipated, the estimate should be adjusted accordingly.

In estimating revenues, a basic principle in budget planning is to *be conservative*. Generally, an inflated revenue estimate is a much graver sin than padding the expenditure estimate.

Swimming Pool Receipts

	1981 Actual	1982 Actual	Estimated	Actual 6/30	1983 Estimated-Balance of Year	Estimated Total	1984 Estimate
Season tickets							
Family	$10,000	$9,000	$11,500	$10,000	$1.200	$11,200	$13,300
Adult	3,000	3,000	2,500	2,300	200	2,500	3,500
Child	2,000	1,500	1,500	1,000	200	1,200	1,500
Admissions	15,000	12,500	14,000	11,000	3,000	14,000	13,500
Registration fees—							
lessons	5,500	5,000	6,200	2,000	4,000	6,000	7,000
Concessions	4,000	2,400	5,500	2,000	3,600	5,600	6,000
Towel-locker rental	2,000	1,000	2,000	600	1,500	2,100	2,200
Miscellaneous	2,000	1,000	1,800	700	1,200	1,900	2,000
Total	$43,500	$35,400	$45,000	$29,600	$14,900	$44,500	$49,000

Figure 5.3 Estimated Receipts for Swimming Pool, 1984.

Classification of Expenditures

After the cost items (expenditures) have been estimated for each program in the budget, they should be grouped according to the object of expenditure classification system adopted by the taxing district or local governmental jurisdiction. A standard system of objects of expenditure should be used by all agencies throughout the governmental jurisdiction.

With the development of line item or object of expenditure budgeting in the early 1900s came the listing of objects or cost items and the establishment of objects of expenditure classification systems. An object has been defined as the article purchased or a service obtained, that is, supplies, equipment, salaries, electricity, and telephone. In the early years of this approach to budgeting a detailed listing of all objects was included in the budget. This was found to be unnecessary and later a grouping of like items was made and line item categories were developed, that is, personal services, supplies, and other services and charges.

Public agencies vary as to the type of system that is employed. Efforts have been made by public officials and organizations to standardize the systems used throughout the country. The National Municipal League has given leadership toward developing a unified system. Many local governments have adopted the original or a slightly modified form, however, the goal of establishing one system has not been achieved.

Objects of expenditure are generally classified on two different levels of detail. The major categories that are often found in budget summaries include the following.

Personal services.
Supplies.
Other services and charges.
Capital outlays.

A more detailed classification system of these major categories is used when the cost items are listed under each program. This is necessary to enable agencies to develop budget estimates for performing the work functions to carry out each program. For example, personal services is often subdivided into salaries and wages, employee benefits, and other personal services. Supplies might include office supplies, operating supplies, repair and maintenance of supplies, and other supplies.

States mandate the type of classification systems used by cities, counties, and special districts. The classification system required for all cities in Indiana, revised in 1981, is found in Appendix C, page 142.

Objects of expenditure classification systems include a numbering or coding of each object that serves as the basis of establishing an accounting system, as well as an identification of objects. The numbering of objects makes possible the transference of cost information to matching accounting systems and data processing. Coding of the fund, function, and objects is essential if the information is to be transferred from time slips, vouchers, and requisitions to appropriate accounting ledgers. In this manner the cost items are charged to the appropriate agency and function, thus enabling the agency to ascertain the actual cost of each function performed by the agency.

Classification of Revenues

The recording of sources of revenues and the development of an appropriate classification system for revenues performs a similar function to that of objects of expenditure classification systems. Such a system provides detailed information as to the types and amount of revenues received, which is essential for estimating revenues in the budget planning process.

Quality of Performance

The extent and quality of conducting programs varies from local government to local government, as well as within each local jurisdiction. A park, swimming pool, or camp may be run in an "a number one" fashion or may be conducted in a less desirable manner. For example, financial conditions may require an agency to place common laborers in a park to carry out supervisory as well as maintenance responsibilities. Different conditions may make it necessary to add park police, recreation leaders, uniformed park receptionists or other types of specialized personnel in the park. The addition of these types of personnel would definitely increase the standards of operation and quality of service performed.

Whether to mow a park or recreation area once a week, twice a month, or once a month would be a decision that has to be made and recommended to the official body for approval. The real question is, "What is the proper maintenance standards for a park, playfield, or zoo?" Are there minimum and maximum standards of operating programs? How many life guards are needed to provide supervision for the public pool?

Some standards (facility and personnel) have been developed and are used in justifying leisure service programs. However, the need for establishing standards that can be used in justifying budget requests and as yardsticks for measuring the adequacy of leisure services is urgent and long overdue. Such standards are necessary guideposts for professionals to follow in developing work programs; they also serve as performance indicators to measure the success of program services.

There are a growing number of park and recreation professionals who feel that public agencies should strive to operate quality programs even if this means the elimination of low-priority programs. The principle here is to do fewer things, but to do them better. For years Oakland, California, has received wide recognition for the Children's

Fairyland and Animal Zoo, which is an example of running a leisure service program on a "first-rate" basis.

Americans spend between $200 to $300 billion on recreation, which indicates that they are willing to spend money for leisure activities. The response of the American public to Disneyland and Disney World, both operated on a quality basis, is well known. Private and commercial agencies providing leisure services have spent huge sums of money in developing creative and quality programs in an attempt to attract the general public. Public and semi-public leisure agencies, which are competing with television and commercial agencies in attracting the public to their facilities and programs, should realize that the public is willing to pay for and participate in quality leisure programs.

It is widely recognized that the level of financial support generally affects the quality of the service provided. In an era of fiscal constraints, inflation and reduced budgets have resulted, in many instances, in the watering down of the quality of maintenance, leadership, and service provided. If an agency continues to conduct programs and facilities at the same level with less dollars, it is evident that the quality of performance will inevitably decline. During the 1970s the heavy dependence of local agencies on CETA workers had allowed most agencies to continue services that otherwise might have been cut. The National Urban Recreation Study found that the use of CETA workers had produced a variety of adverse effects on the quality of services offered the public.

A decision must be made on whether to continue to offer the same level of services for less money, or to offer fewer services but with a higher level of performance. In the long run the leisure service agency will be judged by the standards of service that is being provided.

Determining Alternatives

A practice that currently prevails in many of the newer approaches to budgeting is the preparation of alternative budgets. In zero-base budgeting, one facet in preparing a decision package is developing alternatives for each program to be performed by an agency. These alternatives, normally three, are then prioritized along with alternatives developed for all other programs offered by an agency so that top management may allocate the finance resources available in a systematic and efficient manner. Rather than presenting only one estimate for operating a program, the alternatives give the reviewing body several choices from which to choose, and politicians like choices.

Literature on zero-base budgeting points out that there are two classes of alternatives.

1. Different ways of performing the function.
2. Different levels of effort in performing the function.

Program planners should always be alert in exploring different ways of performing either the work or the function. If the contracting out for work to a private firm is the most effective and efficient manner of operating, this should be incorporated in the budget planning and not left to legislative determination. It is in the scope of the function or the level of effort where alternatives should be developed.

Local government officials generally establish the levels of service that should guide the budget planner in preparing alternatives. These often include:

1. *Minimum Level.* Reduce level below the previous fiscal year.
2. *Base Level.* Represents a continuance of current service level.
3. *Increase Level* Resources required to meet increased workload, improvement, or expansion of the function.

In examining budgets from several cities that have developed alternatives, we find that there appear to be several distinct approaches used by administrators in preparing alternatives. All these approaches were utilized by park and recreation budget planners in Memphis, Tennessee, and Lakewood, Colorado (see Figure 5.4).

If financial resources are limited and legislative officials must make the tough choice of budget reduction, professionals in all fields of public service should prepare alternatives that represent reduction in services performed rather than cutting down the quality of the program. The general public appreciates good quality services and is often willing to pay for the service that is operated well. If the agency elects to offer programs that lack quality, the image of the agency and the acceptance of the program will ultimately suffer.

Along with the alternatives recommended, a decision package also includes the benefits of the funding and the consequences of not funding the decision package. One of three decision packages presented as a part of the budget for the swimming pool season offered by the parks and recreation department in Phoenix, Arizona, is found in Appendix D-5, page 148. This example represents a minimum level of service or a reduction from the previous fiscal year.

Capital Improvement Programs and Budgets

One of the priority problems identified by HUD in its 1978 study of local governmental finance was, "There is a need for capital improvement programming which accurately reflects the total priority capital needs of communities and the impact on the operating budget."[6]

HUD's study found that capital planning and budgeting are often not integrated with the municipality's annual operating budget. As a result:

planning for capital facilities is fragmented, and neither the policy makers nor citizens fully understand the decision making process and the implications for future operating costs. Taxpayers' resistance tends to become even more intense in the face of requests for large capital expenditures that have not been explained or adequately justified.[7]

Gaining approval for the yearly operating budget for the ongoing and accustomed programs is test enough of the administrator's professional talents. However, the real challenge comes in selling and interpreting large expenditures for capital items—acquiring land, developing open space areas (parks), or the construction of buildings and recreation facilities. The development of a capital program and a capital budget requires the best planning and administrative talents of the budget maker. Before further discussion of the subject, a brief look at the two preceding terms might be in order. Moak and Killian, who authored one of the most complete and comprehensive texts on the subject, define these two concepts as follows.

A *capital program* is a plan for capital expenditures to be incurred each year over a fixed period of years to meet capital needs arising from the long term work program.

A *capital budget* is a plan for capital expenditures to be incurred during the budget year from funds subject to appropriation by the governing body of the concerned government for projects scheduled in the capital program for the first year thereof.[8]

It should be noted that the key word in both definitions is "plan." In preparing a program type operating budget the emphasis is placed on planning—setting goals and objectives, program planning, and determining priorities. For capital improvement pro-

[6]*Local Government Financial Management Capacity Sharing Program Plan,* U.S. Department of Housing and Urban Development, draft report, Washington, D.C., July 1978, p. 12.
[7]Ibid.
[8]Lennox L. Moak, and Kathryn W. Killian, *Capital Programming and Capital Budgeting,* Municipal Finance Officers Association, Chicago, 1964, p. 3.

Approaches to Alternatives

A. *Quality of performance[1]*

Maintenance of parks
1. Reduced: Package gives a 21-day clean-up and service level. No weekend service.
2. Maintenance: Would provide 14-day cycles and some weekend work.
3. Increase I: Would provide 14-day cycles and complete weekend work and increased clean-up.
4. Increase II: Would give 10-day mowing cycle and increased clean-up.

B. *Programs and services[2]*

Zoo
1. Reduced Level I: Will provide only 8 major exhibit areas—will close the Carnivore Building, Tropical Bird House, Primate Building, Elephant House, Contact Area and Tortoise Building, and close public access to the Education Building.
2. Reduced Level II: Will provide only 11 major exhibit areas instead of 14, which will close the Carnivore Building, Tropical Bird House, and Contact Area.
3. Maintenance: Provide 14 major exhibit areas and facilities of the modern-day urban zoological garden and aquarium.
4. Inc. Level I: Promote the Memphis Zoological Garden and Aquarium locally, regionally, and nationally.

C. *Combination—quality and services[3]*

Playgrounds
1. Reduced Level I: Playgrounds open eight weeks—lose one week service—only one worker per playground.
2. Reduced Level II: Playgrounds open eight weeks—lose one week service—two workers per playground.
3. Maintenance Level: Playgrounds open nine weeks—full normal service—two workers per playground.

D. *Elimination of complete program[4]*

Community events (cultural programs)

[1]Memphis 1979 budget (Vol. 3), pp. 7–10.
[2]Ibid, p. 167.
[3]Ibid, p. 17.
[4]Lakewood, Colorado, 1979 Budget, pp. 148–149.

Figure 5.4 Approaches Used for Preparing Alternatives.

---

gramming and budgeting long-range comprehensive planning is a must. Planning for capital projects for open space and recreation should be carefully integrated with other community needs and functions (schools, transportation, industrial growth, housing, etc.) of the city and region. A city or county master plan, and in many cases a regional plan, provides the essential guidelines and priorities for which the open space and recreation needs are projected for the overall development of the community or region. It is unfortunate that many local governments do not manage their community growth and development by using good capital improvement planning strategies. One of the findings reported in the National Urban Recreation Study (1978) was, "Most recreation plans do not set priorities or implementation strategies, and are not linked to capital improvement programs. Plan implementation is limited by fiscal constraints and inadequate public support in many cities studied."[9] As a result of the financial problems facing local governments and the lack of good planning, new capital projects are often abandoned in deference to the daily operating concerns.

Another concern is evident. As local financial resources fail to keep pace with inflation and tax limitation measures are creating a fiscal crisis in many communities, local governments have turned to the federal government for financing local capital improvements. A number of federal assistance programs (revenue sharing, Land and Water Conservation Fund, and Community Development Block Grants) have been responsible for providing matching funds for land acquisition and capital improvements. If the local park and recreation agency looks toward the federal government for funding, it must

[9]*National Urban Recreation Study,* U.S. Department of Interior, Washington, D.C., 1978, p. 79.

have a comprehensive plan in order to be eligible for such funding. It is interesting that those local governments that have tied their planning process directly with the budget process were those that have been most successful in gaining federal support for capital programs.

Cities and departments vary as to their approach to capital improvements programs and budgets. In larger jurisdictions the forms and instructions for preparing these budgets are often formulated by the central budget agency. Generally, two formats are found in the capital improvement budgets—a summary of the agency's project requests and detail for each individual project request. The capital improvement budget in Montogomery County, Maryland, provides an excellent example of the information that should be presented in a capital budget. The summary of the agency's project estimates is found in Figure 5.5. The status of each project based on a six-year plan gives the reviewing body an overall picture of the funding plan for each project. The capital budget for the current budget year is also given.

Moak and Killian suggest that the following information should be included for each capital project.

1. Identifying information—project number, title, and type of projects—i.e., replacement, alternation, or new facility.
2. Narrative description of project.
3. Justification of need.
4. Priority ranking of the project.
5. Total funds expended or to be expended.
6. Sources of project financing.
7. Status of the project site—city owned, not yet acquired, condemnation ordered, and so on.
8. Status of project plans.
9. Estimated total cost.
10. Annual operating and maintenance cost.
11. Revenues anticipated.[10]

Most of the information suggested by Moak and Killian can be found in the Montogomery County's capital improvement program for Old Germantown Local Park, revealed in Figure 5.6.

THE BUDGET DOCUMENT

Just as the approach to the development of the budget is specified by state statutes and local ordinances, the resulting budget document is also determined by legal provisions. The form and content of the budget document varies from state to state and local government to local government. Budgets differ

in terms of format, length, amount of detail, arrangement, and approach to the data included.

The budget document varies from a one- or two-page listing of object items for a park and recreation department to a more comprehensive presentation of the budget information, which is often contained in one or several volumes. A careful analysis of budgets from local governments of all sizes indicates that certain information is common to most budget documents. The format, sequence of materials, and content of a meaningful budget document should include: budget message, budget summary, estimates of expenditures and receipts for functions and programs, and supplemental data to support the budget data that are being presented.

Budget Message

The budget message serves as the "state of the agency" or the executive's formal letter of introduction to the budget being presented to the legislative body. In a most limited sense the budget message serves as a letter of transmittal to the agency's immediate superior, indicating the agency's response to the higher authorities' mandates, instructions, and guidelines for developing the budget proposal. It does have an important function in setting the stage for the review of the detailed budget that follows. The message should focus on these concerns.

- Highlight some of the significant changes in programs or levels of service that are being proposed in the new budget.
- Indicate some of the major problem areas that are facing the agency.
- Point out areas where significant increases or decreases in expenditures and receipts take place.
- Reveal notable accomplishments of the agency during the previous year.
- Mention some of the needs and problems anticipated in the future.
- Comment on the impact of major capital improvements on budget projections for the new budget year.

The overall purpose of the budget message is to prepare the budget reviewing body and the public about the salient features of the proposed budget that will help explain and justify the budget data that follows. The budget message should be concise, well written, and designed to maintain the reader's interest. It also provides an opportunity for the executive to acknowledge the individuals and groups that have contributed to the success of the program.

Many executives include graphs, figures, tables, and other illustrations, either as a part of their budget message or placed immediately after the message, to amplify the text and budget figures.

[10]Moak and Killian, *Capital Programming and Capital Budgeting*, p. 61, 63.

The Maryland-National Capital Park and Planning Commission
EXPENDITURE SCHEDULE

PROJECT LISTING

ALL FIGURES IN THOUSANDS

MAP REF NUM	PDF PAGE NUM	PROJECT NUMBER	PROJECT NAME	EST TOTAL COST	EXPEND THRU FY 77	EST EXPEND FY 78	TOTAL SIX YEARS	EXPENDITURE SCHEDULE						APPROP THRU FY 78	BUDGET REQUEST FY 79
								YR 1 FY 79	YR 2 FY 80	YR 3 FY 81	YR 4 FY 82	YR 5 FY 83	YR 6 FY 84		
			COMMUNITY RECREATION AND URBAN BEAUTIFICATION PARK PROJECTS (CONTINUED)												
A05K	4061	777879	John Haines Neighborhood Park	60		5	55	55						9	51
D15R	4062	777886	Kemp Mill Urban Park Addition	40	2	1	37	37						3	37
D15Q	4063	717434	Kensington Heights Neighborhood Park	325	234	3	88	88						237	88
D16M	4064	697461	Kentsdale Local Park	200*		4*	12				5*	3	4		
A06I	4065	717462	Kings Local Park	200*			196		3	3	190			7*	120
D15L	4066	727464	Lake Normandy Estates Neighborhood Park	132	2	10	120	60	60					12	
D17S	4067	717468	Long Branch Local Park	1,250	1,087	15	148	5	143					1,107	
B09Q	4068	777988	Longwood Local Park	143	3	80	60	60						83 (+33)	
B08M	4069	717469	Maple View Local Park	170*			7*					5*	2		27
D14S	4070	747785	Meadowood Local Park	312	282	30								312	
D17R	4071	777885	Metro Urban Park	400		165	235	235						388	12
A09J	4072	757424	Middlebrook Road Local Park	170*			10*				5*	2	3		
D13R	4073	707472	Middlevale Neighborhood Park	77	7	5	65		3	62				12	
D16R	4074	757426	Montgomery Hills Neighborhood Park	235	151	4	80	3	77					155	3
B09P	4075	707754	Mount Zion Local Park	229*	229	*								229*	
D17S	4076	717475	New Hampshire Estates Neighborhood Park	454*	362		42*	2*	40					364*	
D130	4077	727477	North Gate Local Park	632	464		191	95	96					464	
D12S	4078	767680	Notley Road Local Park	310	114	5	200		4	3	3	190		120	190
D11P	4079	727478	Oakdale Local Park	200	80										
A10I	4080	727463	Old Germantown Local Park	246	80		166				3	3	160	80	
B10Q	4081	697479	Olney Southeast Local Park	170*			7*					5*	2		
B10P	4082	757428	Olney Square Neighborhood Park	120	65	55								120	
C11J	4083	717485	Orchard Local Park	170*			170*			5*	5*	3	160		
A09E	4084	717494	Owens Local Park	323	275	8	40		2	38				283	
D13S	4085	777884	Peachwood Local Park	170	2	3	165	2	3	160				7	
D17L	4086	697481	Persimmon Tree Local Park	170*			170*		3	5*	2	3	160		
D17R	4087	777880	Philadelphia Ave. Urban Park	42*			4*				1*	1	2		
D16S	4088	757423	Pinecrest Local Park	140		10	130	7	123					17	
A09K	4089	707483	Plumgar Local Park	448	428	20								448	
C12J	4090	787138	Quince Orchard Knolls Loc. Park	35		35								35	
C11N	4091	717413	Redland Local Park	310	114	4	192	2	82	108				120	
D17R	4092	717489	Rosemary Hills Local Park	280*	145	55	80*	80*						200	80*
D16N	4093	767675	Scotland Neighborhood Park	135	110	25								135	
D17S	4094	777881	Seven Oaks Neighborhood Park	65		2	63	1	2	60				5	
D17S	4095	777882	Silver Spring Intermediate Neighborhood Park	120	78	42								120	
D17S	4096	727499	Sligo Ave. Neighborhood Park	362	265	97								362	
A10J	4097	707500	South Gunner's Branch Loc. Park	170	2		168		4	4	160			2	
C12E	4098	707501	South Poolesville Local Park	200*			5*						5*		

Figure 5.5   Summary of Capital Improvement Program in Culture and Recreation 1979–1984, Montgomery County, Maryland.

A. IDENTIFICATION AND CODING INFORMATION

1. Project Number	Agency No.	Update Code	2. Date September 15, 1977	7. PREL. PDF PG NO. 4088
727463		Change		

3. Project Name — Old Germantown Local Park

5. Agency — M-NCPPC

4. Program — Culture and Recreation

6. Planning Area — 19 Germantown & Vicinity

B.

EXPENDITURE SCHEDULE (000'S)

Cost Elements	(8) Total	(9) Thru FY 77	(10) Estimate FY 78	(11) Total 6 Years	(12) Year 1 FY 79	(13) Year 2 FY 80	(14) Year 3 FY 81	(15) Year 4 FY 82	(16) Year 5 FY 83	(17) Year 6 FY 84	(18) Beyond 6 Years
1. Planning, Design and Supervision	15	4		11				3	3	5	
2. Land	76	76									
3. Site Improvements and Utilities	75			75						75	
4. Construction	75			75						75	
5. Furniture and Equipment	5			5						5	
6. Total	246	80		166				3	3	160	

C.

FUNDING SCHEDULE (000'S)

05 State Aid	76	76									
06 P&P Bonds	170	4		166				3	3	160	

D. DESCRIPTION & JUSTIFICATION   PROJECT NO. 727463   PROJECT NAME Old Germantown Local Park

1. DESCRIPTION: This project will provide development of an existing 8-acre local park portion of an 18 acre park-school located south of Clopper Road and east of Route 118. Development may include: (1) a recreation shelter with restrooms and recreation storage space; (2) control plaza; (3) athletic fields; (4) lighted tennis courts; (5) play equipment; (6) parking area; (7) drinking fountain; (8) benches; (9) bicycle rack; and (10) landscaping, upon approval by the local citizens association(s). Capacity: The park should accommodate approximately 200 people with recreational programming space as required by the Recreation Department. Service Area: The southwest portion of the Germantown and Vicinity Planning Area. This is one of 17 local use parks which will be acquired in the Germantown and Vicinity Planning Area by 1984, at which time the projected planning area population will be 24,700.

2. JUSTIFICATION: Plans and Studies: The current Germantown and Vicinity Master Plan. Currently adopted CIP. Specific Data: Presently the area is predominantly rural. It is anticipated that as the area becomes more fully developed demand for this facility will increase.

3. STATUS: Acquisition: Land already in parkland status: Development: Conceptual stage.

4. OTHER: This project was formerly designated Kingsview Local Park.

E. ANNUAL OPERATING BUDGET IMPACT (000's)

Program Costs:	Staff	0
	Other	0
Facility Costs:	Maintenance	16
	Debt Service	17
Total Costs		33
Offsetting Revenue or Cost Savings		(0)

F. APPROPRIATION AND EXPENDITURE DATA (000's)

Date First In Capital Program		FY 72
Date First Appropriation		FY 73
Initial Cost Estimate		224
Present Cost Estimate		246

Cumulative Appropriation	Expenditures and Encumbrances	Unencumbered Balance
80	80	0

Appropriation Request, Budget Year FY 79	0

Supplemental Appropriation Request	
Current Year FY 78	0

G. RELOCATION INFORMATION

Families 0   Individuals 0   Businesses 0

H. MAP   Map Reference Code: A101

I. COORDINATION INFORMATION

The development plan is to be coordinated with the community, Montgomery County Public Schools, and the Montgomery County Recreation Department.

PDF 7/77

Figure 5.6 Capital Improvement Budget for Old Germantown Local Park, Montgomery County, Maryland.

Budget Summary

The budget summary that follows the budget message serves as the connecting link between the message and the detailed summaries of expenditures and revenues for programs that follow. It is simply the budget reduced to outline form. The budget summary, normally limited to one or two pages, gives the budget reviewer an overall picture of the revenues and expenditures of past years and the current year with those projected for the coming fiscal year. As a result, significant increases and decreases in the proposed budget can be readily identified.

The content of a budget summary generally includes sources of revenues by funds, expenditures by department or program, revenues according to major sources, and object of expenditures by major categories. An example of the format and contents that is included in the budget summary for the parks and recreation department, Lakewood, Colorado, is found in Appendix D-1, page 144.

Program Budget Estimates

For each program identified in the budget summary the next section of the budget document should contain information on the proposed program and a summary of estimated expenditures and receipts for the program. The type of information included is greatly influenced by the type of budget that is used by the local government. Newer concepts of budgeting, that is, program, program performance, and zero base, each require different kinds of information in this step of budget development.

The program budget (see Appendix D-2, page 145) normally gives a brief description of the program, followed by a summary of the object of expenditure costs. The identity of detailed work programs and plans is not included until later in the budget document. The program performance budget identifies the program and a brief description of the program as found in the aforementioned program budget and also identifies performance objectives, indicators of performance, and an analysis of the changes that will take place in the plan that is presented (see Appendix D-3, page 146). The program budget format developed in 1980 by the Hennepin County Park Reserve District, Minnesota, (see Appendix D-4, page 147) incorporates many of the features of the Lakewood, Colorado, program performance budget.

The budget planner, in following the guidelines of zero-base budgeting, would utilize the format and procedures adopted by the city or county. The main differences from other types of budgets would be the

development of decision packages that identify alternatives and the consequences of accepting each package. The decision package, illustrated in Appendix D-5, page 148, is just one of three alternatives that were presented in the Phoenix, Arizona, budget for the swimming pool program.

In the basic development and planning of the budget detailed planning often takes place for each function, that is, swimming pool. When the budget document is prepared by an agency, often all swimming pools in the system are consolidated into one program budget estimate. This is especially true when the park and recreation budget is incorporated as a function in a city's budget document. The identity of many of the smaller functions are lost; otherwise the budget would become too bulky and cumbersome for the legislative body to review.

Moak and Killian suggest that the following items should be included in the budget document presented to local governmental officials.

1. A narrative explanation of the functions of each department, sub-organizational unit, and activity, and a separate section for comments on the major changes proposed in each activity.
2. A listing by major objects of expenditure of the overall cost of conducting each department and sub-organizational unit; and a detailed listing of the costs required to carry out each activity and identification of proposed change.
3. The personnel complement assigned to each department, listed by position title within the various activities, showing the changes proposed.
4. Identification of the workload volume being undertaken in conjunction with each activity.[11]

The first item indicated, "A narrative explanation of the function of each department," would be included in this section of the budget document. The other items mentioned would be placed in the supplemental budget detail that follows.

Supplemental Budget Detail

In addition to the information already discussed, additional supporting data are often provided in the budget document itself or prepared in a separate document that accompanies the budget. If not included as a part of the budget, this information can be retained by the director and staff to be used in answering questions during the budget conference.

[11]Lennox Moak and Kathryn Killian, *A Manual of Techniques for the Preparation, Consideration, Adoption and Administration of Operating Budgets,* Municipal Finance Officers Association, Chicago, 1973, p. 234.

The amount of detail and the kind of information requested varies greatly among communities. Thus the budget maker will need to follow the mandates of the chief executive and legislative body as to what should be included as a part of the budget document.

Most cities request supporting detail to accompany each program estimate. Information that could accompany the program, program/performance, and the Hennepin County budget estimate previously mentioned is found in Appendix D-6, D-7, and D-8, pages 149 to 151. It provides the budget reviewer with further breakdowns, which help to explain the summary figures given in the program estimate.

This kind of data gives park and recreation personnel information that is essential for the management of the agency, as well as an excellent interpretive aid that can be used to justify budget requests. Supporting schedules and detail provide the decision maker with information that relates directly to the quantity and quality of the services or program provided. This kind of detail should be beneficial in changing public officials' attitudes that budgets are padded and wasteful.

In addition to budget data that support each program provided by the agency, other types of supporting data are often found in budget documents. As salaries and wages consume the largest percentage of the agency's expenditures, a summary of the full- and part-time positions is often included in the budget proposal. This summary provides a listing of authorized positions within the department, along with the salaries and wages for these positions. Names of individuals filling the positions generally are omitted. Salary figures for the positions for past years, the current year, and the amount recommended for the new budget are included (see Appendix D-9, page 152). Also, included as a part of the personnel summary are the costs of fringe benefits, that is, retirement, insurance, and medical payments.

Most budgets also include a summary of expenditures by the agency, which identifies line item detail separate from the object costs identified under each program (see Appendix D-10, pages 153–155). Because the kind of supporting data varies greatly, it is almost impossible to discuss all the approaches used. A perusal of numerous park and recreation budgets reveals that several additional types of descriptive information have been incorporated into budget documents: projected goals and objectives; work program data; planning detail, unit costs and performance data; capital improvement information; statistical data on program needs and results; and salary scales.

Summary

The preparation of the budget is influenced by state statutes, mandates from local legislative officials, and the procedures introduced by the park and recreation administrator for providing staff involvement in the budgeting process. The preparation of a program type budget, which is basic to most modern approaches to budgeting, involves the following steps: (1) determining the program (planning), (2) determining the work programs; (3) determining the personnel, supplies, and equipment, (4) estimating expenditures needed, and (5) estimating the receipts that will be taken in by each program.

Program planning involves establishing agency goals and objectives, performance objectives, and performance measurement indicators, as well as a detailed program plan for accomplishing each function. Also, budget planners must carefully study ways to improve work methods and to assure efficient operation of programs. Determining standards of performance, alternatives, and priorities are important aspects of newer approaches to budgets. Integrating capital budgeting and programming with long-range comprehensive planning is basic to receiving acceptance of capital improvements.

The budget document varies greatly from state to state and local government to local government in terms of format, length, amount of detail arrangement, and approach to the data included.

Selected References

Budgeting, A Guide for United Ways and Not-For-Profit Organizations, United Way of America, Alexandria, VA. 1975, 51 pp.

Lehan, Edward A., *Simplified Governmental Budgeting,* Municipal Finance Officers Association, Chicago, 1981, pp. 39–66.

Moak, Lennox, L., and Albert M. Hillhouse, *Local Government Finance,* Municipal Finance Officers Association, Chicago, 1975, pp. 81–89, 95–118.

Rosenberg, Philip, and C. Wayne Stallings, *A Capital Improvement Programming Handbook for Small Cities and Other Governmental Units,* Municipal Finance Officers Association, Chicago, 1978, 76 pp.

Rosenberg, Philip, and C. Wayne Stallings, *An Operating Budget Handbook for Small Cities and Other Governmental Units,* Municipal Finance Officers Association, Chicago, 1978, pp. 5–72.

Chapter 6

Presentation and Adoption of Budget

Gaining approval for the agency's budget proposal involves public officials, legislative boards, citizens, and in some cases, higher governmental groups such as county and state reviewing bodies. The overall complexity of this process depends largely on the fiscal status of the agency, whether it has fiscal dependence or fiscal independence. The success or failure achieved in securing approval of the budget request hinges on the fiscal and political climate confronting the agency and the effectiveness in which the budget is presented.

The fiscal climate that local governments are confronting as they operate in the 1980s, discussed in Chapter 2, has created a fiscal stress on legislative bodies at the local level. There exists a wide gap between the needs and expectations of citizens and the ability of local government to generate adequate revenues to fund the programs and services demanded by the public. In this era of limits the leisure service administrator is placed in a most untenable position of competing for the declining tax dollar. A situation such as an expansion of programs and services, no growth, or even a cutback of agency operations will have a major impact on administrators' strategies in coping with the presentation of the agency's budget proposal for approval.

This phase of the budget process is not only a legislative one; it is also an opportunity to interpret agency functions to the public at large. The administrator will have many audiences with which to deal. The approach taken in presenting the budget to each audience must be carefully planned and adapted or tailored to each public with which the agency must work.

The professionalism of the budget document that is presented to the legislative body will also considerably affect the success achieved in this phase of the budget process. A well-planned and conceived budget that identifies programs and services to be performed will serve as a meaningful interpretive tool for legislative approval. If the public and legislative officials are involved in the planning process, they will view the presentation in a much clearer and receptive light. The professional expertise that the administrator and staff exhibit in preparing the budget is perhaps their best weapon in gaining approval of the budget.

BOARD REVIEW/APPROVAL

If an agency is administered by an official park and recreation board, the budget must be presented to this body. It is the responsibility of the board to establish a sound fiscal plan to achieve the agency's goals. Boards must have the final approval over the budget and exert fiscal control over all expenditures.

Review of the budget generally takes place over a long period of time, in fact, budgeting is really a year-long process. The administrator and staff should be interpreting needs and problems continuously to avoid making major decisions hurriedly during the relatively short budget review period. If board members are constantly informed and involved in agency operations, they are generally receptive to the program plans that are developed in the budget planning and presentation process.

Some park and recreation executives have found that it is unwise to submit the overall agency budget to their boards at one time. Because a number of budget work sessions are normally necessary to discuss the budget, the director and staff present separate parcels of the budget at each session. After each part of the budget is described in detail, the budget is then assembled and the overall document is presented and discussed. In the work sessions, most of which are informal, it is important that there is a good dialogue between staff and board members.

If the board has the power to adopt the budget, public hearings must be held and public notices regarding the budget and anticipated rates are generally required by law to inform citizens of the proposed budget. Public involvement, as will be discussed later, is essential if the general public is to accept the agency's plans and activities. The relationship that executives have with their boards greatly influences the informality or formality of the budget meetings that are held.

PRESENTATION TO LOCAL GOVERNMENTAL OFFICIALS

In local governments where the park and recreation agency is responsible to a professional manager or mayor and a municipal council, the budget review process is considerably different from the case where the budget is reviewed only by an administrative board. The normal process then is to submit the budget proposal to the chief executive or the budget officer. In larger local governments where budget divisions are involved, budget officers play a significant role in analyzing budget requests. They work closely with the chief executive in recommending revisions in the budgets submitted by the various departments or agencies and a tentative working strategy is established. At this time it is generally known whether the budget requests can be financed by the anticipated revenues or whether budget reductions must be made. The latter is most often the case.

The chief executive, budget officers, and often members of the legislative board serve as a review committee and budget hearings are scheduled with all department or agency heads to discuss the proposed budgets. At this time the park and recreation executive and the board's representative (often the president or chairman of the board), if appropriate, have the opportunity to discuss and interpret the park and recreation budget request. The administrator must be prepared to justify the increases and changes that are projected in the budget proposal. The need for offering programs, the explanation of work programs, and possible sources of alternative funding are topics that are often considered.

During these budget workshop sessions local governmental officials generally suggest making reductions or cuts. The department or agency head should be prepared to respond to these requests with corresponding program reductions and the consequences of such reductions in funding. If the reductions are significant, the director may want to go back to the staff and board to discuss the adjustments and changes that might be made in order to provide the best services to the public for the available revenues anticipated.

PUBLIC HEARINGS

After the proposed budget has been reviewed and revised in the work sessions attended by public officials, public meetings, mandated by state laws, are held to seek public reactions to the proposed budget. These meetings are designed to increase citizen participation and to ensure that governmental agencies are responsive to citizen needs and interests.

It is unfortunate that the public at large, who turned out at the polls in unexpected large numbers in the late 1970s to vote against tax referendums and tax limitation measures, fail to take advantage of this opportunity to express their approval or concerns about the budget that greatly infuences their local government and community. Some believe that the public's lack of interest in attending hearings results from little or no involvement in the budget development process. Citizens often feel that everything has already been decided through the private budget sessions and therefore their expressions and concerns will not change the action previously taken on the budget proposal. The relatively small attendance at these meetings is generally composed of individuals representing taxpayer's groups, the Chamber of Commerce, the local press, and a few interested citizens who represent special interest groups or concerns. Supporters of the local park and recreation programs are often absent. Those present generally have a cause to present or come to protest the elimination of programs or services that may have been cut earlier from the budget.

It is recommended that the agency head and the board president or chairman be present to answer the questions from the local governmental officials or general public. After the preliminary public hearing, the approved budget is published in the local newspaper and a final hearing is held, at which time the budget is formally adopted.

CITIZEN PARTICIPATION

Public hearings are just one instance where citizens may participate in the budget process. The lack of public interest at these hearings has led some communities to structure other ways of stimulating citizen involvement. As previously mentioned, Lakewood, Colorado, conducts citizen opinion surveys to determine the needs and interests of local citizens and to assess the performance of various programs. Lakewood citizens are also asked to give input to goal identification and resource allocation at special hearings and neighborhood planning meetings. In Plainfield, New Jersey, the city established a citizen's budget advisory committee and conducts a city-wide survey as citizen participation mechanisms.

It is generally accepted that providing increased means of citizen participation in public affairs will increase public trust and confidence in local government, which should result in making its programs and services more effective.

PRESENTING BUDGET TO OTHER AUDIENCES

Leisure service administrators not only have the responsibility to present their budgets to the various public officials and legislative bodies but should avail themselves of every opportunity to "interpret their budget" to the media, taxpayer and civic organizations, labor unions, and the general public. The type of presentation must be tailored to each group.

In one community the superintendent of parks and recreation was asked to speak frequently to luncheon groups in his community and prepared a "budget in brief" place mat that could be placed before each person in attendance. The city of Prescott, Arizona, publishes a citizen-oriented "Budget-in-Brief" in newspaper tabloid form, which has proved to be an economical and easy way to inform the public of the city's budgetary plans. The eight-page publication contained the city manager's budget message; brief summaries of departmental budgets; goals and objectives; "pie" drawings showing the sources of revenue; and the functions and activities of all city departments. Clark County, Nevada, and the city of San Diego, California, have also been successful in using "Budget in Briefs" for informing the public about their budgets.

STRATEGIES IN PRESENTING BUDGETS

The strategies that are used by the leisure service executives in presenting their budgets vary substantially according to the fiscal climate, type of budget proposed, the individual or reviewing body, and the ability of the presentor. Many of the budget review sessions are informal and lend themselves to a good discussion of the programs and projected budget costs. Other sessions can be highly political and partisan and offer a real test of the administrator's skill, knowledge, and patience. There are times when a presentation of new and innovative programs is warranted and an increase in funding enables growth in programs and services. In recent years budget sessions are dominated with a need for holding the line or cutting the operation of the agency.

Despite the situation that the administrator is in, many worthwhile suggestions have surfaced from professionals in the field in presenting their budgets for approval.

- View the presentation of the budget as an opportunity to sell or interpret the needs, programs, and problems facing the agency.
- Focus the presentation on highlights of last year's programs, goals and objectives for the coming year, and how they fit into the agency's overall master plan.
- Indicate the steps that have been taken or contemplated to make the agency more efficient, productive, and effective.
- Give suggestions for new and innovative approaches to alternative funding.
- Use an approach that is proactive rather than reactive to the mandates of the presentor's superiors.
- Have sufficient supplementary data available to provide information about the agencies and programs.
- Cut out the surprises. Inform decision makers of major changes prior to budget time so they will not have to defend their ignorance in public at the budget hearing.
- Be prepared to justify increases or major changes. This is particularly true in line item budgets where the budget format dictates concentrating on increases in salaries, supplies, and so on from last year's budget to the proposed budget for the new year.
- Respond to budget cuts with several alternatives (choices) for cutdown management, if attempts to supplement declining fiscal resources by alternative funding methods or raising fees and charges fail. Be in a position of explaining what programs or services will have to be reduced fully or partially—if the budget is reduced.
- Explain, interpret, or justify the budget information presented. Administrators do not need to defend their budget proposals.
- Avoid arguments with budget reviewers. Presentors should keep calm and hold their tempers.
- Be prepared to "tell your story" quickly and effectively. Administrators sometimes find themselves in a situation where time is limited. Public officials have many more budgets to review.
- Remember, selling the budget is a year-round job.
- Consider having a lay citizen (board president) make

the presentation. Often he/she may be more effective in presenting the agency's budget than the professional who is sometimes viewed as building an empire.

The success that leisure service administrators achieve in getting their fair share of the limited tax dollar is based on the professionalism displayed during the budget presentation period.

BUDGET ADOPTION

The official adoption of the proposed budget is the culmination of an exhaustive review of the agency's budget proposal by the park and recreation authority, city administrative officials, and the legislative body. After taking the various steps in the review process, informal and formal, internal and external, the chief executive and budget officer have the responsibility of modifying the proposed budget based on the directives of the legislative body. The legislative body must then take final action on the budget by passing an appropriation ordinance or resolution. The action by this body establishes a spending ceiling for the governmental unit for the fiscal year but allows a certain degree of flexibility to agency administrators in operating their programs.

In some states further approval must be obtained before the final adoption of the budget. In Indiana, for example, local jurisdictions (city, county, and school districts) must gain approval from two additional reviewing bodies: the county tax review board and the state tax board. Both governmental bodies have the power to approve or revise the budgets that have already been adopted by the local governmental units.

Most fiscal and governmental authorities agree that the final adoption of the budget should take place before the beginning of the new fiscal year. Sometimes approval of the budget is not finalized until two or three months into the new fiscal year. This situation creates many problems and uncertainties for agencies as they undertake their programming for the new fiscal year.

Summary

The fiscal and political climate facing park and recreation agencies and the professionalism in which the budget is prepared and presented greatly influence the chances of gaining approval of the proposed budget. A well-conceived and well-planned budget that identifies programs and services to be performed will serve as a valuable interpretive tool in gaining legislative approval.

It is during this phase of the budgetary process that administrators and staff should be prepared to interpret the agencies' plans and functions to their boards, public officials, and the general public. This chapter gives a number of strategies that have been used by professionals in the field in presenting their budgets to reviewing bodies.

Selected References

Lehan, Edward A., *Simplified Governmental Budgeting*, Municipal Finance Officers Association, Chicago, 1981, pp. 69–72.

Moak, Lennox L., and Kathryn W. Killian, *A Manual of Techniques for the Preparation, Consideration, Adoption, and Administration of Operating Budgets*, Municipal Finance Officers Association, Chicago, 1963, pp. 242–276.

Chapter 7

Budget Implementation

With the final adoption of the budget, the focus of the budgetary process is shifted back to the operating departments or agencies that have the responsibility for conducting the programs and implementing the work plans that were presented in the budget. The administrator and staff are not only challenged to carry out the plans that have been laid down in the budget requests but must conduct operations within the financial limits approved by the legislative body. The overall success of this phase of budgeting will ultimately be determined by both the relationship established between the agency and the chief executive and legislative body and the teamwork exhibited by the administrator and the staff. These relationships play key roles in the organization's success or failure in carrying out the objectives incorporated in the approved budget.

Usually, central administration is responsible for establishing an overall budgeting control and accountability. If the primary objective is "control for control sake" and the system is not viewed as a joint venture, budget administration will shift from the role of one of assistance and support to that of actual hindrance to and interference in an agency's operation. It is essential that the accounting system, cost records, cash management, authorization policies and procedures, and financial reporting be developed jointly so that both parties benefit.

Budget administration within an agency is largely influenced by the type of budget adopted, that is, scope of programs and work plans developed, and the involvement of staff in preparing the budget. If budget preparation was a cooperative venture between the administrative and supervisory personnel and

their subordinates, carrying out these plans will be readily accepted as an overall agency responsibility ans challenge. It is up to the entire staff to put the plans into operation and to seek ways of operating in the most efficient and effective manner.

At the beginning of each fiscal year the agency head must set into motion the implementation of the new budget. The remainder of this chapter discusses the various management strategies and devices used in administering the park and recreation budget.

ALLOTMENTS

The use of allotments has proved to be a useful tool in agency management. In local governments that utilize the allotment process, agency heads are asked to make monthly or quarterly projections of expenditures for each of their programs. This information can then be used to monitor the fiscal status of the agency or to serve as a control device.

First, the actual expenditures made by the agency can be plotted against the amount estimated (allotment) to determine whether the spending program is on track. When the estimated expenditures are used as a control device, the agency is prohibited in spending funds in excess of the amount allotted. If conditions require spending more money, the agency would be required to gain approval from the city administrator or budget division. Since most cities and departments prepare monthly reports, it would seem advisable that allotments be made on a monthly rather than a quarterly basis. Having more frequent check points gives administrators more up-to-date information with which to guide the operations of their agencies. Monthly allotments would allow administrators to monitor their fiscal operations more closely and if deviations were found, immediate corrective action could be taken.

One of the primary reasons for using an allotment system is to prevent overspending. Supervisory staff is responsible for developing work programs and estimating costs for carrying out these plans. Budget planners who identify programs or activities and work programs with their spending plans are in an excellent position to project their expenditures on a monthly time frame. When this is accomplished, the allotment system can be used as a monitoring device. This approach to fiscal management should enable the agency to carry out their programs throughout the entire year, thus avoiding overdrafts in the budget or year-end deficiencies.

Allotments are also valuable in providing essential information that can be used in implementing an effective cash management program for the agency. Management of the fiscal affairs of an organization calls for expertise in determining carryover balances, projecting cash flow, planning short-term borrowing, and investing idle funds. All these management concerns require data concerning the estimated monthly expenditures.

Leisure service administrators know that their agencies do not spend the same number of dollars each month. Many of the programs that they offer are seasonal and therefore expenditures will be influenced by the timing of these programs. Most of the expenditures for a summer resident camping program, for example, will be concentrated in a two- or three-month period. Actually, there are few agencies that require an absolute uniform apportionment of expenditures throughout the twelve-month period.

In developing a program-type budget, the budget planner first prepares a detailed program plan and work schedule and then determines the cost items that are needed to perform the work. With this kind of information, it is not difficult to break down the expenditure plan into monthly estimates. Note that allotments are only estimates of the probable rate of expenditures. To the degree that these estimates are carefully planned and based on an analysis of past experiences, the estimate is a valid management tool that can be used to guide the operation of an organization. As with work programs and programs that are subject to varying responses and external forces, plans are also subject to change; therefore expenditure time schedules should be considered internal and can be exceeded or adjusted in actual operation.

Allotments do provide a guidepost, however, to judge spending funds in an agency.

In some jurisdictions expenditure allotments are based on the agency's historical pattern of expenditures for each month or quarter. Actual expenditures for each month are obtained and translated into a percentage of the yearly budget. Analyzing this information over a period of time (i.e., five years), an average percentage estimate for each month is obtained. When the budget for the new fiscal year is approved, the allotments can be quickly figured by using the monthly percentage that has been developed. If the monthly percentage method is employed, agency heads would need to adjust their estimates for any significant changes in work programs or programs projected in the new budget that would alter the past performance figures. For example, the cancellation of an after school recreation program offered in past years during the spring months and the transfer of these funds to a summer camp for the handicapped would necessitate an adjustment in the allotment estimates for the new year.

The spending programs of an organization should not only be monitored, but there is also a need to analyze the receipts for each program. The same rationale used in establishing an allotment system for expenditures can be made regarding receipts, that is, comparing the actual receipts against the amounts approved in the budget. If an agency finds that actual receipts are lagging behind projected estimates, the staff can take steps to increase receipts for future months or inform the budget office that conditions indicate that the amount estimated in preparing the budget will not be obtained. A shortfall in receipts might make it necessary to adjust spending plans.

The agency's role in estimating receipts was discussed in Chapter 5 as one of the steps in preparing a budget. It is now the responsibility of the budget planner to estimate the amount of money that will be received each month. As previously mentioned, programs and work programs are often seasonal and because receipts coincide with these programs, they will not be the same each month during the fiscal year.

The historical approach used in estimating expenditures can also be used in figuring monthly allotments for receipts. Any significant changes in programs or policies relating to revenue should be considered with a corresponding adjustment in the estimated allotments.

Figure 7.1 reveals the expenditures and receipts allotments figured for a swimming pool. If allotments are to be used as a monitoring device, accounting controls should be established.

Swimming Pool—*Allotments, 1984*

	January	February	March	April	May	June	July	August	September	October	November	December	Total
						Operating Period—May 26–Sept. 6							
						15 weeks							
Expenditures				$1,500	$8,630	$15,620	$19,525	$15,620	$3,905				$64,800
Receipts					13,000	19,600	8,200	6,560	1,640				49,000

Figure 7.1 Monthly allotment of expenditures and receipts for swimming pool, 1984.

ACCOUNTING CONTROLS

After the budget has been adopted by the legislative body, the budget estimates, expenditures, and receipts should be transferred to accounting ledgers. Records should be kept for each agency program so that the financial status of each agency operation can be analyzed every month. Actual expenditures and receipts can then be compared with the estimated allotments in monitoring the fiscal operations of the department.

The final aspect of fiscal control is reporting the financial status of an agency to the various publics concerned with its operation. Daily statements of transactions and balances that indicate the current status of budgetary accounts are often provided by the finance office to each agency. Monthly reports are submitted to administrative boards and city officials.

For these reports to be meaningful the actual expenditures and receipts that are taken from the accounting ledgers should be compared with the estimated allotments. Without this information, the reader would not know whether the amount spent or received during the past month was over, under, or on target with the budget approved by the legislative body.

Financial reports are one of the prime methods of providing accountability to governing boards and the general public. They also give directors and their staff timely information on the operation of their agencies. Fiscal control and accountability are obviously important aspects of such reporting; however, they are also internal guideposts in analyzing agency operations.

Budgetary accounting and financial reporting are discussed in more detail in Chapter 8.

TRANSFER OF FUNDS

In preparing a budget, one finds it virtually impossible to anticipate the spending needs of an entire agency. Because the response to parks and recreation programs and services is questionable and is based on the general acceptance of the public, it is evident that alterations or adjustments to the approved budget will be needed. It is inevitable that programs and work plans might be modified throughout the year in response to changing community needs and social and economic changes in society. Inflation alone might make it necessary for an agency to make adjustments in its budget so that its operation can respond effectively to these changes. Even a well-planned budget must have some degree of flexibility in actual operation. Most local jurisdictions must make budget modifications and allow transfers within the budget document.

Local budget ordinances, appropriation ordinances, and state statutes often regulate an agency's ability to transfer funds. In some local governments charters or budget ordinances regulate the transfer of funds between agencies and within an agency budget. Normally, transferring funds between agencies that are funded by appropriations from a general fund may be permitted only by approval of the legislative body. Minor adjustments within the agency's budget may need the approval of the budget officer or city administrator.

If the budget appropriation ordinance passed by the legislative body is broad and allows a lump sum appropriation to the agency, generally, there is some degree of flexibility in transferring funds within the agency budget. If, however, the ordinance is specific and identifies programs and objects in detail, transfer of monies may require legislative approval. Despite the laws in effect that regulate this facet of budget execution, agencies should have the flexibility of modifying their budgets and in transferring funds within their budgets.

Some of the generally accepted types of transfers include the following.

- Transfer funds to the agency's budget from the local government's contingent fund because of emergencies.

• Transfer funds from one program or activity to another, that is, from golfing to the swimming budget.
• Transfer between major objects or expenditure categories, that is, from personal services to supplies. In some states this is not permissible; in others, approval of such a transfer must be obtained from the budget officer, chief executive, or legislative body.
• Transfer money between minor objects within the same major objects of classification, that is, from the surplus balance in office supplies to an overrun in the telephone budget category.

After approval is received for transferring funds within the budget, the appropriate changes should be made in the expenditure accounting ledgers.

BUDGET AMENDMENTS

Circumstances often arise that require agencies to amend their budgets during the fiscal year. Increases or decreases to the approved budget may be required and normally these changes must be approved by the budget officers, the chief executive, and/or the legislative body.

In most instances the initiation of a budget reduction comes from the central administration. The need for a budget reversion often results from a shortfall in tax collections or other anticipated revenue and the local government is unable to fund the budgets that were approved. As one solution, the chief executive, at the mandate of the legislative body, can request a budget reversion for each of the operating agencies. It is usually up to the agency to determine where the budget will be amended and from what source funds will be derived.

If there is a need for increased funds to cover situations that were unforeseen when the budget was planned and approved, the agency may seek money from the local government's unappropriated surplus or from revenues in excess of the amount that was originally estimated. Once again, legislative approval is generally needed.

Within the parks and recreation agency, the actual carrying out of the programs planned in the budget may need to be adjusted based on actual conditions encountered. As recreation is voluntary and the response to the programs cannot always be ascertained a year or two in advance when the budget is being planned, there may be a varying degree of response and general acceptance to the programs offered. Some programs may not be so successful as anticipated. Others may draw many more participants than planned. Pressures may be received for new or expanded programs and the agency must be responsive to the ever changing society.

If funds that were appropriated for one program were not needed or entirely consumed, they may be shifted to another area where the demands are heavy. Even if the budget is planned and approved for various programs, it is imperative that the agency has the flexibility and freedom to amend its programs in order to meet the needs of the public. Normally, administrators would keep their boards informed as to the progress of programs and any anticipated needed change. If an agency is under an administrative board, the board would have the power to approve changes in programs and shifting the funds. In other instances approval may have to be received from the budget officer or chief executive.

MEETING EMERGENCY NEEDS

Emergencies often occur during the year that may require unanticipated expense that cannot be met with the approved budget. Generally, the crisis confronting an agency is of such a magnitude that adjustments in the budget would be disruptive to the operation of an agency and therefore additional funds are needed to solve the problem. There are two approaches that can be used in meeting emergency needs: a contingency fund or short-term borrowing.

Most local jurisdictions are permitted to establish a contingent fund as a part of their budget. Such funds are controlled by the chief executive and the legislative body. If an emergency situation arises in the park and recreation agency, a proposal is made to the chief executive for funds to cover it. The chief executive would then recommend to the legislative body that appropriate funds be taken from the contingent fund.

If contingent funds have already been drained and adequate funds are not available to meet the agency's request, the agency may have to take out a short-term loan to meet the financial crisis. In order to liquidate the loan, the agency would have to include the money in the next year's budget to pay the principal and interest obligated by it in borrowing the money.

CASH MANAGEMENT

In an era of rising costs, revenue shortages, and increased demands for more public services, public officials are forced to seek solutions to their financial problems. Even as these conditions exist, many units of local government have been found to have an ineffective management of their financial resources. One solution that is receiving more attention among local governmental units is that of better management of cash resources. The primary objective of cash management is to increase the governmental unit's revenue by investing "idle funds" that are not needed to meet current obligations. If this objective is to be attained, Haskin and Sells feel that local officials responsible for implementing a cash management program may need to upgrade their skills in the following areas.

- Understanding the present cash flow, its nature, timing and sources. The cash manager must see it as cash received or disbursed, not in terms of debits or credits to funds used in the accounting records.
- Estimating the pattern of future cash flows. If the cash manager has a good understanding of past cash flows, this is half the battle.
- Identifying and becoming familiar with short-term money markets where funds can be invested to earn income until the cash is required to pay municipal bills.
- Arranging for the short term investment of idle cash. To get the best return on this investment, the cash manager must schedule maturities so that:
  —Bills can be paid when they are due without selling securities before they mature.
  —Full advantage is taken of higher yields which may be available if longer maturities are purchased.
  —Idle cash is held to a predetermined minimum.[1]

Before idle cash in invested in short-term securities, agency officials should be familiar with state or local legal constraints that regulate the type of investments allowed.

Cash Flow

With the information derived from the allotment system, cash flow estimates can be determined for each time period (month). Allotments reveal the expenditures estimated for each month and the anticipated receipts. The net cash flow can be calculated by subtracting the expenditures from the receipts. If receipts are greater than expenditures for the time period, then a positive cash flow results. Conversely, if the estimated expenditures are greater than the anticipated receipts, a negative cash flow occurs. If the budget officer or administrator have accurately figured cash flow estimates for the entire fiscal year, they are in a better position to administer the financial affairs of the agency. By determining accurate cash flow estimates, several of the functions of a cash management system can be attained.

[1]Haskin and Sells, *Implementing Effective Cash Management in Local Goverment: A Practical Guide,* Municipal Finance Officers Association, Chicago, 1977, p. 2.

Meeting Current Obligations

One of the responsibilities of a manager of a cash management system is to have funds available to meet the current operating expenses of the organization. Because one of the main sources of revenues (tax collections) is normally received on two occasions during the fiscal year (in Indiana, May and November), generally, an agency has to develop a plan providing for an adequate positive cash flow to handle monthly expenses. Two methods are commonly used to handle this situation: carry-over balances and short-term borrowing.

Carry-over balances are built into the agency's previous year's operating budget so that an operating balance will be carried over into the new fiscal year. Because property taxes in Indiana are due in May, they are not collected and distributed to the local units of government until June. The amount of the carry-over balance is based on the amount that the expenditures exceeds the revenues during the first five months of the new year, the time period from the beginning of the fiscal year to the month that the property tax collections are received by the agency.

In Figure 7.2 the net cash flow for the first five months totals $41,500. With a carryover balance of this amount, the agency is in a good position to meet current operating expenses until June, when the property tax revenues are received. This planned method of fiscal management negates the need for short-term borrowing, which would be necessary if the carryover balance was not allowed or planned.

If the previously discussed method is not allowed or a negative cash balance occurs during the fiscal year, short-term borrowing in the form of a bank loan may be needed to bridge the gap until tax monies are received. The ultimate cash management program will minimize the costs of short-term borrowing, placing the manager in a position to consider the investment of surplus funds so that nontax revenues might be increased.

Investment of Idle Cash

The primary objective of a cash management program is short-term investment of idle funds. Once the cash flow needs of an agency are met, the cash manager must determine the minimum cash balance that is needed to meet the current obligations of the governmental unit. As investments are subject to local and state legal constraints, cash managers must make sure they conform with the legal restrictions that regulate the handling of public funds.

There are a number of investment alternatives

Cash Budget

	January	February	March	April	May	June	July[1]	August	September	October	November	December[1]	Total
Expenditures	$15,000	$16,000	$16,000	$16,500	$35,000	$38,000	$40,000	$39,000	$20,000	$18,000	$18,000	$17,000	$288,500
Receipts	7,000	8,000	10,000	12,000	20,000	24,000	29,000	29,000	14,000	13,000	13,000	7,000	288,500
						51,250						51,250	
Receipts less disbursements	(8,000)	(8,000)	(6,000)	(4,500)	(15,000)	37,250	(11,000)	(10,000)	(6,000)	(5,000)	(5,000)	41,250	—
Cash at beginning of month	41,500	33,500	25,000	19,500	15,000	—	37,250	26,250	16,250	10,250	5,250	250	
Cumulative cash position—end of month	33,500	25,500	19,500	15,000	—	37,250	26,250	16,250	10,250	5,250	250	41,500	

[1]Property tax revenues received

Figure 7.2 Cash Budget for a park and recreation agency.

that are available to local goverment officals. Various forms of investments include commercial bank savings, time deposits, certificates of deposit, and banker's acceptance, to mention only a few. In choosing the type of investment, one should consider important factors such as risk, liquidity, and yield. High-risk or speculative investments are seldom recommended. Obviously, consideration should be for obtaining the highest yield possible. Liquidity of the investment is equally important; this refers to the ability of investors to cash in their investments quickly without loss of principal or accrued income. After all, the agency is obligated to pay its bills on time and money must be available.

Generally, short-term investments are handled by the local government's finance officer; however, park and recreation agencies that are fiscally independent need to operate a cash management program within their operation. When the local government operates such a program, it pools idle cash from all agency budgets, which results in larger sums for investing, and thus permits greater flexibility in the selection of investment alternatives. Several states operate investment pools that are of help to smaller communities.

A cash management program will not only enable communities to make money from investment opportunities but there are other management strategies that will improve the agency's management of its fiscal affairs. These strategies should also include other efficiencies in the operation of the agency, such as

- Keep the number of checking accounts within the department to a minimum.
- Deposit receipts collected by the agency the same day that the money is received.
- Delay payment of bills until the last possible date that they are due.
- Pay bills within the discount period if invoices offer attractive discounts.

MONITORING PROGRAM ACCOMPLISHMENTS

The real test of budget administration is for the director and staff to carry out the programs and work programs that were approved in the budget. Thus far most of the discussion on budget implementation has stressed fiscal controls and keeping within the financial limits of the approved budget. Management strategies must be initiated for performing and controlling the work that must be done.

The success that will be achieved in this phase of budgeting is largely dependent on the planning that has gone into the development of the budget. If the planning job was a detailed and cooperative effort involving both administrators and staff, carrying out these plans should be relatively easy and meaningful. The old saying "Plan your work, work your plan" has relevance here. Implementation of program plans normally considers the following steps: assigning responsibilities for performing tasks, establishing monthly plans of work, setting deadlines, executing supervisory control, and reviewing and evaluating activities.

After the budget has been approved by the legislative body, the leisure services manager discusses with the staff the approval, revision, or deletion of the program that resulted from the presentation and adoption of the budget. The supervisors or division heads are then given the responsibility for carefully studying the budget document and developing monthly plans of work for carrying out the functions in their division or agency. As a part of the monthly work plans, deadlines should be established for completing them.

Once this phase of the planning process has been completed, the staff is responsible for putting their plans into action. The manager is responsible for making sure that the program conforms to the program plans developed in the budget. Administrative and supervisory personnel are responsible for monitoring agency activities and work programs. It is good public relations to invite board members and elected public officials to as many of the park and recreation activities as possible and program accomplishments should be incorporated as a part of the monthly report. Progress reports on programs and possible adjustments or necessary changes can be given at weekly staff meeting. Periodic evaluations of long-term programs are essential and final evaluations of seasonal programs should follow the completion of the activity. It is important that program accomplishments be measured against performance standards and predetermined goals and objectives.

The Elmhurst Park District, Illinois, has developed a prototype operation in using goals and objectives in its budgetary process. Each year goals and objectives are developed by the director and appropriate staff. These are categorized into five groups: administration, facilities, recreation programs, planning, and personnel. A listing of the 1982–1983 goals and objectives developed for the recreation division is found in Appendix B, pages 139–141. The goals and objectives represent advanced planning and forethought and serve as a guide for the operation of the park district for the year. This approach to planning provides direction to the staff and gives specific deadlines for accomplishing objectives. Each year the status of the goals and objectives are summarized by group to determine whether the objective is (1) completed, (2) started, but not completed, (3) not started, or (4) dropped. In 1981–1982, 53 goals with 200 objectives were developed by the administrator and his staff and were adopted by the Board of Commissioners. At the end of the fiscal year it was found that 63 percent of the objectives were completed, 15 percent were started, 4 percent were not started, and 8 percent of the objectives were dropped. This use of goals and objectives not only provide direction for the staff for implementing their budget

but it also gives accountability for producing the programs that were planned.

Summary

Upon adoption of the budget, emphasis in the budgetary process shifts to the agency or department for budget implementation. Accounting controls are established and allotments are utilized for monitoring the budget. Often administrators are confronted with budget amendments, emergencies that must be met, or necessary transfer of funds. Another important aspect of budget administration is cash management. By an efficient management of cash resources, cash flow estimates are determined, thus enabling an agency to meet current obligations and to invest idle cash.

Finally, and, perhaps most importantly, management strategies must be initiated for controlling the work that must be done and implementing programs. A careful monitoring of agency operations makes the administrator and staff accountable for producing the programs that were included in the budget and meeting the goals and objectives established by the leisure service agency.

Selected References

Aronson, J. Richard, and Eli Schwartz (eds.), *Management Policies in Local Government Finance,* International City Management Association, Washington, D.C., 1981, pp. 328–345. (Chapter 14—Cash Management)

Haskin and Sells, *Implementing Effective Cash Management in Local Government: a Practical Guide,* Municipal Finance Officers Association, Chicago, 1977, 59 pp.

Moak, Lennox C., and Kathryn W. Killian, *A Manual of Techniques for the Preparation, Consideration, Adoption, and Administration of Operating Budgets,* Municipal Finance Officers Association, Chicago, 1963, pp. 28–330.

Rosenberg, Philip and C. Wayne Stallings, *An Operating Budget Handbook for Small Cities and Other Governmental Units,* Municipal Finance Officers Association, Chicago, 1978, pp. 79–93.

Chapter 8

Financial Record Keeping

The budget is transferred to finance record-keeping ledgers after its final adoption. Effective management and control of an organization relies heavily on the availability of financial information. Accurate, up-to-date information provides the administrator and staff with the essential data that is critical for planning, decision making, and program implementation.

During budget preparation the staff often relies on past financial information in estimating new budget data. An analysis of former practices, operational procedures, and program costs provides the basis for projecting new estimates and programs. Also, daily and monthly financial reports keep the staff informed of current operations and the financial status of an agency. Agency or department heads and board members use the data to oversee or monitor the operation of an agency.

More detailed cost records give information on the performance of agency personnel and the costs of providing programs and services. Finally, the agency is accountable to its board, public officials, and the general public as to how well it has carried out the programs approved in the budget. An effective accounting system serves as an "information retrieval system" to provide the data necessary for these management functions.

The approach that park and recreation administrators take in developing accounting systems for their agencies is greatly influenced by the size and complexity of local governmental units and the type of budgeting and accounting systems endorsed by these jurisdictions. State controls over the budgeting and accounting processes of local government often mandate the system used.

HUD's study of local financial management needs (see Chapter 4, page 44) stressed the importance of integrating budgeting, accounting, and performance in order to hold local agencies accountable in terms of services provided. Some local jurisdictions, notably smaller ones, were found to have inadequate budgeting and accounting systems. Where line item budgeting was used, the jurisdiction's accounting system was often ineffective in relating costs to programs and services rendered. In recent years the program, program performance, and zero-base budgets have been instrumental in establishing an automated, integrated financial management system with the capability of measuring performance and program costs.

Most finance experts feel that the minimum standard for budgeting and accounting is to establish budgets and financial records for each of the agency's programs and services. Since I recommend the preparation of a program budget that can be incorporated in most of the newer concepts of budgeting, the establishment of the financial record-keeping system in the agency should match this minimal concept of budgeting. With the increasing emphasis on performance measurement and evaluation, park and recreation managers should consider utilizing a more comprehensive cost analysis system that will become easier to operate with the use of electronic data processing equipment.

Most of the larger cities, counties, and special districts have finance departments or officers that have the responsibility for establishing and controlling the financial administration of the local governmental unit. The system of local governmental accounting established should conform to the accounting principles and procedures recommended by the National Committee on Governmental Accounting (NCGA). Naturally, agencies functioning under the control of local units of government and centralized finance departments must operate under the system adopted by the central administration. It is not uncommon, however, to find park and recreation agencies operating a more detailed internal accounting system to supplement the overall system in operation. These additional financial data can be used in budget development and the management of the agency.

If the park and recreation agency is fiscally independent and thereby functions independently from a city or county, it must develop its own accounting system. For these agencies, a professional accountant should be hired or retained as a consultant to establish and operate the fiscal records of the agency. Fiscally independent organizations must conform to the same accounting principles and procedures as any other local governmental unit.

There are several principles or guidelines recommended by the NCGA that should be followed in establishing an accounting system.

1. The central accounting system should be on a double entry basis.
2. Separate accounting records should be maintained for each fund.
3. The accounting system should be developed on an accrual or modified accrual basis.
4. Budgetary accounting should reflect encumbrances or obligations of the funds and appropriations.
5. Financial reports should be prepared at least monthly with actual receipts and expenditures compared with the amounts budgeted.
6. Cost accounting systems should be established wherever costs can be measured.

Governmental accounting emphasizes two approaches to accounting—fund accounting and budgetary accounting.

FUND ACCOUNTING

Local units of government offer a wide variety of functions or programs that are financed by a number of sources. In order to analyze, control, and report on the financing of these functions, finance experts recommend that separate fund accounting systems should be established for recording the financial transactions for each of these functions. This assures that the money received from specific revenue sources will be used to finance specific functions.

The NCGA suggests the following types of funds for local units of government.

1. *General Fund.* The largest of all funds, the general fund accounts for revenues devoted to finance general services of government or all functions that are not supported by a special revenue fund.
2. *Special Revenue Fund.* Accounts for revenue raised for a purpose, that is, establishing a fund raised by a special tax for parks and recreation (discussed in Chapter 2, page 13).
3. *Special Assessment Fund.* Accounts for the financing of special improvements or programs that directly benefit certain property owners.
4. *Debt Service Fund.* Accounts for the financing of interest and principal of a long-term debt.
5. *Capital Projects Fund.* Accounts for the financing of capital improvements financed primarily from bond issues or federal funds.
6. *Trust or Agency Fund.* Accounts for resources held by the local jurisdiction under specific trust purposes. A special trust fund may be established to account for gifts or donations to the local park and recreation agency that are designated for park acquisition or development.
7. *Enterprise Fund.* Accounts for park and recreation activities that are operated as a businesslike enterprise, that is, golf courses, marinas, swimming pools, and tennis centers.
8. *Internal Service Fund.* Accounts for services rendered to departments within the local government jurisdiction, that is, motor pools, central purchasing, or duplicating services.

BUDGETARY ACCOUNTING

Budgets are of little value unless the actual expenditures, receipts, and performance can be monitored in relation to the approved plan. Budgetary accounting provides a system for the monitoring, controlling, and reporting of the financial status of an agency and the programs and services offered. The accounting system adopted must be integrated with the budget format in operation, as well as conform to generally accepted accounting principles, mentioned previously. Just as a good budget identifies programs and services performed by an agency, the budgetary accounting system must be developed in a similar manner.

Accounting controls can be established by the central administration or at a divisional or department level, or by both. In some local jurisdictions agency ledgers are more detailed and may be more current than those operated by the local government. This additional duplication of work or increased costs should not be tolerated if the fiscal reports prepared

by the local government are up to date and distributed to departments on a daily or monthly basis and are of adequate detail. Modern bookkeeping machines and data processing systems have proved to be valuable in cutting down the reporting time and in keeping the information current.

It is important that the accounting classification structure and the coding system adopted permit the appropriate financial data required by management to operate the agency effectively. The accounting system should focus on budgetary control of both expenditures and revenues.

Expenditure Accounting

In preparing an accounting system for recording expenditures, the ledgers should contain information on the agency, division, programs or services, and objects of expenditure. Codes must be assigned to each component part of the classification structure. Figure 8.1 illustrates a classification system that could be established for a park and recreation agency.

Expenditure Ledgers. For each departmental or divisional function, expenditure ledgers should be developed to record the actual expenditures. A ledger should be established for each of the objects of expenditure included in the budget for each program.

As I believe that an allotment system should serve as a monitoring device rather than a control mechanism, an expenditure ledger based on the overall appropriation would provide the information needed to monitor expenditures. The amount spent each month can then be compared with the anticipated spending in the monthly financial report. If the expenditures each month exceed the allotment, action can be taken, if necessary, to control the spending of the agency.

One of the guidelines recommended by the NCGA is that budgetary accounting should reflect encumbrances or obligations of the funds and appropriation. Expenditure ledgers should allow for the posting of encumbrances. For example, an entry should be made in the ledger that records a purchase order or contract that is made to purchase goods or services. When the items are received and paid for, the encumbrance should be removed and the actual expenditure recorded.

An illustration of an expenditure ledger showing the various types of transactions that can be made is found in Figure 8.2. This ledger would be just one of several that would need to be established for a swimming pool budget. By using the expenditure classification found on pages 86–87, Figure 8.1, the expenditure designation and coding for office supplies for the ledger includes the following.

Organizational unit	- Parks (51)
Program	- Swimming pool (.20)
Object of expenditure	- Office supplies (21)
Approved budget for object	- $500

Assuming that the budget goes into effect on January 1, the first step would be to post $500 in the appropriation column. On May 2 a purchase order was issued to Rogers Company for the purchase of office supplies at an estimated cost of $45. This creates an encumbrance (increase column) of $45, which is subtracted from the appropriation, creating an unencumbered balance of $455.00. In mid-May a central stores requisition is submitted to obtain duplicating supplies at an estimated cost of $15. This creates a total encumbrance of $60 and an unencumbered balance of $440.

On May 30 the secretary or accountant submits vouchers and receipts to the local governmental finance department to reimburse the petty cash fund. A voucher of $8.50 was included for supplies for the swimming pool and an expenditure of this amount was recorded in the expenditure column and the unencumbered balance is reduced to $431.50.

In June two additional encumbrances are recorded—a $200 blanket order to Indiana Office Supply Company and an order for $140 to the book store for miscellaneous supplies. Both entries were made in similar fashion as the previous transactions.

The office supplies ordered on May 2 from Rogers Company are received and a bill of $48 is submitted. The encumbrance ($45) is canceled and an expenditure of $48 is posted. Since $45 was already subtracted from the appropriation, an additional $3 would need to be subtracted from the unencumbered balance.

The supplies received from the central stores cost the agency $12.50, which was less than the amount encumbered. The amount encumbered was canceled, $12.50 was recorded as an expenditure, and the difference, $2.50, was added to the unencumbered balance.

The final transaction in the expenditure ledger involved the receipt of an invoice for $120 for supplies ordered on the blanket order issued on June 1. An amount of $120 is deducted from encumbrances and recorded as an expenditure. No change should be made in the unencumbered balance.

Revenue Accounting

Anticipated receipts, as well as expenditures, should be monitored in the implementation phase of the budgetary process. Matching the actual receipts with

Parks and Recreation
Expenditure Classification System
(Coding Expenditure Accounts)

10—General administration	
20—Courts	
30—Community development	
40—Fire	
50—Parks and recreation	Governmental functions
60—Police	
70—Public works	
80—Sanitation	
90—Other	

50—Parks and recreation	
51—Administration	
52—Division of parks	Organizational unit
53—Division of recreation	

52—Division of parks	
.11—Administration	
.12—Parks	
.13—Beaches	
.14—Botanical gardens	
.15—Golf courses	
.16—Nursery	
.17—Marinas	
.18—Outdoor skating rinks	
.19—Parkways	
.20—Swimming pools	
53—Division of recreation	Programs
.41—Administration	
.42—Athletics	
.43—Aquatics	
.44—Community centers	
.45—Community events	
.46—Fine arts	
.47—Outdoor recreation	
.48—Senior citizens	
.49—Programs for handicapped	
.50—Supervised playgrounds	

1 Personal services	
11—Salaries and wages	
12—Employee benefits	
13—Other personal services	
2 Supplies	
21—Office supplies	
22—Operating supplies	
23—Repair and maintenance supplies	
24—Other supplies	
3 Other services and charges	
31—Professional services	
32—Communication and transportation	Object
33—Printing and advertising	of
34—Insurance	Expenditure
35—Utility services	
36—Repairs and maintenance	
37—Rentals	*(continued)*

Parks and Recreation
Expenditure Classification System
(Coding Expenditure Accounts) (Continued)

38—Debt service
39—Other services and charges
4 Capital outlays
41—Land
42—Buildings
43—Improvements other than building
44—Machinery and equipment
45—Other capital outlays

Figure 8.1 Expenditure Classification System for a Park and Recreation Agency.

those budgeted provides essential information for the cash management program. Revenue data on past operations also give the budget planner realistic information for making projections in planning the budget for the coming year. A system for accounting actual revenues should be established in much the same manner as for expenditures.

The same classification and coding system used in expenditure accounting (organizational unit and programs) can be used in revenue accounting, except that a coding for sources of revenues should be substituted for objects of expenditure. In Figure 5.3, found on page 63, the sources of revenue for the swimming pool were indicated. An appropriate coding for the anticipated revenues for this program would be as follows.

52 - Division of Parks
    .20 - Swimming Pool
        10 - Season Tickets
            11 - Family
            12 - Adult
            13 - Child
        20 - Daily Admissions
        25 - Registration Fees
        30 - Concessions
        40 - Towel and Locker Rental
        50 - Miscellaneous

Revenue Ledgers. Ledgers should be established for the anticipated revenues for each program offered by the agency. If the revenue accounting system is to be consistent with the budget structure developed in Chapter 5 for the swimming pool operation, separate revenue ledgers should be established for each source of revenue indicated in the budget. This would necessitate eight ledgers for the swimming pool budget. An example of a ledger developed to record the actual receipts for family season tickets is found in Figure 8.3.

PETTY CASH FUNDS

Most leisure service organizations find it feasible to establish a system for facilitating cash payments for small cash items. A petty cash fund is established to make money available to purchase these items, because it is not economical or practical to write checks or to follow the normal purchase routine for small cost items.

Not all administrative officials favor the establishment of petty cash funds. Arguments against such funds are that if you allow employees to purchase emergency items, they will not plan ahead and purchase supplies or materials in large volume, thus receiving better prices. Such a system makes it "too easy" for employees to shop for these items.

On the other hand, advocates of petty cash funds feel that small amounts of cash are necessary to operate effectively. For example, if recreation leaders are conducting a social event in their recreation center and are in the need for a door prize that costs under $5, it is not feasible to follow normal purchasing procedures to obtain the item. Or if an employer needs a receipt book ($2.50) for recording cash payments, he/she could easily purchase the item to meet an emergency situation.

If the park and recreation board authorizes the use of a petty cash fund, then a system for verification, authorization, and accountability for cash payments must be established.

Policies and Procedures

The initiation of a petty cash fund should be preceded by the adoption of certain policies and procedures by the board.

Amount of the fund. The total amount of the fund varies greatly, from $50 to $500. The number of funds in an agency, amount of expenditure allowed

Parks and Recreation
Enterprise, U.S.A.

Expenditure Ledger

Function: Swimming pool (.20)   Object: Office supplies (21)
Department: Parks (51)   Year: 198_

| Date | Explanation | Encumbrances | | | Expenditures | | Appropria-tion | Unen-cumbered Balance |
		Increase	Decrease	Balance	Amount	Total		
1/1/8_	Appropriation						$500.00	
1/28/8_	Petty cash #1				$8.50	$8.50		$491.50
5/2/8_	Rogers Co.— P.O. #40	$45.00		$45.00				446.60
5/15/8_	Central stores— #22	15.00		60.00				431.50
6/1/8_	Indiana Office Supplies— blanket order— P.O. #52	200.00		260.00				231.50
6/10/8_	Book store— P.O. #58	140.00		400.00				91.50
6/15/8_	Rogers Co.— P.O. 40		$45.00	355.00	48.00	56.50		88.50
6/18/8_	Central stores— #22		15.00	340.00	12.50	69.00		91.00
6/30/8_	Indiana Office supplies— P.O. #52		120.00	220.00	120.00	189.00		91.00

Figure 8.2 An expenditure ledger for office supplies in a swimming pool budget.

Parks and Recreation
Enterprise, U.S.A.

Revenue Ledger

Function: Swimming pool (.20)   Source of revenue: Season tickets
Department: Parks (51)   Account No.: 11—Family
                                        Year: 198_

| Date | Description | Receipts | | | Estimated Receipts | Unrealized Balance |
		Number	Amount	Total		
1/1/8_	Approved budget				$13,300	
May 15	50 season tickets	15	$1,500	$1,500		$11,800
May 20	100 season tickets	20	3,000	4,500		8,800
May 24	60 season tickets	24	1,800	6,300		7,000

Figure 8.3 Revenue ledger for swimming pool.

per purchase, need and use for purchasing supplies, and so on, all influence the amount that would be approved by the board. If the fund approved needs to be replenished each week, perhaps the amount should be increased.

Accessibility. The size of the local government and the division within will influence the location of the petty cash fund(s). In smaller local jurisdictions the fund is located in a central office. In larger jurisdictions the funds may be decentralized and placed in district offices, recreation centers, and/or maintenance depots. If the philosophy is to make them easily available and to aid employees in their jobs, funds should be made more accessible. The abuse or overuse of these funds or the excessive bypassing of normal purchasing procedures may influence the administrator and board to make the fund more difficult to utilize.

Dollar Purchase Limit. A limit on the amount of each purchase is usually set, the amount varying from $5 to $50. In large local governments with large budgets, the amount may be much greater than in smaller units of government.

Authorization. Control over the access and use of the fund is vitally important. An individual is appointed custodian of the fund. Employees wishing to purchase supplies under the policies established, must obtain approval to purchase small cost items. The two most common methods of controlling the use of these funds are:

1. *Voucher Authorization.* The employee would need to receive approval to purchase items by completing an authorization voucher. A receipt for the purchase is generally attached to the voucher.
2. *Verbal Approval and Receipt.* Perhaps the most common procedure used, the employee merely gains approval from the custodian of the fund and submits the receipt for the item for reimbursement.

Payment Charged Against Account. Expenditures for petty cash payments should be charged to the account, program, and object of expenditure classification in the budget. These expenditures are similar to purchasing supplies and materials through the normal purchasing procedures, only the amount of the purchase is smaller and the manner of obtaining these items are different.

Operating the Fund

After the park and recreation board has approved the establishment of the fund and the policies for operating the petty cash system, the fund is placed in operation by the receipt of a check, that is, $100, payable to the custodian of the fund. The check is written by the finance officer of the local government. The employee cashes the check and places the money in a cash box or safe. Having cash in a departmental office is subject to theft and the safeguarding of these funds is of utmost importance.

An entry of $100 is made in the receipts column of a petty cash book (see Figure 8.4), which is established to record petty cash transactions. When an employee needs to use the fund for purchasing a small item, he/she receives approval from the custodian of the fund by filling out a petty cash voucher (see Figure 8.5). A purchase is made, the vendor initials the voucher that a payment was received, and a receipt is attached to the voucher. The person in charge of the fund, upon receipt of the voucher and receipt, reimburses the employee for the money spent. This procedure is followed until such time that the fund is almost depleted and the money spent must be replenished. At all times, the money in the cash box, plus the amount represented by the vouchers and receipts, should total the amount of the fund.

In preparation for "cashing in" the vouchers for payment, the secretary records each voucher and the amount paid for each transaction in the petty cash book. A description of each payment may be written in the description column, however, this is really not necessary as a complete description of each transaction can be found in the petty cash voucher attached to the petty cash book. Also recorded in the petty cash book are the code numbers that identify the appropriate accounts where each expenditure should be charged.

Entries should be made in the appropriate expenditure ledger. When more than one voucher is to be charged to the same program and expenditure ledger the amount is consolidated and only one entry is made. For example, in Figure 8.4, two vouchers were entered in the petty cash book for the swimming pool account (0.20) for office supplies (36). An entry of $8.50 should be made in the expenditure column of the ledger (see Figure 8.2, page 88).

The amount expended from the petty cash fund, effective January 28, 198_, was $91.30. The petty cash book, No. 1, along with the vouchers and receipt slips are sent to the finance officer where appropriate charges are made to the program and expenditure ledgers. A check for $91.30 is returned to the agency where the check is cashed and the fund is back to its original balance. The appropriate entries in the next petty cash book, No. 2, are illustrated in Figure 8.6. The process for operating the petty cash fund previously discussed is again continued.

Parks and Recreation
Enterprise, U.S.A.

Date: January 28, 198_   Page No. 1

Petty Cash Book

Date	Voucher No.	Description	Receipts	Expenditures	Program	Object
January 1, 198_		Check	$100.00			
January 4	1	Central office supplies		$4.00	.20	36
January 6	2			8.75	.18	24
January 10	3			3.00	.11	24
January 12	4			4.50	.20	36
January 14	5			7.30	.11	36
January 20	6			9.25	.18	26
January 20	7			8.00	.14	25
January 21	8			7.00	.12	41
January 23	9			9.85	.18	36
January 24	10			8.65	.11	36
January 25	11			6.50	.12	41
January 25	12			5.10	.18	36
January 26	13			3.25	.12	43
January 27	14			6.15	.12	43

Total expenditures $91.30

Cash balance on hand $ 8.70

Submitted by

Figure 8.4   Petty cash book.

Parks and Recreation
Enterprise, U.S.A.

Petty Cash Voucher

No. 1   Date   January 4, 198_

Paid to   Central office supplies   Est. Amt. $ 4 / 00

For   Office supplies

Expenditure classification   P & R   Swimming pool   36
                            Fund   Function   Object

Amount received $ 4 / 00   Marie Jones
                                    Authorized by

Payment received   J. Peterson
                Vendor

Figure 8.5   Petty cash voucher.

Parks and Recreation
Enterprise, U.S.A.

Date: _____

Petty Cash Book

Page No. <u>2</u>

Date	Voucher No.	Description	Receipts	Expenditures	Program	Object
January 28, 198—		Balance	$8.70			
February 5, 198—		Check	91.30			
	15					
	16					

Total expenditures _____
Cash balance on hand _____

Submitted by

Figure 8.6 Petty cash book (No. 2).

INTERNAL FUNDS

Leisure service agencies offer a number of programs that are partially or completely self-supporting and are, in many cases, administered by those engaged in the program. These include clubs and interest groups that are operated by their own officers and that have their own treasurer and separate bank accounts.

Although these activities are under the general sponsorship of the agency and are an integral part of the overall program, they are not financed by budgeted funds. In most instances the revenues collected by these groups by membership fees, money-raising projects, and self-imposed fees and charges, actually belong to the group and are not the agency's funds. Because these organizations do receive money and expend funds, agency administrators and boards may find it advisable to establish a system of internal accounts that would include proper fiscal procedures for the effective operation of these groups.

Internal funds can also be used for other purposes. For example, participants in arts and crafts classes generally pay for the costs of their instruction and the supplies and materials consumed. Youth and adult groups pay admission fees to help defray the costs of their bands or instrumental groups. Sport teams may pay entry fees to participate in city leagues that are used to cover the expenses of officials and sports equipment. To add these expenses to the regular budget would distort the financial picture with respect to the money available for expenditures by the department.

It should be noted, however, that revenues procured from golf courses, swimming pools, marinas, indoor skating rinks, and other similar facilities which are estimated in the agency's budget, are not included in internal fund accounts.

Local and state governments have established revolving fund accounts to handle the fiscal operations of such organizations and activities. These accounts, often referred to as trust funds, activity accounts, clearing accounts, or internal funds, involve the receipt and expenditure of money outside the regular financial transactions directly related to the budget. As an example, Indiana University operates a Student Organization Accounts Office (SOA) to handle the financial accounts of student organizations. In 1979–1980, almost 500 student organizations spent over a million dollars for their various operations and educational activities in purchasing food, supplies, equipment, gifts, and other items. The SOA has proved to be valuable in expediting, coordinating, and controlling the payment of organization obligations to local merchants. It also serves as a focal point for local vendors who must deal with this large number of organizations, which are constantly changing in membership. The public relations value alone makes the consolidation of these organizations worthwhile.

Many of the recreation clubs and interest groups that are eligible for internal fund accounts maintain their own financial records and individual banking accounts. Consolidating these accounts into one general fund can benefit the organizations as well as the agency. The merit of grouping several bank accounts into one account is a justification in itself. A larger

Parks and Recreation
Enterprise, U.S.A.
Activity Fund

General Journal

Page No. 1

Date	Entry	Account No.	Receipt No.	Check No.		Receipts	Disbursements	Balance
1/1/8_	Balance 12/31/8_	All						$3025.00
1/6/8_	Membership	2	1		√	$120.00		3145.00
1/8/8_	Entry fees	1	2		√	75.00		3220.00
1/10/8_	Martin Printing Co.	2		1	√		$72.00	3148.00
1/12/8_	Mr. Vellar	3		2	√		30.00	3118.00
1/14/8_	University Sports Co.	1		3	√		105.00	3013.00
1/21/8_	L. S. Ayres	2		4	√		10.50	3002.50
1/26/8_	Bake Sale	2	3		√	38.75		3041.25

Figure 8.7 Activity Fund—General Journal.

bank balance eliminates bank charges, permits investment of funds, and results in a more efficient and less costly operation. The agency is in a position to verify the organizations that they sponsor and can offer assistance to the organizations and local businesses in purchasing supplies and equipment.

Internal funds require separate management. One or more persons should be given the responsibility for assisting clubs and interest groups in conducting their business affairs.

Policies and Procedures

The office responsible for managing internal funds must establish a system for controlling, accounting, reporting, and auditing these funds. The system that is being presented is designed to meet generally accepted principles of accounting, purchasing, and handling of receipts. The following steps and procedures are recommended for the establishment of an internal accounting system for a park and recreation agency.

Administration of Fund. An individual or, in some larger jurisdictions, an office with several employees should be given the responsibility for operating the internal fund system. The individual serving as treasurer should be bonded, the amount of which should be set by the local governmental finance office.

Accounting. In establishing books for the accounting of the funds, a general journal and account ledgers for each activity should be developed. All financial transactions, revenues received or expenditures, should be recorded in the general journal and then in the appropriate activity ledger (See Figure 8.7—General Journal, and Figure 8.8 for three activity account ledgers—Sports Association, Senior Citizens Club, and Square Dance Club).

Receipt of Funds. When funds are received, an official receipt form should be completed and given to the club treasurer by the custodian of the fund (see Figure 8.9). An entry should be made in the general journal and the activity account ledger, and the money should be deposited daily to the agency's internal fund account in the bank.

Disbursement of Funds. When a person representing one of the organizations or activities is interested in purchasing supplies or other items, an authorization voucher (see Figure 8.10) should be completed and signed by the club treasurer and an agency representative. The purchase is charged and a receipt is attached to the voucher indicating the items that have been received. This information is submitted to the treasurer of the fund and a check is written for payment of the purchase. This transaction is posted in both the general journal and the activity account ledger.

The treasurer of each of the clubs should keep an activity account ledger so that an up-to-date record of the financial status of the club or account is available.

An alternative to the use of an authorization voucher is a credit authorization card. This procedure is used by the SOA office at Indiana University. The treasurer/advisor of each student organization is

Parks and Recreation
Enterprise, U.S.A.

Acct. No. 1

Sports Association
Activity Account

Date	Entry	Receipt No.	Check No.	Receipt	Disbursements	Balance
1/1/8_	Balance 12/31/8_					$1800.00
1/8/8_	Entry fees	2		$75.00		1875.00
1/14/8_	University Sports Co.		3		$105.00	1770.00

Acct. No. 2

Senior Citizens Club
Activity Account

Date	Entry	Receipt No.	Check No.	Receipt	Disbursement	Balance
1/1/8_	Balance 12/31/81					$800.00
1/10/8_	Martin Printing Co.		1		$92.00	728.00
1/21/8_	L. S. Ayres		4		10.50	717.50
1/26/8_	Bake Sale	3		$38.75		756.25

Acct. No.3

Square Dance Club
Activity Account

Date	Entry	Receipt No.	Check No.	Receipt	Disbursement	Balance
1/1/8_	Balance 12/31/81					$425.00
1/6/8_	Memberships	1		$120.00		545.00
1/12/8_	Mr. Vellar		2		30	515.00

Figure 8.8 Activity fund—activity account ledger.

issued a Credit Authorization Card (see Figure 8.11). The SOA lists the following advantages for the use of CA cards.

- Ready and quick identification of authorized purchasers of the organization concerned to the local merchants.
- Elimination of charge sales to individuals in the name of the organization who are not authorized by the advisor of officers of the organization to make purchases.
- Benefits of sales tax exemptions on charge sales that are normally not available to the organization in making cash purchases by an individual.
- Ready availability of the *correct* name and SOA account of the organization to the merchant making the charge sale.

The CA card does place financial responsibility on the organization and its officers and provides local vendors the assurance that the purchaser and organization is an authorized student organization and that a prompt payment of the obligations made by the organization will be made.

Financial Report. A monthly report is often prepared and distributed to the administrative officials and to each organization represented in the internal fund system. This report should be distributed no later than the tenth day of each month for the preceding month. The information that should be included is found in Figure 8.12.

The final procedure to be followed is the cash reconcilement of the financial status of the account with the bank. This is accomplished in the form illustrated in Figure 8.13.

Parks and Recreation
Enterprise, U.S.A.

Activity Fund   No.   1

Receipts

Enterprise, Indiana _____   Date   Jan. 6, 198_ _____
          city-state
Received from   Square Dance Club $120.00

The sum of   One hundred and twenty and 00/100   Dollars

For Deposit to the credit of_____#1_____ Account

Source   Memberships   Marie Jones
                                              Treasurer

Figure 8.9   Activity fund, receipt form.

Parks and Recreation
Enterprise, U.S.A.

Activity Fund   No.   1

Authorization Voucher

Name of Account   Senior Citizens Club   Date   1/10/8_

Pay to   Martin Printing Co.   Amount $72.00

Address   1982 Lake, Bloomington

For   Printing—Membership Cards

Material received: _____   Approved by _____ C. Beeler _____
                                                   Sponsor-Treasurer

----

Paid by Check no.   1   Amount $72.00

Date: 1/10/8_   _____ Marie Jones _____
                                            Treasurer—Activity funds

Figure 8.10   Activity fund, authorization voucher.

The proper handling of money received by agency clubs and interest groups can prove to be a troublesome problem for a leisure service agency. The mishandling of these funds, sometimes referred to as "slush funds," can result in an improper image for the administration and agency. Fiscal accountability is an essential part of sound management. The establishment of the system discussed can result in better community relations and a better image.

The internal fund system is subject to approval by state government; therefore the forms and records established should be approved by the state. Also, in most states the operation of internal funds is subject to public audit.

```
Indiana University                          No. 9007
  SOA Credit                             Valid thru
  Authorization                    August 31, 1981
  Card 1980–1981,
                              State Sales Tax Exempt
```

Charge to:_____
　　　　Name of Organization/Account　　Account No.

The bearer of this Credit Authorization Card is identified to merchants as an official purchaser of the above-named organization. Merchants are authorized to extend credit to this organization upon presentation of this card subject to the terms and conditions on the reverse side.

Unauthorized use of this
C.A. Card shall subject
the user to university dis- _____
ciplinary action and civil　　Student Organization Accounts
liability for monetary　　　　Room 101, Student Services Bldg.
damages.

Figure 8.11　Credit authorization card used by Student Organization Accounts Office, Indiana University.

ENTERPRISE FUNDS

Enterprise funds are used to account for the administering and operating of park and recreation revenue-producing facilities and concessions. These funds are separate from the agency's special recreation tax or general fund accounts and serve to account for the revenues generated through those fees and charges of the enterprise that are allowed to be retained for the operation of the particular facility or operation.

These funds operate much the same as private enterprise, with the profit motive or self-supporting concept as one of the major goals. If the facility's operation is based on the revenue generated, it is essential that a cost tracking system be established to produce accurate data on the cost of the operation. The expenditures of self-operated revenue-producing operations are tied closely to dollars earned; therefore fees and charges must be continually analyzed and adjusted to meet rising costs of operation if the facility is to be self-supporting.

If the actual cost of the provision of goods and services is to be ascertained, the debt service, administrative overhead, and depreciation costs should be included, and also the operation costs should be accounted for. By segregating park and recreation operations that have the potential of being self-supporting into separate enterprise funds, which are based on businesslike accounting systems, agencies are in a better position to make profit or loss determinations on these programs.

The enterprise fund approach has been used successfully by many park and recreation agencies throughout the country. In 1975 the Department of Parks, Montgomery County, initiated a Park Enterprise Facilities Division to finance, operate, and maintain facilities and services that were entirely or

Parks and Recreation
Enterprise, U.S.A.

Activity Fund

Financial Report

From <u>January 1, 19xx</u> to <u>January 31, 19xx</u>

Activity Accounts	Balance Beginning of Period	Receipts During Period	Total Receipts	Expenses During Period	Balance at End of Period
1. Sports Association	$1800.00	$75.00	$1875.00	$105.00	$1770.00
2. Senior Citizens Club	800.00	38.75	838.75	82.50	756.25
3. Square Dance Club	425.00	120.00	545.00	30.00	515.00
Total	$3025.00	$233.75	$3258.75	$217.50	$3041.25

Figure 8.12　Activity fund, financial report.

Parks and Recreation
Enterprise, U.S.A.

Activity Fund

Cash Reconcilement of Financial Statement

From <u>January 1, 19xx</u> to <u>January 31, 19xx</u>

Bank <u>Monroe County Bank,</u>   <u>Bloomington</u>   <u>Indiana</u>
                                                          City   State

Bank balance per <u>1/31/19xx</u>			$3081.75
Plus			+
Total cash on hand and in bank			$3081.75

Less outstanding checks (below)

Date	Number	Amount
1/12	2	30.00
1/21	4	10.50

| Total of outstanding checks | $40.50 |
| Balance in general journal per _____ | $3041.25 |

Figure 8.13 Activity fund, cash reconcilement of financial statement.

predominately self-supporting enterprises by user fees. The goal of the division is twofold: (1) to be responsive to the public needs and desires and (2) to be responsive in such a manner that does not necessitate the utilization of tax monies from the general fund.[1]

In 1982 the Park Enterprise Division administered and managed the following park-operated revenue-producing facilities: three golf courses, two golf pro shops, two golf cart operations, one air-inflated indoor tennis facility, one boating facility, the Armory Place, a hay management program, and coin-operated outdoor lights for tennis, handball, and basketball courts. The proposed budget for operating these facilities was $2,064,913, which included allocation of administrative expenses. The revenue anticipated was $2,201,425.

As enterprise funds are nonreverting funds, revenues over the operating expenses (profit) can be retained each year in the fund. The retained earnings are thus allowed to accumulate and may be used for capital improvements or to support other special user-fee recreation facilities that are not completely self-supporting. In Montgomery County, the retained earnings from their revenue-producing facilities,

[1]*Proposed Annual Budget FY 1981–82,* The Maryland National Capital Park and Planning Commission, Silver Spring, Md., 1981–1982, p. 77.

over a four-year period, provided the funds necessary to build a nine-hole executive golf course and to purchase much needed heavy equipment for supporting other phases of parks operation within the overall organization.

Because enterprise fund accounts rely heavily on identifying the full costs of services rendered, a cost accounting system must be used to determine direct and indirect costs. This goes hand in hand with establishing fees and charges. In an era of fiscal restraint, effective, business-oriented, enterprise approaches provide effective management of many park and recreation facilities.

COST ACCOUNTING

The budgetary accounting system already discussed, which includes the accounting of expenditures and revenues for each program, is considered to be the minimum system applicable to any agency. If more complex, complete, or useful data are needed in the management of an agency, the budgetary accounting system can be extended to include the cost tracking of all costs, direct or indirect, of performing a program or work function. In order to obtain this additional information, one must establish a system of cost accounting.

Cost accounting has been widely used in business;

however, it was not until the 1950s that it was adopted by public agencies. In the mid-1950s and 1960s performance budgeting was introduced as a more meaningful and useful budgeting and management approach. It was the performance budget that used the previously accepted program budget and added an additional feature, the figuring of unit costs. This created the need to establish a cost analysis system so that the cost of units of work performed could be obtained and compared with standard costs.

There is little question as to both the value of obtaining this kind of information and its use as a management tool in operating an organization. Cost analysis has long been considered essential in the business world; however, it has met resistance and a less than enthusiastic acceptance by public agencies. In many local jurisdictions the process of establishing and operating a cost accounting system was found to be unnecessary, complicated, too costly, and time consuming. The translating of cost figures to units of measurement often seemed of little value in some of the public agencies. To know the exact cost of producing an automobile is essential, but the figuring of the cost of each participant on a playground or in a swimming pool did not have the same value.

During the period when performance budgeting was at its peak, I conducted an extensive study of the use of cost analysis in parks and recreation agencies throughout the country. Visits were made to 27 cities and counties in the United States and Canada. These cities and counties were recognized by city managers and finance officers as having excellent budgeting systems and were in the process of changing or had already changed to performance budgeting in their jurisdictions. An example of several of the cities and counties visited were: Vancouver, British Columbia; Los Angeles and Oakland, California; Dade County, Florida; Dayton, Ohio; Peoria, Illinois; and Milwaukee County, Wisconsin. The study revealed many adaptations to the use of cost analysis in these local governments. In some jurisdictions a rather complete use of the system was found, whereas in others only periodic cost studies were made. Most of the local governments were just beginning to initiate their cost system in selected departments or divisions within their jurisdiction.

Several administrators expressed doubts about adapting cost analysis to the field of parks and recreation. Concerns were expressed regarding the cost involved and the administrative time spent in operating the system. Also, problems existed in developing units of measurement, standard costs, and in how the data were used or often times misused. A number of city officials used the data to compare one city with another. Doubts were also expressed about evaluating the quality of the program and their objectives with units of measurement. Many of these observations and concerns are still relevant today.

On the positive side, executives felt that the information gained from the cost systems was of value in making management decisions; that is, Is it more economical to lease concessions or operate them by the agency? or What are the best work methods and equipment in maintaining a park? There appears to be little disagreement that park and recreation agencies do benefit from the data obtained from this more complete accounting system. Knowing the costs of programs and work performed are essential for evaluating programs, establishing priorities, preparing budget estimates, and making management decisions.

With expanded use of the computer in public enterprise, the laborious, time-consuming work of maintaining detailed cost records and making meaningful and timely reports substantially diminish. The operation of park and recreation systems on a more businesslike basis will enhance the agency's image with the public. With expanded use of enterprise funds, the need for establishing cost tracking systems will increase. Accountability for agency operations and programs and the demand for more productive and efficient public agencies will stress the need for more businesslike management tools.

Some administrators question using unit costs and standards of measurement as a part of the budgeting process. They do, however, feel the necessity of compiling cost data of programs and agency operations for evaluating programs and various operational procedures. When there appears to be a need to decide whether it is better to operate concessions on a contractural basis rather than operating them by agency personnel, a thorough study can be made if sufficient cost information is available. Periodic cost studies are conducted by agencies that are concerned with efficient management of the organization.

If operational analysis is to become an important function of management, more detailed cost data are needed. A cost system extends the normal accounting system by:

- Keeping separate records for each facility or area.
- Using a more detailed object of expenditure classification than the simple one already presented.
- Distributing all administrative costs to the separate functions and facilities.
- Levying interchanges between administrative units.

In actual operation many adaptations of collecting and recording the preceding have been used. Management must determine the kind of information that is needed and what use will be made of this data. The structuring of a costs system that is too burdensome and costly in relation to its purpose will result in being a disruptive influence on overall administration.

Coding Expenditure Accounts

Cost data that must be accumulated expands the expenditure classification accounting system (see Chapter 8, pages 86–87) used for program-type budgets, which included administrative unit, program, and object of expenditure, to keeping records on specific functions, subfunctions or activities, and work performed.

The expansion of the classification system used in program budgeting begins with the further breakdown of specific functions. For example, the general function, outdoor skating rinks and swimming pools, can be extended to list each skating rink and swimming pool operated by the department (see Figure 8.14). For each specific function a further breakdown is made to include subfunctions or activities performed at each rink or pool. It is here that the costs of the hockey league or swim team can be recorded. The next breakdown of the cost system identifies the work that is performed to carry out the activity and function. In examining the work programs listed for the outdoor skating rink and swimming pool, one can readily see that work programs vary for each of the functions and activities that are provided.

Basic to all accounting systems is the object of expenditure classification, that records the specific cost items—labor, supplies, equipment, and materials. An example of the information needed to account for the swimming pools operated by a parks and recreation agency is found in Appendix E, pages 156–157.

Cost Items

The costs, both direct and indirect, that are incurred in operating a park and recreation agency fall under four general classes: labor, materials and supplies, equipment, and overhead. By using the more detailed system, one can identify these cost items and charge them to the appropriate function, activity, and work program. A functional data collection system must be developed to gather this information; it is essential that these data can be easily recorded, stored, and retrieved when needed.

Data Collection

A data collection system can be extremely complex and complete. A careful analysis of just what information is really needed should be made. It is important to note that an accounting and record-keeping system's primary function is to provide answers for the staff to assist in the decision-making process, which is more than a complex collection of books, forms, ledgers, and reports. The literature on cost analysis is full of cautions about making the system too complicated, too costly, and gathering more information than is needed or ever used. The steps that will be discussed are intended to provide the minimum data that are needed to assist the administrator in analyzing agency operations.

Labor Costs. The first consideration for gathering cost data is to identify labor costs and to charge these costs to the appropriate function and work being performed. For full-time professional and staff personnel who hold general adminstrative or supervisory positions, their personnel costs can be charged to overhead, which is later prorated with all other administrative charges and charged to the various agency functions.

Direct labor costs of employees paid on an hourly basis are recorded on daily and weekly time slips. The daily slip (see Figure 8.15) is completed by the employee or supervisor and includes the work assignment, place where work is performed, and hours.

The information recorded on the daily time slip is next transferred by the supervisor or secretary to the weekly time slip, which includes the coding of the function, activity, work, and equipment (see Figure 8.16). These data can be taken from the field report and are keypunched on computer cards for information storage and retrieval.

Another important cost item to consider is indirect costs resulting from employee fringe benefits, that is, vacations, sick leave, and workmen's compensation. Often a rate or percentage of the salaries and wages is figured and included in the overhead expenses or in the hourly wage charged to each function.

In the column entitled "Pay Type" found in Figure 8.16 the number that should be recorded is based on the following information.

01 - Regular time—work done at regular hourly rate.
02 - Overtime—any work done in addition to an 8-hour day or 40-hour week. Seasonal or part-time employees are not eligible for overtime rates.
03 - Sick leave
04 - Vacation
05 - Personal business leave
06 - Bereavement—in case of death in immediate family
07 - Military leave
08 - Holiday
09 - Leave without pay
10 - Union business

Equipment. The daily time slip compiled by each employee also includes the equipment used, the code number, and the hours of operation (see Figure 8.15). This information is also transferred to the

Expenditure Classification System
Cost Analysis
Coding Expenditure Accounts

General local governmental functions
10—General administration
20—Courts
30—Community development
40—Fire
50—Parks and recreation
60—Police
70—Public works
80—Sanitation
90—Other
50—Parks and recreation
   51—Division of parks
   52—Division of recreation

General Functions
51—Division of parks
   .11 Administration
   .12 Parks
   .13 Beaches
   .14 Botanical gardens
   .15 Golf courses
   .16 Nursery
   .17 Marinas
   .18 Outdoor skating rinks
   .19 Parkways
   .20 Swimming pools
52—Division of recreation
   .41 Administration
   .42 Athletics
   .43 Aquatics
   .44 Community centers
   .45 Community events
   .46 Fine arts–cultural activities
   .47 Outdoor recreation—camping
   .48 Senior citizens
   .49 Programs for handicapped
   .50 Supervised playgrounds

Specific functions
.18 Outdoor skating rinks
   181—Olympia Park
   182—Norwood School
   183—Monument Park
   184—Brooks Field
   185—Lawson Park
.20 Swimming Pools
   201—Bryan Park Pool
   202—North West Pool
   203—Mills Pool
   204—South Pool
   205—Olcott Pool

Subfunctions—activities
181—Olympia Park Rink (Outdoor Skating Rink)
   01—Open skating
   02—Hockey league
   03—Hockey classes—instruction
   04—Figure skating—lessons
   05—Figure skating—club

201—Bryan Park Pool (swimming)
   01—Open swimming
   02—Swimming lessons
   03—Life saving classes
   04—Swim team
   05—Water carnival
   06—Handicapped program
   07—Water polo
   08—Group use—rental
Work
181—Olympia Park Rink
   301—Maintenance—flooding rink
   302—Maintenance—snow removal
   303—Maintenance—grading rink
   304—Maintenance—warming house
   305—Maintenance—flood lights
   310—Heating—warming house
   315—Instruction—figure skating
   316—Instruction—hockey
   320—Supervision
201—Bryan Park Pool
   401—Administration
   402—Coaching—swim team
   403—Instruction—swimming lessons
   404—Instruction—Life saving classes
   405—Instruction—handicapped program
   406—Coaching—water polo
   407—Supervision—open swimming
   408—Maintenance—building & locker rooms
   409—Maintenance—pool
   410—Maintenance—parking lot
   411—Maintenance—grounds
Object
1 Personal Services
   11—Salaries and wages
   12—Employee benefits
   13—Other personal services
2 Supplies
   21—Office supplies
   22—Operating supplies
   23—Repair and maintenance supplies
   24—Other supplies
3 Other services and charges
   31—Professional services
   32—Communication and transportation
   33—Printing and advertising
   34—Insurance
   35—Utility services
   36—Repairs and maintenance
   37—Rentals
   38—Debt service
   39—Other services and charges
4 Capital outlays
   41—Land
   42—Buildings
   43—Improvements other than building
   44—Machinery and equipment
   45—Other Capital outlays

Figure 8.14 Expenditure Classification System for Cost Analysis Accounting System.

Parks and Recreation
Enterprise, U.S.A.

Daily Time Slip

_____   _____   Employee's Name (Print)
Supervisor's Signature   Date

_____
Employee's Signature

Work Assignment	Place	Hours	Equipment	No.	Hours
Mowing grass	Olcott Pool	4	Toro 21″	408	4
Mowing grass	South Pool	2	Toro 21″	408	2
Repair window	Mills Pool	2	Ford Bronco	203	2

Figure 8.15   Daily time slip.

_____   Parks and Recreation   _____
Supervisor's signature   Enterprise, U.S.A.   Employee's name (print)

Weekly Time Slip   _____
Employee's signature

Parks Division

_____$5.00/hr._____
Rate

Function			Work		Equipment				Hours Worked						
General No.	Specific No.	Activity Account No.	Code	Explanation	No.	Hours	Rate	Pay Type	M	T	W	T	F	S	S
.20	205		411	Mowing grass	408	4	0.25/hr	01	4						
.20	204		411	Mowing grass	408	2	0.25/hr	01	2						
.20	203		408	Repair window	203	2	1.50/hr	01	2						
.20	205	01	407	Life guard				01		8					
.20	205	01	407	Life guard				01			6				
.20	205	04	402	Coach-swim team				01			2				
.20	205	01	407	Life guard				01				8			
.20	205		409	Clean pool				01					1		
.20	205		407	Life guard				01					7		
									8	8	8	8	8		

Figure 8.16   Weekly time slip.

weekly time slip with the charge, cost per hour or mile, being added.

Local governmental central equipment garages have the responsibility for keeping all equipment in good working condition and for maintaining cost records on all vehicles and equipment. Usually, rental rates are used to distribute the direct and indirect costs of maintaining each piece of equipment to the program or work program. An example of cost of equipment that would be charged to each agency and function is found in Figure 8.17.

Materials and Supplies.   The accurate accounting of costs for supplies and materials is an important

Parks and Recreation
Enterprise, U.S.A.

Equipment Coding and Charge

No.	Type	Rate
	100—Automobiles	
101	1976 Ford Sedan	0.15/mi
102	1977 Plymouth Wagon	0.15/mi
103	1978 Olds Sedan	0.15/mi
	200—Trucks	
201	1967 Chevrolet ½T Pickup	1.50/hr
202	1972 Ford 2T Stake	4.00/hr
203	1976 Ford Bronco	1.50/hr
204	1977 Dodge 1T	3.00/hr
	300—Tractors	
301	1971 Case 430	3.00/hr
302	1973 John Deere 300	3.40/hr
303	1973 Case 580 Back hoe	5.25/hr
304	1974 John Deere 30	3.40/hr
	400—Mowers	
401	1969 Ford Flail	.75/hr
402	1969 Wards	.75/hr
403	1970 Jari-sickelbar	.50/hr
404	1970 Toro Trojan II	0.75/hr
405	1971 Toro Trojan III	0.75/hr
406	1972 Toro 31"	0.50/hr
407	1973 Toro 50"	0.70/hr
408	1975 Toro 21"	0.25/hr
	500—Chain Saws	
501	1971 Homelite XL12	0.90/hr
502	1972 Homelite Super XL	0.90/hr
503	1973 Homelite XL12	0.90/hr
	600—Other Equipment	
600	1970 Air Compressor	3.25/hr
601	1971 Snow Plow	2.00/hr
602	1972 Hydraulic Sprayer	1.75/hr

Figure 8.17. Equipment costs.

aspect of costing of a program. This may require the establishment of a central stores system and a stores clearing account. Cost items are purchased, usually in large volume, and stored in a central stores until they are needed. The central stores is operated by either central government or each agency.

When supplies are needed in performing a job or conducting a program, the department submits a stores requisition for the items needed, the supplies are issued, and a charge is made to the appropriate job or program. Overhead costs for operating the central stores operation are normally added to the costs charged to the agency.

Overhead Costs. Administrative or overhead costs are often budgeted as a separate account or function. If the true cost of providing services to the community is desired, then the overhead costs should be prorated back to the programs and services performed.

It is not uncommon for local governments to frown on the reassignment of overhead costs to agency functions. Some governmental units feel that administrative concerns should be identified and carefully analyzed and it is irrelevant to assign these costs to the programs.

True cost analysis prescribes that overhead costs should be distributed to programs and services, and if the agency is interested in obtaining actual and realistic costs, some method or approach should be used to distribute these costs. This may be done on a percentage basis at the end of each month or at the end of the fiscal year.

Interdepartmental Charges. Often work is performed for the park and recreation agency by another agency in the local government. Costs for providing these jobs or services should be recorded and an interdepartmental billing should be made to charge the agency for the cost of conducting the work. If this is done, a more valid picture of the actual costs for providing programs is revealed.

Cost tracking or cost analysis provides management with valuable data in operating an organization. This information can be used in a number of ways, some of which are presented as follows.

- Is a basis for evaluating work programs and methods of doing work.
- Provides data that are essential for determining fees and service charges.
- Provides information on equipment utilization and is useful in giving justification for procuring new equipment.
- Is useful in determining the efficiency and productivity of agency operations.
- Is important for estimating costs of work programs in planning the budget.

EQUIPMENT COST RECORDS

The mechanization of parks and recreation operations and the use of more complex and specialized equipment requires the establishment of an accounting and management system for these types of equipment. The modern, efficient agency needs trucks, tractors, mowers, chain saws, air compressors, stump removers, to mention only a few examples, to maintain its park and recreation areas. Efficient and effective utilization of motorized equipment has become mandatory if scarce funds are to be properly used. The efficient operation of equipment depends to a large degree on the management and accounting system established for controlling this equipment.

Several different approaches appear to be available to leisure service agencies in managing motor equipment operation.

1. A central garage that purchases, maintains, and rents equipment to various agencies.
2. Garages operated by the agency with equipment purchased by the agency.
3. A cooperative venture where by the local government maintains the large equipment units and the park and recreation agency maintains the smaller specialized park equipment.
4. Maintenance of park and recreation equipment performed by private garages in the community.
5. Lease of equipment from private companies. The company owns the equipment and usually maintains the equipment as a part of the lease or rental agreement.

Local governmental administrative officials and finance officers have long advocated central, area-wide, garage operations, stimulating the growth of centralized control of local governmental equipment in recent years. Proponents of this approach have offered a number of arguments in favor of centralized control of equipment.

1. More equipment can made available to agencies.
2. Maximum utilization can be made of equipment avoiding unnecessary duplication of specialized equipment.
3. One garage in a local jurisdiction can be better equipped to maintain equipment than several garages operated by individual agencies.
4. Better maintenance personnel can be made available that results in a higher quality of maintenance operation.
5. More effective designing of a preventive maintenance program will result that is normally not possible in small agency garages.
6. Charging of equipment to the operating agency on a rental basis makes it easier for agencies to prepare their budgets.

Administrators who operate under a central motor pool differ as to the merits of the arguments discussed. Comments are often made that, in many instances, safety vehicles, fire and police, are given top priority in maintenance services that tend to extend the "down time" of park equipment. This is extremely critical during the heavy use demands of the spring and summer season. In some instances park equipment was transferred to other departments, causing a shortage of equipment for park purposes. Other park officials felt that the centralized motor pool provided the most efficient operation of their equipment.

Traditionally, many agencies were responsible for maintaining their own equipment and the transfer of this responsibility to a central operation meant loss of control of their maintenance operation. The consolidation of this maintenance function into central mechanized units is gaining momentum and park and recreation agencies must learn to function effectively under this concept of managing equipment.

The main components of an accounting system for motorized equipment, established either on a local government basis or by the agency, can be summarized as follows.

• The garage should operate as a staff rather than as a line function in providing efficient service for agency operations.
• A revolving or clearing account or fund should be established with the expectation that the operation is run on a "break even" or no profit basis. Actual cost should be charged to agency functions on a rental or charge basis.
• Cost records should be maintained to reveal all expenses for operating each piece of equipment. Cost items include: gas, oil, lubrication, repairs, insurance, license fees, overhead of central motor pool, and depreciation.
• A reserve fund for depreciation should be established to provide for the systematic replacement of equipment.
• The rental charge, based on per hour/per month or per mile rate, should be calculated on "all costs" for operating each piece of equipment. This should include actual cost items, overhead, and depreciation of equipment.
• Records should be maintained on the actual use of equipment, that is, hours operated, miles driven, and work performed, so that the operating costs (per mile/per hour) can be determined and the intensity of equipment use can be ascertained.

Gathering performance data on equipment has definite values for the park and recreation manager. These data provide comparative cost figures on the operating efficiency of various brands of equipment, that is, Toro, John Deere or Case tractors, or Homelite, Stihl, or McCullough chain saws. Also, unit cost data are basic to the sharing of costs for cost analysis, enterprise funds, or program/performance budgeting. Information relative to high cost or worn-out pieces of equipment provides justification for trading in the equipment and purchasing new equipment.

The accounting system for a motor equipment operation can become quite detailed and comprehensive. In smaller local jurisdictions a manual records system may be adequate. However, in most agencies the basic forms that are needed (equipment master record forms, equipment maintenance forms, work order forms, gasoline issue slips, etc.) require an efficient data transmission system. Most garage records are now being recorded by electronic data processing equipment.

FINANCIAL REPORTING

One of the major responsibilities of managers and fiscal officers is the preparation and distribution of periodic reports to their legislative bodies, administrative officials, staff, and the general public concerning the financial status of the organization and the progress that is being made toward reaching agency objectives. These reports are a part of two management responsibilities of an administrator, fiscal control and accountability.

Fiscal control is concerned with assuring the appropriate bodies that the money appropriated is being spent properly and within the amount and time frame approved in the budget. Administrators are committed to staying within their budgets unless conditions make it impossible, in which case they would need to gain approval for overspending or adjusting their budgets. Monthly financial reports represent management's stewardship for the funds that have been allocated for operating the agency.

Another aspect of stewardship is reporting the progress that has been made toward achievement of the organization's objectives. Agencies that are operating under some approach to management by objectives (MBO), program performance, or zero-base budgeting are committed to the evaluation of the effectiveness of agency resources in the management of the organization. Monthly and annual reports should also emphasize the agency's success or failure in administering its resources and carrying out its programs and services.

Although fiscal control, internal planning, and accountability are important functions of financial reports, administrators should also realize the public relations value of these reports. Each organization has several different publics that they must work with and for. These publics may be internal—staff, park and recreation board, administrative officials, and the legislative body—or external—civic and business interest groups, the news media, and the general public. In reporting to these various publics, one should realize that the type and purpose of each financial report should be designed and directed toward the specific public that it is intended to inform. Also, a number of states have rules and regulations regarding the production of these reports.

Types and Format of Reports

Financial reports may be classified into four main groups. They should be designed for: agency or divisional personnel, city and administrative officials, the legislative body, and the general public. Each type of report serves a particular purpose and is directed to one of the four groups mentioned. The format, detail, and content should vary to meet the needs and interests of each of the publics. Also, the timing of the report, whether monthly, or annual, influences the purpose and data provided.

Despite the kind of report issued, it is essential that the following types of information are included as a part of each report.

- *Indicated Type of Report.* The type of fund should be identified—general, special revenue, enterprise. Also, identify the type of financial statement being presented—actual and estimated expenditures and encumbrances, or actual and estimated revenues.
- *Who Issued Report.* The title of the report should include the name of the agency.
- *Period of Time Covered.* A monthly report should include the fiscal year, as well as contain the month that is covered (January 1, 19xx to December 31, 19xx). Without this information, the data included under column "Total to Date" or "Year to Date" would be meaningless to the reader.

It is important to note that reports lose much of their value if they are not issued promptly after the end of each period covered, that is, month or year. Unfortunately, studies made by several finance professional organizations reveal that local governments that publish financial reports are often lax in the timely publication of their reports.

Reports can be prepared by the central accounting division or by the park and recreation agency. If the central accounting report is sufficiently detailed and timely, the duplication of having the park and recreation agency preparing a report might be questioned. However, many maintain even more comprehensive cost records of agency operations, which are used as monitoring devices by administrative and supervisory personnel within the agency. Reports made from these accounting records may be prepared on a daily, weekly, or monthly basis for the prime purpose of internal management, planning, and evaluation. Reports of this kind often contain more detail than the financial reports prepared for the board and public officials. If agency reports are issued, it is important that some of the basic summary data be consistent with the report issued by the central finance division.

It is recommended that agencies prepare monthly financial reports that will coincide with the allotment projections discussed in Chapter 7. As suggested earlier, budgets and accounting ledgers should be prepared on a program basis, the monthly report should also continue the practice of identifying programs and services.

Parks and Recreation
Enterprise, U.S.A.

Statement of Actual and Budgeted Expenditures (Estimated) and Encumbrances
For Month Ending June 30, 19xx and Year Ending December 31, 19xx

Function and Object (1)	Appropriation (2)	This Month			Total to Date					
		Estimated (3)	Actual (4)	Under or (Over) Estimated (5)	Estimated (6)	Actual (7)	Under or (Over) Estimated (8)	Unexpended Balance (9)	Encumbrances (10)	Unencumbered Balance (11)
Administration Personal services	$60,000	$6,000	$5,800	$200	$28,000	$26,500	$1,500	$33,500	$500	$33,000
Swimming pool Personal services	18,000	5,000	5,200	(200)	6,000	6,100	(100)	11,900	—	11,900

Figure 8.18   Monthly Financial Report on Expenditures and Encumbrances.

Monthly Reports

Monthly reports are prepared mainly for agency use and for keeping the board and public officials informed as to the current financial status of the agency. They should be prepared to monitor the expenditures of the agency as well as the receipts from fees and charges.

Statement of Actual and Budgeted Expenditures and Emcumbrances.

Figure 8.18 depicts the information that is included in the monthly statement analyzing the expenditures of each program of the agency. All the data needed to complete this statement can be taken from the expenditure ledgers established for each program (see Figure 8.2, page 88).

In Column 1 all agency programs and objects of expenditure for each program are listed, with the amount appropriated for each included in Column 2. Columns (3), (4), and (5) compare the actual expenditures for the month with the estimated expenditures that were determined by the allotment process discussed in Chapter 7, pages 76 to 78).

In Columns (6) through (9), total expenditures for the year to date (June 30 in Figure 8.18) is completed. The last two columns show the outstanding encumbrances and the unencumbered balance for each program and objects.

Statement of Actual and Estimated Receipts.

The information found in the financial statement of receipts is obtained from the revenue ledgers established for all programs that have revenue estimated in the budget (see Figure 8.3, page 88).

Sources of revenue for each program are listed in Column (1) (see Figure 8.19). For the purpose of illustration only the swimming pool and the sources of revenue discussed earlier in this chapter, page 87, are listed. Information revealed in the financial statement compares the actual versus the estimated revenue for the month and year to date.

By comparing actual with estimated revenues, one can determine the status of the revenue picture and appropriate action can be taken to stimulate revenues if the situation warrants action.

Financial reports submitted to public officials and legislative bodies can be on a monthly basis but are often in a more condensed form. A summary report of the financial status of the department could conform to the budget summary prepared as a part of the budget (see Chapter 5, page 70). An example of a summary statement of expenditures and receipts is found in Appendixes F-1 and F-2, pages 159 and 160, respectively.

Data Processing.

The use of data-processing systems can greatly assist the agency in the preparation of financial reports and can prove to be of value in solving one of the problems or criticisms found in preparing daily or monthly reports—reducing reporting time. A number of local governments have

Parks and Recreation
Enterprise, U.S.A.

Statement of Actual and Estimated Receipts
For Month Ending June 30, 19xx and Year Ending December 31, 19xx

Source (1)	Total Estimate Year (19xx) (2)	This Month			Total to Date			Balance to be Collected (1)
		Estimated (3)	Actual (4)	Over or (Under) (5)	Estimated (6)	Actual (7)	Over or (Under) (8)	
Swimming pool								
10 Season tickets								
11 Family	$8,000	$3,000	$2,700	$(300)	$7,000	$6,800	$(200)	$1,200
12 Adult	3,000	1,000	1,100	100	2,500	2,800	300	200
13 Child	2,500	600	500	(100)	2,300	2,150	(150)	350
20 Daily admission	12,500	3,000	3,300	300	3,500	3,700	200	8,800
30 Concessions	3,000	600	625	25	700	760	60	2,240
40 Towel and locker rental	1,000	200	230	30	250	260	10	740
50 Miscellaneous	1,000	150	100	(50)	300	200	(100)	800
Total	$31,000	$8,550	$8,555	$ 5	$16,550	$16,670	$120	$14,330

Figure 8.19 Monthly financial report of actual and estimated receipts.

contracted out their accounting and reporting functions and have found that they can receive daily financial statements for the use of agency personnel in managing their programs.

Program/Activity Reports. If the agency is to be held accountable for the performance of programs and services designed to meet objectives, the financial statements must be supplemented or combined with program performance reports. Program reports will emphasize the agency's effectiveness in operating procedures, work programs, and carrying out the programs approved in the adoption phase of the budget.

Annual Reports

There are two types of annual financial reports that are often produced by the local government and/or the park and recreation agency: (1) a detailed statistical report prepared for public officials and legislative bodies and (2) a popularized publication is sometimes developed for distribution to the taxpaying public. Despite the audience or the type of report, the annual report should be issued as soon after the end of the fiscal year as possible. The National Council on Governmental Accounting, in its publication *Governmental Accounting, Auditing, and Finan-*

cial Reporting, strongly recommends that municipalities issue their annual reports within 90 or 120 days of the fiscal year end. Issuing reports after this time period would be of little value to the local jurisdictions, as well as to the individuals or groups that the report is prepared for.

Administrative Reports. Agencies should also prepare annual financial reports covering all funds and financial transactions. As fund accounting is basic to any accounting system, the annual report should first report the financial status of each fund. A balance sheet records the assets included in the fund that are offset by liabilities, reserves, and surplus. In the balance sheet prepared at the end of a year all unrealized revenues must be written off and unencumbered appropriations must be canceled or closed out. A balance sheet for enterprise funds operated by Montgomery County from the 1980 financial report issued by The Maryland National Capital Park and Planning Commission is found in Appendix F-3, page 161.

Financial statements should also be prepared to show the final status of expenditures and receipts for the fiscal year. The information included in the final statement would be similar to that included in the monthly statements, except that the data for each month would be excluded. These reports can either be developed on either a summary basis (see Appendix F-2) or a more detailed breakdown of each agency program and object of expenditure.

In order that financial transactions may be finalized or closed out by the end of the fiscal year, organizations often prohibit the requisition of supplies and equipment after the fifteenth of the last month of the fiscal year. Encumbrances should be closed out or canceled if possible.

At the end of a fiscal year any unencumbered balance reverts back to the general fund or is retained in the special revenue fund. Encumbrances that are outstanding may be placed in a reserve account and recorded in an expenditure ledger so that funds are available to pay the encumbered debts early in the new fiscal year. The amount of the carryover encumbrance is thus added to the approved appropriation for the new fiscal year.

Reports to Public. Increasing attention has been directed to the preparation of popular, understandable annual financial reports for wide distribution to the general public. Popularized annual reports serve much the same purpose as 'Budgets in Brief," which are sometimes issued for public consumption.

Once again, it is important to note the interests and capabilities of the taxpaying public or specialized groups for which the report is intended to serve. Physical appearance, content, and readability are of utmost importance. Graphic presentations in the form of pictures, graphs, diagrams, or pie charts add to the readability and general acceptance of the report.

In 1978 the city of Dallas, Texas, issued its third performance report to the taxpayers and special interest groups. The report contained the city manager's message, operations review, statistical highlights, and condensed, consolidated financial statements. The report highlighted several significant recreation activities: construction of a reunion arena for sports and special activities; public–private cooperation in expanding recreation opportunities for the handicapped; and expanded programs in cultural activities, that is, art exhibits, symphony concerts, and ballet performances. The performance report was not prepared in conformity with the general accepted accounting principles (GAAP). However, the public response to the report was so favorable that city officials agreed to rely more heavily on this type of report and agreed to print fewer copies of the comprehensive financial report, which is prepared in conformity with GAAP. Every municipality or department cannot afford to publish a "Dallas performance report." However, a more modest, less costly, but still attractive and meaningful report could be issued with perhaps equal acceptance from the general public.

Improving Financial Reports

A comprehensive study was made of financial reporting practices of one hundred U.S. cities by Ernst and Whinney. The result of the study[2] published in 1979 revealed two major deficiencies in the financial reports made by cities.

1. The relatively low level of compliance with general accepted accounting principles (GAAP) in current financial reporting by cities.
2. Inadequacies in financial reporting formats and measurement principles that underlie current GAAP for governments.[3]

In preparing financial reports, monthly or annual, local governments should follow the guidelines and principles described in the "bible" of governmental accounting, *Governmental Accounting, Auditing, and Financial Reporting* published in 1968 and reaffirmed by the National Council on Governmental Accounting (NCGA) in 1979.

With the voters increasing lack of confidence in government, the demands for more accountability and disclosure of relevant financial information, public agencies must increase their communication and report efforts to gain public support for governmental programs. The preparation of timely, meaningful, and accurate reports is an important management strategy in gaining this support.

Summary

Park and recreation administrators and staff, in concert with the finance officers of the local jurisdiction, must establish and maintain a meaningful record-keeping and reporting system to serve the financial control and accountability functions in managing their departments. As more agencies are fiscally responsible to some local jurisdiction, that is, city, county, or school district, they must adhere to the budgeting and accounting systems endorsed by their parental governmental unit. In many instances, however, agencies find it advisable to install more detailed cost systems to aid the staff in assessing the effectiveness of the operations of the agency.

Much of the information discussed in Chapter 8

[2]Ernst and Whinney, *How Cities Can Improve Their Financial Reporting,* 1979, 153 pp.
[3]Ibid, p. 1

represents a minimal approach for meeting the budgetary accounting needs of the leisure service agency. The accounting records and financial reports discussed conform with most of the modern concepts of budgeting that use program budgeting as the basis of the budgeting process. Approaches for handling internal funds, petty cash funds, enterprise funds, and cost accounting data are also described.

Leisure service agencies that are fiscally independent are responsible for developing accounting systems that meet the generally accepted accounting principles (GAAP) established by the National Council on Governmental Accounting.

With increasing use of data-processing systems, more effective, detailed, and timely financial data can be made available to local administrators and boards in managing their leisure service agency.

Selected References

Accounting and Financial Reporting, United Way of America, Alexandria, Va., 1980, 195 pp.

An Accounting Handbook for Small Cities and Other Governmental Units, Municipal Finance Officers Association, 1979, 145 pp.

Aronson, J. Richard, and Eli Schwartz, *Management Policies in Local Government Finance,* International City Management Association, Washington, D.C., 1975, pp. 283–302.

Ernst and Whinney, *How Cities Can Improve Their Financial Reporting,* Ernst & Whinney, Cleveland, 1979, 153 pp.

Moak, Lennox, L., and Albert M. Hillhouse, *Local Government Finance,* Municipal Finance Officers Association, Chicago, 1975, pp. 329–357.

Siderelis, Chrystos, "Workload/Cost Tracking" *Trends,* Vol. 15, No. 1, 1978, pp. 32–36.

Chapter 9

Purchasing and Property Control

The effectiveness of an agency's purchasing function can lead to considerable savings and ensure efficiency in the delivery of services. In an era of fiscal stress management personnel must carefully analyze their responsibilities, policies, and procedures for purchasing supplies and services. Cooperative approaches to procurement and alternative methods of acquiring supplies or services, such as leasing these commodities from private vendors or from other governmental agencies, can prove to be profitable. As the storage and control of supplies and equipment are equally important and are closely related to the procurement function, these management concerns are also included in this chapter.

PURCHASING

Next to salaries and wages for employees, the greatest expenditure of funds from the operating budget is the procurement of goods and services from outside vendors. Double-digit inflation has accelerated the costs of these commodities to such an extent that citizens and local agencies must shop carefully to get the best prices for their shrinking dollar. Local government has gradually learned from private enterprise that centralizing the purchasing function will result in the most effective procedures for obtaining quality goods at the lowest costs. Most of the larger local governments have initiated centralized purchasing, with the smaller jurisdictions gradually following suit.

Park and recreation agencies, operating independently of local government, must determine how the purchasing function can best be handled. Normally,

this function is assigned to a purchasing agent operating as a staff function within a particular division in an agency. Regardless of who has this responsibility, it is important to recognize that the primary purpose of a purchasing system is to support and enhance agency operations, resulting in a better delivery of services to the community. In accomplishing this task, the purchasing agent is responsible for providing the proper quality and quantity of goods and services requested by an agency or line unit at the lowest cost and within the time frame desired.

As purchasing by agency staff or even by a purchasing agent within a department of an organization has gradually given way to centralized purchasing, many problems and friction have occurred between the purchasing division and the agency, resulting in what has been often referred to as a "staff-line syndrome." This disruptive element has been caused by purchasing staff assuming greater authority and control than they have had and agency personnel losing control of a function they have had for many years. Under these circumstances centralized purchasing sometimes can actually be a deterrent to agency operations. Purchasing agents should assume the same role as other staff functions, that is, personnel, public relations, accounting, budgeting, and thus, should be viewed as a valuable support service to line operations. Cooperation is a two-way street and both staff and line personnel should work hard at establishing good working relationships with each other. The effectiveness of this relationship is often dependent on the qualifications of the persons involved.

Park and recreation agencies must be guided by

professional personnel if they are to be successful; the same can be said for purchasing divisions. The individual who heads the procurement function should have specialized knowledge, experience, and integrity to guide the operations of the division. The ethics of purchasing agents must be above reproach. The National Institute of Governmental Purchasing has taken the lead in developing standards for personnel in the field of procurement and supply management and in certifying persons who meet the standards established by the institute. Centralized purchasing, guided by competent professional staff, can and should provide the operating agency with valuable support service in obtaining goods and services that are needed for agency operations. Purchasing agents are responsible for providing the following procurement functions.

- Conduct the purchasing for all divisions or agencies according to the policies and procedures established by the legislative body and/or the chief executive.
- Be knowledgeable about all sources of supplies and maintain a file on prices of supplies most often used.
- Establish and operate a formal purchasing procedure utilizing requisitions, purchase orders, bid solicitation, expediting and proper receiving procedures.
- Establish good cooperative relationships with vendors, salespersons and contractors.
- Supervise and/or operate a central stores that utilizes quantity buying of supplies and materials common to all divisions or agencies.
- Work with divisions in planning for and anticipation of their needs so that an orderly acquisition of goods is achieved and emergency buying is minimized.
- Follow through with vendors to expedite shipments so that items are received when needed.
- Be alert to joint cooperative purchasing ventures with other state and local jurisdictions whenever such joint efforts will provide a large reduction in costs and when the sharing of information will enhance good purchasing procedures.

Overall, centralized purchasing should assure better costs on items received, better quality in materials, good public relations with vendors, and the meeting of delivery dates.

The approach and procedures used in purchasing are subject to local ordinances and state statutes. Most purchasing procedures fall under three main categories, with some variation of each found among local governments and states.

1. *Petty cash purchasing.* Involves the purchasing of small cash items where time and cost would prohibit obtaining these items by going through the normal purchasing routine. The operation of petty cash funds was discussed in detail in Chapter 8.

2. *Normal purchasing procedure.* Is commonly used by most organizations, which involves the determination of purchasing needs, solicitation of bids or estimates, the awarding of the contract or business to a vendor, and finally, the receipt and inspection of the commodities received. There are a number of ways to bypass these procedures, especially as they relate to receiving estimates from vendors and to approaches in obtaining materials ordered. Because the normal purchasing system is used by most organizations, a somewhat detailed treatment of this system will be included in this chapter.

3. *Formal bidding procedure.* Is required by most state statutes for purchasing costly equipment and services and in awarding construction contracts. Formal bidding generally requires the preparation of detailed specifications, formal announcement of the agency's needs in local newspapers, submission of sealed bids, and finally, the opening of the bids and awarding of a contract.

Normal Purchasing Procedure

There are several separate and distinct steps involved in the normal purchasing procedure used by most public organizations. Responsibilities of the park and recreation agency and recommendations for establishing good rapport with the vendor and purchasing agent are discussed whenever relevant.

Indication of Agency's Need. Procedures should be established within an agency to allow employees to submit requests for items that are needed in the operation of their program or facility. An informal requisition form is sometimes used whereby staff submit information about the supplies and equipment they need. This form would be given to the person designated as purchasing representative for a particular agency. A purchase requisition is then prepared and signed by the administrator, which would indicate approval of the request and that adequate funds are in the budget for the purchase of the item(s). Two concerns that often lead to conflict between the originating division and the purchasing agent in completing the purchase requisition (see Figure 9.1), are the date on which the items are needed and the specifications describing the items desired by the division. The first concern generally results from the lack of planning or anticipation of needs and consequently one is confronted with an emergency situation and requests that the commodities be purchased "as soon as possible." This situation places a severe limitation on the purchasing agent because sufficient time is not available for contracting vendors or obtaining bids. As a result, organizational personnel often become disenchanted with the purchasing process and

City of Enterprise, U.S.A.

PURCHASE REQUISITION

REQ. NO. _____15_____

ACCOUNT TITLE AND NUMBER		EXPENSE CLASS	DATE REQUIRED
Parks and Recreation (51)		21	3/1/83

STATE COMPLETE DELIVERY ADDRESS (BOTH BUILDING AND ROOM NUMBER)
Administration Building, Room 133

REQUESTED BY	DATE	VENDOR SUGGESTED:
John Doe	1/6/83	Steel Case, Inc.

I CERTIFY THAT FUNDS ARE AVAILABLE WITHIN THE ACCOUNT CHARGED.	DATE	VENDOR:
J. M. Parks	1/7/83	
HEAD OF DEPARTMENT		

OTHER APPROVAL	DATE

SHIP VIA.	F.O.B.	TERMS:

QUANTITY	ITEMS (GIVE COMPLETE SPECIFICATIONS)	ESTIMATED TOTAL		ACTUAL TOTAL	
5	Two—drawer vertical file cabinet, letter size, full suspension, with locks, beige color, @ $ 110.00	550	00		
2	Five—drawer vertical file cabinet, legal size, full suspension, without locks, medium grey color, @ $ 190.00	380	00		
1	Two—drawer lateral file cabinet, legal size, full suspension, with lock, 36" wide, with hanging folder frames, medium grey color, @ $ 180.00	180	00		

ORDER NO.	APPROVED--TREASURER	ACCT. DEPT.

REQUISITIONS FOR EQUIPMENT MUST BE ACCOMPANIED BY SUPPORTING STATEMENT

Figure 9.1 Purchase requisition.

place unjust criticism and pressure on the agent for purchasing items that were "needed yesterday." Therefore the key for successful purchasing in this step is to anticipate organizational needs so there can be adequate time to obtain the materials.

If the purchasing agent is to purchase the right kind of supplies or equipment requested by the staff, good specifications are essential. Moak and Hillhouse suggest that an adequate specification should meet the following major criteria:

1. It must be specific and complete, leaving no loopholes whereby an unscrupulous bidder may evade any of its provisions, thereby taking unfair advantage of the buyer and of the other bidders.
2. It must accurately describe the article specified and the requirements for its physical performance.
3. It must not overspecify—requiring materials of a better quality than are needed for the job or including elements not germane to requirements.
4. It must prescribe the methods of inspection and testing which will govern the acceptance or rejection of the materials.
5. It must be worded as simply as is consistent with clarity.
6. It must stipulate any special methods of packing or marking which are required.
7. It must conform, as clearly as possible, to nationally recognized specifications.[1]

For example, if an agency is interested in obtaining new filing cabinets, the specifications included in Figure 9.1 would enable the purchasing agent to meet the expressed needs and expectations. If management personnel do not have sufficient information with which to develop proper specifications, the purchasing agent is often helpful in preparing item "specs."

Once the purchase requisition is properly prepared, it is forwarded to the purchasing division informing their personnel of the goods and services that are needed. If the agency maintains its own financial records, the estimated cost should be entered in the expenditure ledger as an encumbrance and the estimated cost should be subtracted from the unencumbered balance.

Securing Quotations. If several possible vendors are available to supply the items desired, bid solicitations are normally obtained before the purchase order can be prepared. If the item(s) needed are not too costly or if only one vendor is able to supply the commodity, it is not necessary to take the time or

the expense to obtain estimates. However, competitive bidding does stimulate competition, which is an important element of the purchasing process. When vendors know that other firms are interested in supplying supplies or services, they are generally forced to give their best prices if they are to obtain the business.

One of the most widely used methods of soliciting bids is mailing a request for quotation form to selected vendors who are likely to be interested in supplying a particular item. Purchasing personnel are responsible for keeping an up-to-date card file of vendors, organized according to specific commodity items, that is, sporting goods equipment, craft supplies, office supplies and equipment, and swimming pool supplies. The file should be confined to merchants who have proved to be responsible in submitting good bids, are able to meet deadlines, and have a reputation of servicing their products. The Request for Quotation form is mailed to several vendors, seeking their willingness to supply the needed items and their bid for supplying the materials requested in the purchase requisition (see Figure 9.2).

There are several other more informal approaches for getting cost estimates and bids. If time is limited and the number of items and costs are not too excessive, agency personnel may place telephone calls to at least three vendors requesting bids on the items needed. The quotations given by phone are recorded on a form that aids the agency in studying estimates on individual items and the overall list of supplies (see Figure 9.3). In analyzing the bids received from the four vendors, one would give the total award to the most cost-effective choice, Vendor B, who was low on the majority of items and the overall total. Because of the cost of processing the purchase orders and the receipt and payment of the order, the selection of one vendor, rather than purchasing the basketballs from Vendor A and the bases from Vendor C, is the best choice. It would be wise to have each vendor put his/her verbal bids in writing and forward them to the agency for record purposes.

Awarding the contract. Upon receipt of the competitive bids, the purchasing agent has the responsibility for awarding the contact to the "best bids." To be sure, the lowest bid is important; after all, this is the primary reason for obtaining several bids. However, the following concerns should also be considered.

- The ability of the bidder to supply the goods or perform the services within the time frame indicated.
- The reliability of the firm or contractor in performing the service requested.

---

[1] Lennox L. Moak, and Albert M. Hillhouse, *Local Government Finance,* Municipal Finance Officers Association of the United States and Canada, Chicago, 1974, p. 219.

REQUEST FOR PRICE AND TERMS
(THIS IS NOT AN ORDER—KEEP THIS COPY)

From:

City of Enterprise
Purchasing Department
Purchasing Building
Enterprise, U.S.A.

To:

Steel Case, Inc.
1120 36th St., S. E.
Grand Rapids, MI 49501

P.R. No. ....

NOTE CAREFULLY
Reply must be in by early mail unless specified below

.... 19.............

Unless otherwise understood, there are no restrictions on the number of items or the quantity that may be ordered.
No substitutes will be considered unless a complete description is given.
The right is reserved to reject any offer.
Enterprise is a political subdivision of the state and is therefore not subject to any sales or use tax imposed by the state, or to any excise taxes imposed by the Federal Government.

All shipments to be F.O.B DESTINATION, for shipment to Enterprise, USA via ....

Quantity	Unit	Catalog Number and Description of Article	List Price per Unit	Trade Discount	Total Cost
5		Two—drawer vertical file cabinets, letter size, full suspension, with locks, beige color			
2		Five—drawer vertical file cabinet, legal size, full suspension, without locks, medium grey color			
1		Two—drawer lateral file cabinet, legal size, full suspension, with lock, 36″ wide, with hanging folder frames, medium grey color			
				TOTAL COST	

IMPORTANT: The information and signature requested below MUST BE COMPLETED, or your offer may not be considered.
TERMS OF PAYMENT: Cash discount.................% .... Days—Net .... Days; or ....
Shipment can be made by .... 19......from our stock ...., from factory .... at ....
Offer effective until—Date .... Are the above prices firm if order is placed? ....
Yes or No

If lists accompany this request, keep one copy for your records and return the other copy with the canary sheet.

KEEP THIS COPY
Enterprise, U.S.A. is and Equal Opportunity Employer.

Jack Riggins, Purchasing Agent
signed

Figure 9.2 Request for quotation.

Summary of Quotations

Requisition no. ___60___

Date ___March 16, 19xx___

Items	Quantity	Unit	Vendors (Unit Cost Bid)			
			(A)	**(B)**	**(C)**	**(D)**
Basketballs (rubber)	6	each	$12.20	$13.50	$14.00	$13.25
Softballs (leather)	6	dozen	32.50	30.00	34.00	33.50
Softball bases (rubber)	4	set	33.50	32.00	30.00	32.00
Soccer balls	10	each	14.00	12.95	13.95	14.50
Footballs (leather)	12	each	22.00	19.95	21.00	23.50
Volleyball net (steel)	2	each	34.95	34.00	36.00	35.00
Volleyballs	14	each	18.90	18.00	19.00	18.50
Tennis net	2	each	81.00	79.00	80.00	80.00
Total			$1,302.70	$1,235.90	$1,297.50	$1,324.50

Figure 9.3 Summary of quotations.

- The ability of the firm to service the equipment acquired.
- The quality of the supplies and materials or the performance of the work contracted.

If the lowest bid is not accepted, the reasons for selecting a higher bid must be properly documented and explained. If the bids are deemed unsatisfactory, the agency always reserves the right to reject any or all bids.

After choosing the "best bid" one prepares a purchase order (see Figure 9.4) and sends it to the vendor indicating the interest in purchasing the specific commodities or services. Before the purchase order is sent to the vendor, a copy is submitted to the finance department for its confirmation that adequate funds are available in the agency's budget.

Expediting the Order. One of the important tasks of the purchasing division is to make sure that the goods are received on time or that the service is completed according to the contractual agreement made between the city and the contractor. This often proves to be a very time-consuming and frustrating responsibility. A postcard or telephone call to the supplier often is the first step. If the deadline is not being met and the vendor seems unable to obtain the goods from his/her supplier, the purchasing agent can contact the supplier or factory to find out the status of the order. Effective purchasing agents are those who have established good contacts in the business community and know about the type and amount of pressure to apply. Establishing good rapport with vendors is an important part of a purchasing agent's responsibilities.

Receiving Materials. The vendor has the responsibility for delivering goods to the organization or the central processing center operated by the purchasing department. The items received are carefully checked against the purchasing order and evaluated as to whether they meet the specifications established in the purchase requisition and incorporated in the purchase order. It is up to the originating personnel to approve the goods received. A report is signed and sent to the purchasing division. This report could be in the form of a delivery ticket, packing slip, or a copy of the purchase order. Often substantial discounts are available for prompt payment of the bill, therefore the report should be expedited quickly in order to get these savings.

With the verification of the goods, the purchasing personnel are in a position to make a final evaluation of the transaction. The invoice voucher (see Figure 9.5) indicates the items sent and represents the bill from the vendor. After this is compared with the purchase order and the report of the goods received, a copy of the voucher is sent to the finance department for prompt payment. When the bill is paid, the encumbrance in the expenditure ledger is canceled and the amount paid is recorded in the expenditure column. If the final payment differs from the amount encumbered, the appropriate adjustment is made in the unencumbered balance column.

Formal Bidding Procedure

Most states require a formal bidding procedure to be followed in purchasing costly equipment, services, or contracting major construction projects. Many of the same steps and procedures used in the normal pur-

Enterprise, U.S.A.
Purchase Order

Department	Acct. No.	Class	Building/Room
Parks and Recreation	51	21	Administration Building, Room 133
F.O.B.	Terms	Requision No.	Date
Destination	2%—10 days	15	1-6-19xx

Steel Case, Inc.
1120 36th St., S.E.
Grand Rapids, MI 49501

Ship to: Enterprise, U.S.A.

Purchase order no.   1530

Quantity	Description	Total
5	Two-drawer vertical file cabinets, letter size, full suspension, with locks, beige color	$575.00
2	Five-drawer vertical file cabinet, legal size, full suspension, without locks, medium grey color	380.00
1	Two-drawer lateral file cabinet, legal size, full suspension, with lock, 36″ wide, with hanging folder frames, medium grey color	180.00
	Per special quotation Delivery 3/1/19xx	

Jack Riggins   Buyer

Figure 9.4   Purchase order.

INVOICE VOUCHER

MAIL TO:

Enterprise, U.S.A.

ATTN: **PURCHASING DEPARTMENT**

Date
2/28/83

PAY TO

Name of Firm
Steel Case, Inc.

Purchase	Order Number
	1530

Street Address	City	State
1120 36th St., S.E.	Grand Rapids,	Michigan 49501

Req. Number
51

Above numbers must be given

Terms	F. O. B.
2%—10 days	Enterprise, U.S.A

Firm Invoice Number

**IMPORTANT: Your terms
must be stated above**

Date Shipped	Via
2/28/83	Motor Freight

QUANTITY	ITEMS	UNIT PRICE	AMOUNT
5	Two—drawer vertical file cabinet, letter size, full suspension, with locks, beige color, @ $110.00		$ 550.00
2	Five—drawer vertical file cabinet, legal size, full suspension, without locks, medium grey color, @ $ 190.00		380.00
1	Two—drawer lateral file cabinet, legal size, full suspension, with lock, 36″ wide, with hanging folder frames, medium grey color, @ $ 180.00		180.00

City of Enterprise is free of all excise and state sales taxes. Certificate will be furnished

Date _____ , 19 ____   **X** Mr. J. R. Steelcase

SIGNATURE

SECTION BELOW FOR UNIVERSITY USE ONLY

ACCOUNT TITLE AND NUMBER TO BE CHARGED	Expense Classification	Amount
Parks and Recreation (51)		

Approved for Payment	Account Manager		Date	Check No.
Audited by	Material Rec'd O. K.			
Approved for the Vice Pres. and Treasurer	By			

Figure 9.5 Invoice voucher.

chasing routine are followed here: developing detailed specifications, solicitting bids, awarding the contract, and evaluating the equipment received or services rendered. It is in the area of competitive bidding where the difference occurs.

When the anticipated cost of the purchase or contract is over a maximum of $1000, or some larger amount, local governments are often required to place a notice in two or more local newspapers. Advertising is justified as a safeguard against charges of favored treatment or deliberate limitation of competition. Formal notices do meet legal requirements; however, newspaper ads are not often effective in reaching the suppliers, or contractors who might be interested in bidding on the equipment or the capital improvement project. As a supplement to public notices, the puchasing agent sometimes contacts appropriate firms, inviting them to submit bids.

Public notices notify potential bidders of the items or services desired and where detailed specifications can be obtained. Deadlines are stated as to the place, day, and hour for the receipt of bids. The firms are also informed as to where and when the bids will be opened.

Depending on the nature of the procurement desired, sealed bids are opened by the purchasing agents or at an official meeting of the legislative body or park and recreation board. The public meeting allows bidders or citizens to be present if they are interested. Bids are accepted and referred to the purchasing personnel and the agency for study. Recommendations for acceptance of a bid are made at a future meeting of the legislative body. In some cases bidders are required to submit bid sureties (cash, bond, or a certified check) with their formal bids as a guarantee that the bidder will accept the contract if it is awarded to him/her. Normally, bid sureties are required for large construction contracts.

Shortcuts

The normal purchase procedure discussed is generally viewed as the best approach for procurement of commodities and services. Purchasing agents do allow variations of this procedure when certain conditions prohibit following the more time-consuming purchasing routine. Petty cash funds have already been discussed as an approach used to obtain small cash items. Other shortcuts sometimes include one or more of the following.

Blanket Purchase Orders. When an agency is interested in making many repetitive purchases from an individual vendor, it often is not economical or feasible to place purchase orders for each purchase.

For example, the purchasing of items such as food, gasoline, plumbing, and hardware supplies often cannot be anticipated or planned in advance to take advantage of bulk purchasing. As certain local merchants have served the agency well in supplying these items, a blanket purchase order can be issued to the merchant to supply the agency with supplies up to a specific dollar amount, that is, office supplies—$200. If there are several merchants interested in supplying office supplies, bids can be solicited from several vendors, requesting discounts that they would give to the local jurisdiction.

To implement this procedure, the agency should submit a requisition to the purchasing department seeking approval to purchase office supplies not to exceed $200. If the agency maintains expenditure ledgers, an encumbrance of $200 is posted and a similar amount is subtracted from the unencumbered balance (see Figure 8.2, Chapter 8, page 88). A blanket purchase order would be issued to the vendor, that is, Indiana Office Supplies, authorizing agency employees to obtain supplies up to an amount of $200.

After the blanket purchase order is issued, agency personnel are instructed as to the guidelines for obtaining supplies and minor equipment under this order. Persons authorized to obtain items would be given the purchase order number, the vendor's name, and a dollar limitation (i.e., $50.00) that cannot be exceeded. When employees pick up an item, they inform the vendor of the purchase order number and are given a delivery ticket along with the item received.

At the end of each month, or at such a time when the amount of purchase reaches the amount designated in the purchase order, the vendor submits an invoice covering the costs of the items received. The cash receipts or delivery tickets are checked against the items included in the invoice. If, for example, the Indiana Office Supply submits a bill at the end of the month for $120 for office supplies received, an expenditure of $120 would be recorded in the expenditure ledger (see Figure 8.2, Chapter 8, page 88), the same amount would be deducted from encumbrances, and the unencumbered balance would remain the same. The agency would still have $80 remaining on the purchase order to obtain supplies. Blanket purchase orders are widely used and do provide the agency easier access to small cost items supplied by local vendors.

Walk Through Method. Often, purchasing departments will allow agencies to process emergency orders quickly by using a "walk through" procedure. If the commodity needed is too expensive to be obtained by petty cash procedures and not so expensive as to require bids, the originating department prepares a purchase requisition, indicating the item needed and the vendor where the item can be obtained. The requisition is approved by the administrator and the employee takes it to the purchasing division for approval. The purchasing department either can issue a purchase order or can give the employee a purchase order number that gives the person the authority to purchase the needed item. The item can then be picked up and the counter ticket received is forwarded to the purchasing department. When the vendor sends the invoice for the purchase, the invoice can be sent to the finance department for payment. If this transaction is accomplished immediately, and the exact amount of the purchase is known, the bookkeeper in the department could record the transaction as an expenditure rather than as an encumbrance in the ledger.

Call in Approach. In case of an emergency, the agency may call the purchasing department, indicating the problem and requesting approval for procuring the item. If the amount is somewhat substantial, the employee may be asked to contact three local merchants to gain a quotation. The employee then calls the purchasing department, indicating the verbal bids that he/she has received. The purchasing agent indicates approval and notifies the employee of a purchase number that can be given to the local vendor. The employee picks up the item, and sends the delivery slip to the purchasing department for further processing and payment.

It should be realized that emergency purchasing does tempt agency personnel to bypass the normal purchasing system. These shortcuts could result in higher prices and discourage employees from anticipating their needs and following the more time-consuming purchasing procedures. Also, overuse of these approaches does not foster good relationships with purchasing agents.

Central Stores

Many local governments find it advantageous to establish a central stores to stock materials and supplies that are in frequent or constant demand. A central stores operation does eliminate the need for operating substores within agencies or divisions, although some of the larger park and recreation agencies maintain stores for their operations. Many advantages of centralized purchasing can be used in justifying central stores. By standardizing the specifications of commodities used by all agencies or divisions, quantity buying is possible. It is not feasible or necessary for each agency or division to use different brands of office and maintenance supplies or to have their own personalized letterhead stationery. Having certain items available for quick acquisition by agencies or divisions is an additional plus factor, because it often eliminates the need for emergency buying.

One of the keys to successful central stores operations is not to overstock large numbers of items but to limit stock to items that are in heavy demand. Good management and stock control are required to prevent overstocking or loss of items and to assure the proper charging of goods to the agency or division and the program or function.

In obtaining items from central stores, a stores requisition is prepared by the originating department or, in the case of a departmental stores system, by an employee seeking supplies for his/her program or division (see Figure 9.6).

Upon receipt of the items, the employee signs the requisition and the cost is charged to the appropriate department, program, or cost account by the use of an intramural invoice voucher.

Cooperative Purchasing

Cooperative purchasing programs between state and local governments, among local jurisdictions within a community, and between municipalities themselves have received increased attention in recent years. By pooling the needs of several organizations one can do large volume buying, which often results in considerable dollar savings. A number of states, for example, Illinois, New York, and Florida, through their Departments of General Services, utilize a highly competitive bidding process to contract with vendors for standard items that are needed by most governmental units. Also, in a number of states, the state league of municipalities has developed cooperative purchasing programs for local communities. Local units of government may take advantage of these state contracts if they so desire.

In the Chicago metropolitan area approximately 50 park districts joined together in initiating a cooperative purchasing project. From a modest beginning of purchasing only pool supplies, the project expanded to include custodial and turf supplies. A workshop session was held at the Great Lakes Park Training Institute in which the pros and cons of this joint venture were discussed. The procedures followed in implementing this project involved: (1) determining interested agencies, (2) establishing ground rules and areas of interest, (3) developing specifications, (4) developing a bid list of vendors, (5)

Enterprise, U.S.A.

Central Stores Requisition Form

Department ___Recreation (53)___	Deliver to	
	bldg. ___Administration___	
Account no. ___.11___ (program)		
	Received by	
Object class ___21___		
	_____	
Requested by ___Marie Jones___		
	Requisition no. ___60___	
Authorized by ___J. T. Johnson___		
	Date ___Jan. 15, 19xx___	

Stock No.	Quantity	Description	Cost
B 81 00010	10 each	Calendar refills @ $1.04	$10.40
B 81 91200	2 boxes	Duplicating masters-spirit	
		@ $3.81	7.62
B 82 27450	2 boxes	Envelopes—#10 regular @ $4.30	8.60
B 85 80110	10 each	Notebooks-stenographers @ 0.37	3.70
B 87 55210	3 pair	Scissors-office, 8 in. @ $1.50	4.50
Total			$34.82

Figure 9.6   Central stores requisition form.

establishing a memorandum of understanding among park districts, (6) sending specifications to bidders, (7) opening bids at a meeting of representatives of districts involved, and (8) having individual districts send purchase orders to a central point where they were then forwarded to the suppliers. Like any cooperative venture involving a large number of agencies, problems were encountered; however, it was felt that the park districts did receive better prices from large volume buying.[2]

Joining together local public jurisdictions (city, county, school districts, libraries, and special park districts) for cooperative purchasing has proved successful in many parts of the country. City officials in Milwaukee, Wisconsin, reported that their purchasing department coordinated the purchasing efforts of 20 local governmental units, resulting in a good dollar saving for each unit involved.

The advantages of cooperative purchasing far exceed some of the drawbacks that are sometimes expressed, such as bypassing local vendors, agreeing on specifications, and so on. If one of the primary purposes of purchasing is getting quality goods at the best possible price, agencies should explore this approach to purchasing.

[2]*Proceedings of the Great Lakes Park Training Institute*, Department of Recreation and Park Administration, Indiana University, 1978, pp. 177–178.

LEASES AND CONTRACTURAL AGREEMENTS

The use of contracts, informal and formal, are important aspects of the purchasing function already discussed. The purchase order represents a contract to purchase supplies, equipment, or services from a vendor. For the acquisition of costly equipment and capital improvements, formal contracts prescribe the terms, specifications, and condition of the transaction. The procurement of supplies and materials from business firms is a well-established and approved practice. The contracting of private enterprise to provide public services is a somewhat newer and more controversial alternative strategy. Also, a new trend is the leasing of public assets (parks, golf courses, recreation buildings) to individuals and organizations outside the agency to operate. This practice, however, has not received much popular support from park and recreation administrators and boards. With recent widespread emphasis on public agencies to cut the rising cost of services and to operate more efficiently and effectively, the expansion of contracts with private business agencies is being considered as a possible alternative for providing services.

Contracting of Services

The provision of public services by the private sector through contractual or lease agreements is not new.

Some local units of government have contracted out such services as garbage collection, road repair, public transit, snow removal, off street parking, sewage treatment plants, and hospital and health services, rather than utilize public employees for these tasks. Arguments favoring private operation of public services are generally twofold: cost effectiveness and reduction of the public work force, whose size and composition are difficult to change as needs evolve. Fiscal restraints are forcing more cities to investigate this method of providing new services and even to consider contracting established functions.

Cooperative relationships and contractural agreements between park and recreation agencies and other governmental units have been in existence for years. The purchasing of supplies, materials, and equipment; the design and construction of areas and facilities; the joint use of school facilities; the leasing of concession operations; and contractural services for maintenance of equipment and buildings from outside vendors are practices common to most agencies. The contracting with private agencies to deliver services traditionally performed by park and recreation employees is somewhat new and is under question. Many professionals feel that they are losing control of their primary function, the provision of programs and services, by allowing outsiders to perform these functions conducted for years "in house" by agency employees. Because of the mixed response of park and recreation professionals regarding the contracting of public services, the Heritage Conservation and Recreation Service (HCRS) conducted a study on this subject, which resulted in a *Contract Services Handbook*. This handbook is designed to aid administrators in responding to increasing pressures for contracting private agencies to provide public services.[3]

Although the amount of money budgeted for contractural agreements with private agencies is relatively small, there appears to be increasing demands on government officials to consider new alternatives for providing services. It is interesting to note that the data resulting from a survey conducted by the International City Management Association in 1976 show that 59 percent of the 404 cities responding to the survey had "privatized" (transferred to the private sector) at least some public services.[4] Privatization is becoming a well-discussed term among park and recreation professionals, and the profession

should study carefully its ramifications on local delivery of services throughout the country.

For leisure service agencies considering the contracting of the operations of facilities to private entrepreneurs, it is imperative that rules and guidelines be established so that the facility will remain accessible to the public, as well as for those individuals who are able to pay the price to participate. If these conditions are not set at the outset, then minorities and the disadvantadged will be excluded from participating in public recreation activities.

The current status of privatization of park and recreation services is not known; however, the HCRS study reported on three studies conducted in the mid-1970s.

- *Performance and Productivity: 1976* showed that only 9% of responding cities nationwide had transferred any park services to the private sector. Only 5% had transferred recreation services.
- A *League of California Cities* survey, of 203 municipalities in 1976, found that only 11% contracted for any recreation programs. An equally small percentage of respondents contracted for golf course operation. Only 5 to 8% contracted for grounds-keeping or building maintenance.
- *Private Provision of Public Services*, a report published in 1978, concludes that with respect to park and recreation services nationwide, the public sector "does surprisingly little contracting with private firms." The authors cite the 1972 International City Management Association survey in which less than 1% of responding governments reported agreements with private firms for the operation of *any* part of their park and recreation facilities (excludes concessionaires).[5]

The studies mentioned were all conducted prior to Proposition 13 in California and other tax reform measures that have been passed recently. Since the passage of Proposition 13 and the budget reduction imposed on park and recreation agencies in that state, agencies have reported an increased use of contracting out some of their services. The studies that have been conducted reveal mixed reactions concerning privatized operations. There are failures, to be sure; however, successful operations were submitted to HCRS.

Case Studies—Successful Operations. Some of the types of contractural agreements reported by agencies reveal a wide diversity of alternatives to the traditional delivery of services.

- In Massachusetts, the Division of Forests and Parks of the Department of Environmental Management contracts with the nonprofit Massachusetts Audubon Soci-

---

[3]*Contract Services Handbook*, Heritage Conservation and Recreation Service, U.S. Department of Interior, Washington, D.C., 1979, 64 pp.
[4]*Performance and Productivity: 1976 Survey*, International City Management Association, Washington, D.C.

[5]*Contract Services Handbook*, p. 6

ety to *recruit manager interpretor interns for five islands* in the Boston Harbor Island State Park. Rule enforcement, administration, programming and interpretive services are provided at one-third the in-house cost.

- The Fair Oaks Recreation and Park District in California contracts with a private-for-profit firm, formed by the District's own recreation staff, to *operate all recreation programs.*
- The City of Plano Parks and Recreation Department in Texas leased a floodplain to a private business for the *construction, operation and maintenance of a golf course* for public use.
- The Missouri State Parks System contracts with a local motorcycle club for the *operation and maintenance of some multiple use areas* requiring extensive upkeep.
- The Detroit, Michigan recreation department has contracted for *renovation and operation of existing tennis courts,* as well as *construction of additional courts.*[6]

Contracting for Maintenance and Service Functions

Although the operation of programs has been a relatively recent innovation, agencies for years have been contracting with outside firms for maintenance of park and recreation areas and facilities. Several examples of this kind of contractural agreement reported to the HCRS include the following.

- The Hayward Area Recreation and Park District in California contracts for *janitorial work at small buildings.* The janitors, who work between 12 midnight and 4:00 A.M., also act as a deterrent to potential vandals.
- The Livermore Area Recreation and Park District in California contracts with the local soccer club for *maintenance of playing fields used by the club.*
- The East Bay Regional Park District in California saves over $50,000 a year by contracting for *garbage pick-up.* Another example: For a savings in time and travel, District vehicles used at outlying parks are serviced through contracts with service stations.
- The Weaverville-Douglas City Recreation District reports savings through contracting for *accounting and bookkeeping services.* This small agency cannot fully utilize a full-time staff person.[7]

Pros and Cons. Arguments for and against privatization have been made by professionals in the field. Advocates feel that private agencies perform the work cheaper, exhibit better managerial practices, have better equipment, and have lower personnel costs. Private companies often operate with non-unionized employees, pay lower wages, and offer fewer benefits.

Culver City, California, reported savings of 25 to 40 percent on tree trimming and island mainte-

nance by using private contractors. The City of Hawaiian Gardens (California) contracted out building maintenance at $12,000 versus $26,000 by using city employees.

Negative concerns expressed include the feeling that the department loses control of its operations, private agencies are more interested in making money than serving the public, and finally, the unions will react negatively to the loss of public sector jobs.

Lease Agreements

Leisure service agencies often find that leasing is a feasible alternative to the purchase or sale of equipment or property. Current fiscal constraints faced by cities are creating problems in financing capital outlays and in purchasing costly equipment. It is becoming quite common for local agencies to turn to lease agreements for solving facility and equipment problems and many people view leasing as the wave of the future.

Leasing can be defined as a contractural agreement between two parties where one party conveys property to another for a period of time on a rental basis. Park and recreation agencies may find it advantageous to be a leasor, or a leasee, or both. Harrell, in his article "Governmental Leasing Techniques,"[8] discusses three approaches to lease agreements: (1) a straight operating lease, (2) lease–purchase agreements, and (3) lease–sublease agreements.

Straight Operating Lease. In using the straight operating lease, the agency simply leases land, facilities, or equpiment to another agency for a period of time. An automobile, for example, may be leased from a local vendor on a yearly basis, where land may be leased on a long-term basis, that is, 99 years, for use as a park. The property leased reverts back to the owner at the termination of the lease. Many agencies find it cheaper to rent a costly piece of equipment and fully utilize it when it is needed rather than purchase the equipment and only use it periodically during the year. Often, office equipment and computers are leased with the maintenance of the item built in the lease agreement. The high obsolescence factor of computers is reason enough to lease this equipment rather than to purchase it. The high initial purchase cost of some types of equipment prohibits many smaller agencies from direct purchase and ownership. If the agency owns property, it

---

[6]Ibid, pp. 8–9.
[7]Ibid, pp. 8, 12.

[8]Rhett D. Harrell, "Governmental Leasing Techniques," *Governmental Finance* Vol. 9, pp. 15–18, March 1980.

may be desirable to lease the building or major piece of equipment to another governmental unit or private firm on a rental basis to utilize the property more fully and also to receive revenue for the upkeep of the facility or equipment. Leasing property is the same as a family renting a home; a down payment and high mortgage costs are eliminated; however, the renter does not accumulate equity in the property.

Lease–Purchase Agreements. This type of contractual agreement is actually purchasing on an installment plan. Rather than direct purchase, the lease allows the leasor to spread the payment of the cost of the property (principle and interest) over a period of years or for the time of the lease. At the conclusion of the lease agreement the ownership of the property is transferred to the leasee. Lease purchase agreements are often used in lieu of bond issues or in cases where the agency cannot afford the high initial cost of the property desired. Harrell suggests that lease agreements can be more efficient and less expensive than bond issues for two reasons: practicality and economic feasibility. He suggests that

The practicality of the lease–purchase contract is demonstrated in a number of ways, such as (1) elimination of the expense and delay caused by a bond referendum; (2) the capacity it has for use by small governments which have limited access to the capital markets; and (3) its ability to finance relatively small capital needs that are too large to be funded from current revenues, yet too small to even be considered for bond financing.[9]

Private businesses are most receptive to lease–purchase agreements because federal regulations provide for a tax exemption of the interest portion of the lease.

Lease–Sublease Agreements. A lease–sublease may be beneficial to local governments if a governmental unit desires to lease a community building to another agency and then to lease back a portion of the building for its own purposes. The agency leasing the building is required to pay for the maintenance and operation costs of the entire building while the payment of rent for the building provides a good source of revenue for the governmental agency. The governmental agency maintains the portion of the building needed for its own needs and allocates the remaining portion of the building, not needed for its program, to the leasing agency in need of the remaining space in the building. There are a number

of city–county relationships where a lease–sublease agreement might be advantageous to both parties. With the closing of a number of schools in recent years, a lease–sublease approach between the school corporation and the park and recreation department could prove to be a meaningful solution to the school board in disposing of surplus school buildings and a way park and recreation departments may expand their programs without financing the building of new community centers.

PROPERTY CONTROL

The acquisition of supplies, materials, and equipment represents a sizable investment of funds for most park and recreation agencies, and thus the accounting and control of those physical assets becomes extremely important. Most agencies keep records of supplies and materials in their central office, central stores, or maintenance divisions. For the more costly capital equipment a property control system should be established for accounting for these assets. For smaller jurisdictions, costly equipment may mean items valued at $100 or more. Indiana University recently revised its property control system and found that it was not feasible or practical to inventory equipment under $500. Despite the lower cost limit decided on, certain information should be kept regarding the capital equipment owned by the agency.

The primary purpose of a property control system is to safeguard the physical assets of an agency against loss by fire or theft, to provide documentation for insurance purposes, and to assure proper utilization of equipment. Records and procedures should be established to record the acquisition of the property, to maintain control of agency equipment that is often widely distributed throughout the organization, to record transfers or loans between departments, and to record the final disposition of the equipment. Property control is concerned with the more permanent type of property that has a normal life expectancy of two years or more. Examples include vehicles, park maintenance equipment (tractors, mowers, graders, etc.) gymnastic equipment, electric typewriters, computers, and so on.

Finance or purchasing departments are normally charged with the responsibility of property control. It is important to note that the officer and staff of the property control office does not regulate or influence the agency's use of the equipment; its primary function is to assure proper accounting

9Ibid, p. 17.

records and agency accountability for its physical assets.

In initiating a property control system, considerable time and effort may be involved at first in conducting an inventory of the equipment already owned by the agency. Once this is accomplished, the system should be relatively easy to maintain because entries or changes in the records are made infrequently. Information should be kept for each piece of equipment that is recorded manually on record cards or processed by data-processing equipment. Specific information that often is included follows

A. Identification
Description
Manufacturer's name, model, and serial number
Property control number
Equipment code
Standard life of equipment
B. Location
Department or division
Building and room number
C. Acquisition
Date of acquisition
Type: purchase, gift, fabrication, or lease
Source of funds: budget, gift, grant (i.e., federal government)
Value: actual cost less trade-in
D. Disposal
Sold or traded in
Discarded—equipment damaged beyond repair
Loss: theft or fire

A uniform coding system should be developed for identifying items. Often the coding may coincide with the general accounting system used for budgeting and accounting purposes, especially if the classification coding includes a breakdown by departments, programs, buildings, facilities, and objects of expenditure. This kind of information is generally contained in cost accounting systems.

A property control number is assigned to each piece of equipment and placed on the item by a prenumbered decalcomania, metal tag, stencil, or some other relatively permanent method. The number will remain with the item until it is disposed of. As new capital equipment is acquired by purchase, gift, lease, or fabrication, the property control office should be informed, record cards completed, and property control numbers affixed on the newly acquired items. These procedures will allow the office to keep up-to-date records on all property owned or leased by the agency.

Proper procedures should also be established for removing property from the property control system.

If equipment is sold or used as a trade-in for purchasing new equipment, the purchasing department should be responsible for handling these transactions and informing the property control officer of the disposition of the property. If the department feels that an item is no longer usable and cannot be used as a trade-in, approval must be received from a designated official or body (purchasing officer, park and recreation board, etc.) for the disposition of the property and the property control office is notified to remove the item from the records. If property is lost because of theft or fire, a report should be filed to the police and the insurance agency. After an investigation by the appropriate officials, the property control officer should be instructed to remove lost articles from the inventory.

Once a year an inventory of all equipment owned by the agency is made and the results are reconciled with the property control records. Any differences found between the inventory and the records should be investigated. Because the extensive use of equipment often influences the location, value, condition, and perhaps the misplacement or loss of property, periodic inventories provide accountability for the personal property controlled by departments. Keeping current information on the condition and value of property is often helpful in establishing insurance claims and planning equipment needs when planning the budget.

Summary

Public agencies have followed private enterprise in establishing good business practices in the procurement of goods and services. Since centralized purchasing departments are becoming more commonplace in local governments throughout the country, resulting in an increasing professionalism of the purchasing process, it behooves park and recreation professionals to work cooperatively with the purchasing agents in securing the best prices for the supplies and services needed by the agency.

The normal purchasing procedure used by most agencies includes the following steps: determining agency needs, securing bids or quotations, awarding the contract, expediting the order, and receiving and evaluating the materials received. Also, agencies usually follow various shortcuts to the normal purchasing procedure, that is, petty cash purchasing, central stores, blanket purchase orders, walk through and call in approaches, which offer some flexibility to agencies in meeting emergency needs.

Cooperative purchasing programs between various units of government provide for large volume buying, which results in considerable dollar savings. In addition, contractural agreements with private agencies have proved to be a possible alternative for local government for operating programs and maintaining areas and facilities.

Because supplies and equipment represent a considerable investment of taxpayers' money, park and recreation agencies have the responsibility for accounting for and control of these costly physical assets. A property control system enables agencies to safeguard these assets against loss by fire and theft and helps to assure proper control and utilization of these properties.

Selected References

Contract Services Handbook, Heritage Conservation and Recreation Service, U.S. Department of Interior, Washington, D.C., 1979, 64 pp.

Moak, Lennox L., and Albert M. Hillhouse, *Local Government Finance,* Municipal Finance Officers Association, Chicago, 1974, pp. 209–238.

Purchasing and Cooperative Agreements, Great Lakes Park Training Institute, *1978 Proceedings,* Indiana University, 1978, pp. 170–179.

Schultz, Joe, "Purchasing," *Network,* National Recreation and Park Association, Great Lakes Region, Palatine, Ill., 1981, pp. 1–2, 10–12.

Chapter 10

Other Fiscal Concerns

The major emphasis in this text has been on the financing and budgeting concerns of the park and recreation administrator and staff. I recognize that no single text can adequately cover even these two management functions; however, there are several additional matters that are part and parcel of finance and budgeting that need to be addressed. This book would not be complete without mentioning the auditing and risk management responsibilities of administrative officials. Also, reference has been made many times throughout earlier chapters of the use of computers in managing agency functions; thus a brief discussion of present and future applications of data processing to parks and recreation seems appropriate. The ultimate success that administrators achieve will be influenced by their knowledge and application of these additional concerns, as well as by their ability to implement the management strategies discussed throughout the text.

AUDITING

Organizations of various types, both public and private, have always been responsible for providing a full accounting of their financial status and procedures. Historically, an audit, generally performed by a certified accountant, has had as its main function the checking of financial records and reports to ascertain their accuracy and to determine whether the organization is conforming to local and state laws and regulations. Recently, the audit function has expanded from primarily a technical study of the accuracy of financial records to an accountability of the operations and functions of an organization. The

leader in this movement has been the American Institute of Certified Public Accountants (AICPA), which has been responsible for developing standards and procedures for conducting public audits at the local and state levels.

Auditing of local government may stem from local ordinances, state statutes, or federal laws. The local city council, or the park and recreation board if it is fiscally independent, may require the administrator to conduct an audit of the organization. In 1979 the Council on Municipal Performance, in a publication funded by HUD, reported that 40 states impose audit requirements on at least some classes of local government.[1] Federal intergovernmental grant programs, such as the Comprehensive Employment and Training Act (CETA), Community Development Block Grant (CDBG), Economic Development Act (EDA), and General Revenue Sharing (GRS), impose audit requirements on local and state governmental units receiving grants.

Although there is no unanimous agreement among local governments as to what constitutes a proper audit, the generally accepted auditing standards developed by AICPA recommends that a public audit should consist of three elements.

1. *Financial and compliance*—determine (a) whether financial operations are properly conducted, (b) whether the financial reports of an audited entity are presented fairly, and (c) whether the entity has complied with applicable laws and regulations.
2. *Economy and efficiency*—determine whether the entity is managing or utilizing its resources (personnel, prop-

---

[1]*Local Government Auditing,* Council on Municipal Performance, New York, 1979, p. 30.

erty, space, and so forth) in an economical and efficient manner and (uncovers) the causes of any inefficiencies or uneconomical practices, including inadequacies in management information systems, administrative procedures, or organizational structure.

3. *Program results*—determine whether the desired results or benefits are being achieved, whether the objectives established by the legislature or other authorizing body are being met, and whether the agency has considered alternatives which might yield desired results at a lower cost.[2]

Local governments that have initiated the newer concepts of budgeting—program, program performance, and zero-base—are in a good position to provide information to auditors concerning economy and efficiency and program results. In order to conform to the three elements mentioned, two types of audit can be performed: The financial audit and the performance audit. The financial audit is concerned with answering such questions as to how money is spent, whether reports are accurate, and whether the accounting records and procedures conform to existing state laws. Performance audits address internal concerns such as efficiency and effectiveness and if programs are meeting agency goals and objectives. Just as the newer concepts of budgeting are not universally practiced throughout the country, performance audits also are new to many local governments. Because many of the federal grant programs to local and state park and recreation agencies require an audit on program results, administrators should be prepared to identify goals and objectives, programs, performance measurement, and evaluation, all of which were previously discussed.

There are two approaches of conducting an audit—internal and external. Some of the larger jurisdictions employ their own professional auditor, whereas in other instances an audit committee is appointed from among employees in the organization. These individuals should have appropriate accounting, statistical, and computer skills and knowledges. Also, it is important that internal auditors maintain an independent and impartial attitude so that unbiased opinions and recommendations will be made. The external audit may be conducted by an official from the state or by a private professional accountant. External auditors serve at the pleasure of the legislative body and are independent of the administrative officers of the local governments. Certified public accountants should be employed to conduct the auditing function.

[2]*Standards for Audit of Governmental Organizations, Programs, Activities, and Functions*, U.S. General Accounting Office, Washington, D.C., 1972, p. 2.

It is the responsibility of park and recreation personnel to cooperate fully with auditors in supplying the information and documentation requested. Documents that are often needed include some of the following.

- Charters, ordinances, and other legal documents.
- Minutes of official meetings of the legislative body.
- Administrative manual—including organizational charts, fiscal policies and procedures, and the system of internal control for financial operations.
- Financial accounting ledgers and forms, bank statements, investments, financial reports, payroll registers, and outstanding debts.
- Property inventories and controls.
- Budget approved by the legislative body.
- Federal grants, including proposals, budgets, and supporting schedules.
- Internal funds that are generally not part of the budget.

The primary objectives of auditing are not to probe for irregularities, expose fraud, or uncover the poor management practices of an organization. To be sure, if such conditions exist they should be uncovered and brought to the attention of the proper officials. If weaknesses are found in the internal management of an organization, auditors should be ready to give suggestions for improvement. An outside, independent appraisal can give professional insight on how to operate the department more efficiently and effectively, as well as serve to inform the public of how their tax dollars are wisely and correctly spent and cared for.

RISK MANAGEMENT

For years governmental agencies have been primarily concerned with insuring their real and personal property investments against natural and common perils such as floods, windstorms, fires, collisions, and vandalism. Insurance policies were carried to protect public entities against possible loss. To some extent local governments have always been worried about their legal responsibilities; however, public agencies were somewhat protected by the widely accepted doctrine of governmental immunity, which exempted them from liability. Times have changed and the concept of sovereign immunity has given way to a suit-conscious public, which has filed an increasingly large number of liability claims against public agencies of all kinds.

Today park and recreation personnel are expressing real concern about their management responsibilities of security of their physical assets, personnel safety, fleet safety, and protection from lawsuits against themselves and the agency. Risk management, an outgrowth and expansion of insurance management, is rapidly becoming recognized as an accepted discipline, with a mandate to develop practical solutions to risk problems and to protect agency resources from accidental loss.

Kloman, President and Director of Risk Planning Group, Inc., an independent risk, insurance, and benefit management consulting and research firm, contends that risk management is becoming a developing discipline and mentions that:

the erosion of governmental immunity to third party liability suits, the lack of effective risk controls, the increasing cost of governmental insurance, and the evaporation of the interest of insurance companies to write governmental entities have all led to a renewed interest in risk management.[3]

In order to conserve an agency's resources from possible loss, Kloman suggests that a risk management program should be concerned with the following elements.

(1) uncovering significant exposures to loss, (2) measuring financial risk, (3) applying reasonable and effective risk controls, and (4) insuring that the financial integrity of the governmental entity is not impaired after loss. These concerns are the major responsibilities of the persons responsible for the risk management program of an agency.[4]

Exposure Identification

The expansion of park and recreation areas, facilities, and programs by local agencies in recent years has increased the potential exposures to risk and financial losses. When one adds to these many and varied types of exposures the possibility of inadequate funds for maintenance, the potential for hazardous conditions, the expansion of high risk activities, and, in some cases, the lack of professional leadership and supervision, an agency faces a serious loss potential from its party liability suits. An inventory and inspection of physical assets can be used to identify the potential loss exposures. Also, an analysis of personnel, both paid and volunteer, will reveal the agency's responsibilities to exposure of accidents, disability, and illness.

The most serious loss exposure facing public agencies in terms of potential dollar loss results from liability claims against the agency. With the gradual erosion of governmental immunity and the growing trend toward levying suits against the government,

the potential liability for parks and recreation was predicated on the distinction of whether parks and recreation was considered a proprietary or governmental function. This functional dichotomy has gradually been replaced by a new distinction based on the job or act performed by the governmental official or employee. van der Smissen writes that:

At the beginning of the decade of the '70s, it appears that the primary distinction concerning immunity relates to discretionary and ministerial duties of the employee, in contrast to governmental and proprietary functions of the governmental entity.[5]

This newer dichotomy considers the operational duties of employees (ministerial) as potentially liable, whereas planning duties of public officials and boards (discretionary) are immune from tort liability claims. The ministerial and discretionary distinction concerning immunity is gradually becoming the basis of governmental tort liability.

In recent years many states have enacted tort claim acts that have had an effect in abrogating the sovereign immunity doctrine. Most of these tort claim statutes provide for the discretionary exception to liability for the policy and planning acts of public officials and also make the acts of employees subject to tort claims.

The purpose of this brief discussion concerning liability is to alert park and recreation professionals and risk management officials to the liability exposure risks confronting agencies and to suggest that public officials be knowledgeable about judicial and legislative actions currently taking place. In an effort to determine whether park and recreation administrators were sensitive to this new legislation, Morgan conducted a nationwide study to determine to what extent agencies were prepared for potential tort liability. Morgan reported that:

with 133 agency respondents from a sample of 200, 60 (45.1%) indicated that they did not know whether or not tort claims legislation had been enacted in their states. The lack of awareness of tort claims legislation by public recreation and park administrators is surprising considering the potential impact such legislation may have upon the liability of park and recreation agencies.[6]

[3]H. Felix Kloman, "Risk Management: A Developing Discipline," *Governmental Finance* Vol. 6, p. 5, May 1977.
[4]Ibid, p. 6.

[5]van der Smissen, *Legal Liability of Cities and Schools for Injuries in Recreation and Parks—1975 Supplement,* W. Anderson, Cincinnati, 1975, p. 2.
[6]Ann L. Morgan, *A Comparison of the Professional Judgment of Park and Recreation Administrators and the Indiana Tort Claims Act as Doctrine,* doctoral thesis, Indiana University, Bloomington, 1981, p. 23.

Risk Evaluation

After the exposures to risk have been identified, the risk manager must identify the financial loss that is inherent in various types of risks discussed. Because it is neither possible nor desirable to cover the costs of all risks involved, attention is generally directed toward those exposures that might have the greatest financial impact on the organization in case of loss. One approach for gathering information is to study the agency's loss history over a period of five years. In the case of assigning values to buildings and facilities, appraisal by outside experts can be made to determine replacement costs or actual cash values. This approach is used by insurance companies in determining the insurance needs of an agency.

Risk Control

The prevention or reduction of inherent risks within the operation of an agency is an important aspect of risk management. Just as preventive medicine (i.e., good health habits, physical exams, and physical fitness) is basic to prevent illness, risk control programs must be concerned with eliminating the risk of accidents, theft, fire, and vandalism of property. The proper design and maintenance of facilities and good security measures will help to prevent theft, burglary, and vandalism. Fleet safety can be enhanced by good maintenance of equipment, periodic inspections, adherence to safety standards, and employee driver education programs. Safety programs have proved to be valuable in preventing accidents of employees on the job. The Los Angeles County Department of Parks and Recreation, as part of a departmental risk management program, prepared and distributed the *Risk Management Manual* to employees in an effort to educate employees in the matters of safety. In a cover letter to employees, Ralph Cryder, Director, commented that:

This manual is but the beginning of our concern for safety. It should pave the way to a continuous study of the problem inherent in our operations, so that more positive loss control programs may be instituted in all units of our Department. Our first real step is to become more safety conscious and more aware of the heavy cost of industrial accidents, in terms of dollars, efficiency, and human life.[7]

Funding of Risks

In spite of the preventive controls initiated, losses are certain to occur. Therefore steps must be taken to lessen their financial impact. It is up to each

agency to determine the most effective use of their financial resources in meeting losses. Recently, a number of different approaches to handling financial loss have developed; however, insurance still continues to be one of the main approaches.

Insurance. The cost of local governmental insurance has currently skyrocketed because of the changes taking place in governmental liability. Insurance companies contend that insuring governmental agencies is becoming risky business, and as a result, they find it less profitable to renew insurance policies with public agencies. Compounding the problem is the practice of requiring bidding for insurance coverage, which causes insurance agencies to lose interest in short-term coverage. The high insurance costs makes it almost impossible for most communities to finance the full replacement values of their assets. As one possible solution, insurance is used to cover catastrophic losses through large deductible policies, with the agency assuming the risk for smaller claims and losses by self-insurance and other financial resources.

Generally, insurance companies, operating on a profit basis, usually collect $1.50 to $2 for each dollar spent as claims. Consequently, public agencies are more and more turning to self-insurance programs as an alternative or supplement to private insurance coverage.

Self-Insurance. Many local governments, especially larger ones, have established a self-insurance program whereby they assume all or a portion of the risks involved. The money that is normally budgeted for paying insurance premiums is placed into an internal fund to cover the losses that might occur. The amount placed into a self-insurance program varies; however, professional risk managers recommend the following formula for the amount of money a local government should be able to retain.

(1) Up to one-tenth of one percent of its annual operating budget for any one occurrence, and
(2) up to one percent of its annual operating budget for any one year (for all losses).[8]

If the agency feels that it cannot carry all the risks involved, insurance policies with large deductibles can be purchased to cover the possibility of excessive losses that would have a devastating effect on the municipality. Smaller cities or governmental units may find it impossible to develop a self-insurance program. In recent years the practice of risk-sharing

[7]*Risk Management Manual,* Los Angeles County Department of Parks and Recreation, 1980.

[8]*Governmental Risk Management, Elements of Financial Management,* Government Finance Research Center, Municipal Finance Officers Association, 1980, p. 2.

through pooling has been found as a possible alternative to purchasing insurance or self-insurance. Pooling has been tried on a local, regional, and state basis. Kloman predicts that, "some sort of pooling will be probably the most significant development in governmental risk management in the next ten years."[9]

COMPUTERS

The fantastic growth and changes in computer technology in the past thirty-five years have had a dramatic effect on the management of today's organizations. Introduced in 1946, the electronic computer has changed drastically from a huge expensive, temperamental machine to a new generation of faster, more compact, cheaper, more powerful, simpler, and better programmed models. New technological advances have changed the computer from a big city, big business management tool to a device applicable to small communities and organizations, and even the home. For years this electronic marvel carried with it a mystique that was understood only by a small group of computer scientists. In earlier years the extreme cost of computers relegated their use to big industry and large local governmental units. Times have changed and it has been said that:

Computers will become so fast, so compact, so inexpensive, so powerful, so well programmed, and so easy to operate that even the smallest park and recreation departments will be unable to ignore them any longer. Some people feel that day is rapidly approaching. Others believe it has already arrived.[10]

Computerization can no longer be viewed as a thing of the future for governmental organizations. The use of computers by local government has grown rapidly since the early 1950s and today almost all the larger cities and counties are using computers and the smaller units of government are beginning to follow suit. In the larger jurisdictions computers are operated in-house, with equipment that is generally leased or rented. Smaller cities and counties most often make use of outside computing sources. Because computers were first used for accounting and budgeting functions, they were initially housed in the finance department. As the use of data processing increased and computer applications expanded to other managerial tasks, the computer operation has gradually been shifted to an independent department and in some cases to an operating department.

Park and recreation agencies have been slow to jump on the computer bandwagon. Agency personnel were first introduced to computer technology through citywide payrolls, budgets, accounting records, and financial reports. Like other professional personnel, park and recreation executives lacked the knowledge of computer operations and thus were reluctant to investigate the use of data processing equipment for park and recreation purposes. However, recently, a relatively small group of park and recreation professionals have been pioneering the cause of expanding the use of computers in the field.

Since 1976 the National Recreation and Park Association has conducted five national workshops on computers in recreation and parks. Proceedings from these workshops attest that park and recreation personnel are moving away from a feeling of frustration and intimidation by computers toward a more active day-to-day use of data processing in managing agency operations. Case studies of successful computer operations have been increasing yearly, and although the primary use is still for administrative tasks, agencies are slowly exploring computer applications for park and recreation operations. Perhaps one of the reasons for the growth in the use of computers is the increased interest of park and recreation executives toward computer use.

In a paper presented at the 1981 national workshop, Sharpless discussed the findings resulting from a nationwide study conducted by the Leisure Research Institute at Indiana University regarding the attitudes of park and recreation executives toward the use of computers in the field. Executives were asked to indicate their opinion of statements concerned with the present as well as with the future use of computers. It is encouraging to note that executives are becoming more and more convinced about the value of computers in managing their organizations. Results of the study reveal that:

- Over three-fourths (76.1%) of the respondents agreed that computers offer solutions to problems facing parks and recreation.
- A similar portion of the executives (75.9%) felt that computers will greatly improve the way departments do their work.
- An even greater percent (92%) favored greater use of computers in their departments.[11]

[9]Kloman, "Risk Management," p. 9.
[10]Daniel R. Sharpless, and Doyle E. Allen, *The Minicomputer in Parks and Recreation,* Leisure Research Institute, Indiana University, Bloomington, p. 2.

[11]Daniel R. Sharpless, "Attitudes Toward Computers in Parks and Recreation," *Park and Recreation Opinion Poll and Status Survey* (PROPS-8), Leisure Research Institute, Indiana University, Bloomington, 1981.

There appears to be widespread agreement that computers enable organizations to operate many of their business functions more quickly, accurately, and efficiently. Executives must take leadership in promoting data processing in their organizations. In assuming this leadership, they do not necessarily need to know how to program the computer but should have a good understanding of what the computer can do. Nearly all the executives responding to the study (97.3 percent) agreed that an understanding of computer applications to the field would be valuable if they are to exert strong leadership and support for computer use. Also, an understanding of some of the computer jargon is helpful for park and recreation personnel if they are to communicate effectively with computer operators. It is generally agreed that a lack of computer knowledge by agency personnel is one of the major deterrents to greater use of computers in parks and recreation. A majority of today's executives confess that they do not have an adequate knowledge or understanding of computers. More opportunities must be made available through workshops and short courses for park and recreation personnel to obtain skills and knowledges in computer use. Courses in computers should be required of students majoring in parks and recreation. Graduates who possess strong competencies in computer programming are currently, and will continue to be, in great demand.

Standard Business Applications

As early as 1963, William Penn Mott, then general manager of the East Bay Regional Park District, Oakland, California, reported that his district contracted an IBM firm to take over the complete fiscal responsibilities of the East Bay park district. By having available the most modern computing devices at the time, the district was given more accurate, detailed, and timely information. Within 24 hours, detailed cost accounting reports were placed on the desk of each department head in the district.[12]

During this same period, officials in Albuquerque, New Mexico, indicated a versatile use of a computer system. Some of the uses made of the computer included: preparing paychecks, inventoring property, storing information on land use, and keeping sick leave accounts. The report noted that prior to using the computer, it took 44 hours to write a city payroll. The computer cut the task to three and one-half hours.[13]

Throughout the text mention has been made of the desirability of using data processing for enhancing financial procedures in park and recreation agencies. Computers are being substituted for many of the manual approaches of performing business-related tasks. In most local governments and park and recreation agencies, computer use is still by and large directed toward standard business applications. Accounting, budgeting, purchasing, payrolls, inventory, mailing, personnel, and word processing are some of the most common business applications used. In 1979 Sharpless conducted a study of park and recreation agencies in eight Midwest states to find out what agencies were using computers. Seventy-five municipal agencies reported use of computers and of these, approximately 95 percent of the computer applications were for administrative or business tasks.[14]

Because of the wide use of data processing for the standard business functions, computer programs (software) are already available and can be purchased from a variety of sources. If an agency is interested in using the computer for park and recreation applications, computer programs must be custom designed or obtained from agencies that already have a program in operation and then must be modified to meet the new user's specific needs.

Park and Recreation Applications

It is encouraging to note in the case studies presented at recent national computer workshops the increasing number of applications of the computer for park and recreation purposes. Although the applications were first initiated in larger agencies and run on large computers, the advent of the minicomputer has made it possible for smaller jurisdictions to make use of data processing for park and recreation operations. Although the minicomputer is within the price range of even the smaller agencies and can be programmed to do just about every kind of job that a large computer can do, the off-the-shelf programs are not so available for park and recreation applications as they are for business applications. If the computer is to be an in-house operation, a highly skilled programmer must be hired to develop the appropriate software. Because of these problems, a number of park and recreation districts in Illinois have joined forces in standardizing computer operations and in developing and sharing applications for park and recreation purposes. Faculty members in a number of universities have developed

---

[12]William Penn Mott, "Creativity in Parks and Recreation," *Proceedings*, Great Lakes Park Training Institute, 1963, p. 82.

[13]*Public Automation*, Public Administration Series, Chicago, August 1965, p. 4.

[14]Sharpless and Allen, *The Minicomputer in Parks and Recreation*, p. 4.

computer programs for park and recreation applications, which have proved to be valuable sources of software for local agencies.

In the later 1970s case studies of computer applications for park and recreation management have been appearing in professional publications and workshops. The following discussion represents examples of applications currently in use.

Reservations. Just as the computer has revolutionized the reservation process in the airline industry, a number of park and recreation agencies have found that a computerized reservation system is valuable for scheduling users of park facilities and programs. For many years, state, regional and local park systems have enlisted the help of Ticketron, Inc. to handle the reservation system for campsites. Local park and recreation agencies also use reservation systems for users of their park facilities—athletic fields, picnic sites, park shelters, meeting rooms, and gymnasiums.

In 1976 the Department of Parks and Recreation of St. Louis County, Missouri, changed its reservation system from a manual to a computerized system. In 1975, using the manual system, 6273 reservations were issued, serving 461,898 people. In 1978 the department efficiently and effectively issued 28,257 reservations serving 2.1 million people. The system was also used to book services such as tours (outdoor education programs, historic tours, etc.) and special events (i.e., concerts, dances, and plays).[15]

Registrations. One of the most widely used applications is the registration of individuals in programs offered by park and recreation agencies. The processing of large numbers of persons manually can be a real burden to agencies and often an inconvenience to those who must wait in line to enroll in a class or activity. In 1977 Johnson County in Kansas solved these problems with the purchase of a Sperry Univac BC7 Minicomputer. Prior to that time the paperwork and manpower needed to register persons in an ever increasing number of activities and participants became a problem. Registration of recreation classes was often inaccurate, slow, and an embarrassment to the professional staff. In 1978 the department processed 34,378 individual registrations for programs offered by the department, a total that would be almost impossible to process manually by the office staff. The computerized system not only handled the large numbers of participants in an effective, accurate, and efficient manner, but it generated the fol-

lowing information: daily class master report, daily class roster report, daily cash receipts register, seasonal participation analysis report by zip codes, seasonal class master reports, and seasonal class roster reports. Names and addresses of registrants proved to be valuable in planning facility locations for classes and a mailing list and labels were easily prepared for public relation purposes.[16]

Another successful case study presented at the 1979 workshop was the Hassle Free Registration System operated by the Wilmette Park District in Illinois, which serves a village of 32,000 people. After experimenting several years with different approaches to computer service, the district decided to go to an in-house computer, a Basic/Four Corporation Model 400 minicomputer. In a relatively short period of time, the in-house system was programmed to perform accounting, payroll, personnel, and financial reports as well as the registration function. In the first two years of operation the computer system recorded over 37,500 registrants in 1695 program class sections, accumulating over one million dollars in fees. Because of the expanded applications planned by the district, a more powerful Model 410 has been acquired.[17]

Athletic League Management. One of the most comprehensive program offerings conducted by local agencies is the planning and operating of sport leagues. The tasks involved in operating leagues lend themselves to minicomputers and like other applications, a real time saving can be made by computerizing the scheduling and statistical data needed in league management. League master schedule, team schedules, team rosters, and schedules for officials, playing sites, and maintenance can be produced quickly and accurately by the computer. Statistics involved in sport leagues also can be programmed: that is, league standings, team averages, pitching records, bowling averages, and golf handicaps. Park and recreation agencies in Camden, South Carolina, and Tempe, Arizona, have reported successful computerized applications for the management of their athletic leagues.

Cost Tracking/Cost Analysis. Cost analysis is widely accepted in the business field. Introduced to the public sector during the advent of performance budgeting during the 1960s, the establishment of this system in local government, and in parks and recreation in particular, was met with considerable resistance mainly because of the time, effort, and costs of gathering the data. Cost tracking is con-

[15]National Workshop on Computers in Recreation and Parks, *Proceedings 1979,* St. Louis, Mo., p. 13.

[16]Ibid, pp. 51–72.
[17]Ibid, pp. 73–82.

cerned with recording all the costs (labor, supplies, materials, and equipment) of performing management functions. These data can be kept manually; however, in most agencies they are almost prohibitive to keep. By feeding this same information into the computer, one can obtain actual costs, unit costs, and performance reports more easily than by manual efforts. Cost tracking is essential for the implementation of a cost analysis system or for establishing enterprise funds, which was discussed previously in Chapter 8.

Other Applications. The applications previously discussed are those most often mentioned by agencies in the case studies presented at the national workshops. Other applications include: recording participation in recreation activities, land-use planning graphics, recreation needs assessment studies, street tree inventory and management systems, and a Christmas "Letters to Santa" program conducted by the recreation department in Camden, South Carolina.

Management Information Systems. The computer applications for park and recreation purposes previously discussed reveal many of the common applications that have been initiated by agencies throughout the country. In initiating computer applications, many agencies use only one or two applications. For agencies that have advanced beyond this initial effort, more comprehensive management information systems can be developed that will have an overall impact on improving the efficiency of the management process. Two park districts that have pioneered in the development of management information systems (MIS) are the Montgomery County Park Department of the Maryland National Capital Park and Planning Commission and the Hennepin County Park Reserve District, Minnesota.

The MIS program developed by Montgomery County in 1978 is operated by an in-house computer network of two Hewlett Packard Computers and 30 terminals. One of the major problems facing the MIS staff in making this new system operational as well as an effective management tool was the training of the park staff in using the latest computer technology. In the first three years 45 parks personnel were trained in using the computer. The new management system reflects a varied use of the computer in developing information for the planning and management of the department. According to Rich Schroth, management analyst, some of the programs that have been or are currently being implemented include:

Maintenance Cost Tracking System
Utility Cost Monitoring System
Capital Improvements Program Management System
Nursery Management System
Property Management Records System
Park Police Ticketing System
Contract Preparations and Analysis System
Recreation/Park User Analysis Program
Land Record Keeping System
Preventive Vehicle Maintenance System
Botanical Management System
Park Plant Management System
Park Police Operations Support Systems
Park Police Crime Analysis System
Home Vegetable Gardening Program
Operating Budget Projection System
Park Characteristic Mapping Program

In addition to the in-place management programs listed, staff been trained to produce documents on the computer's word processing, statistics, and graphics systems.

Stan Ernst, director, feels that "there are facts which support the improvements in productivity, cash savings to the Commission, improved management decisions and improvement of services to the residents of Montgomery County." Ernst concludes that "in spite of the many lessons we have learned in the development of our new management program, we have only scratched the surface of what should be accomplished."

At the Fifth National Workshop on Computers in Recreation and Parks, held at Indiana University in July 1981, John Christian, Director of Administration, Hennepin County Park Reserve District, reported that in recent years his organization "demonstrated a changing policy direction of its management procedures in controlling costs for all functions within the District's organization." Collectively, the change was coded as a "Management Information System," with many separate and identifiable components as "subsystems." Christian's paper highlighted the following systems that have been instituted by the park reserve district to increase managerial awareness and productivity of their many organizational functions: budget preparation system, daily time card system, budget versus actual system, detail project history system, and equipment management system.

The lessons learned by the administrators and staff of the district are certainly applicable to any park and recreation agency that is considering using a computer.

- Involve the user from the start. . . . And listen closely.
- Beware of the unexpected.
- Get users to use the computer—Build mutual trust

- Everything takes longer and costs more.
- Beware of too much concern with the computer and not enough with people.
- Training of staff is critical.
- Keep applications practical.... If something can't be done, say so.
- Put things back into focus from time to time. In the hurry of everyday activities, it is not hard to lose sight of goals and objectives.
- We are all going to have to depend upon and move toward more sophisticated tools and techniques to become more efficient and productive.[18]

The use of the computer for park and recreation programs, today and in the future, is subject to the imagination, creativity, and competence of the administrator and his/her staff.

MANAGING FISCAL STRESS

Park and recreation executives are being confronted with new management problems as they are faced with the challenge of managing fiscal stress. Chapter 2 discussed the trends in finance and the factors that have created a financial crisis in local government. A brief look back at some of these financing trends would indicate that traditionally most of a public administrator's management strategies have been predicated on the assumption of continuing increase in public expenditures and revenues. The first seventy years of this country might well be called an "era of growth." During this period the country experienced growth in cities, population, programs and services, organizations, and parks and recreation. An organization's success was judged on a continuous and steady expansion and the GNP was used as the prime indicator of the nation's prosperity. Incremental budgeting, which represented *adding* to a secure base, dominated the budget picture. The 1960s will long be remembered as the greatest growth period of this century, for it was during this decade that the greatest increase in public programs, services, and budgets took place. New organizations were formed and programs expanded to meet the needs and demands of a dynamic society, and managerial philosophy was predicated on building and expanding organizational functions. Expanding programs, adding personnel, and increasing the budget all were inherent in this era and they represented the yardsticks for measuring success.

The social, political, and economic events of the 1970s (i.e., inflation, recession, unemployment, and taxpayers' revolts) forced organizations to change gears, to slow down, and to reevaluate their opera-

tions, as organizations were confronted with an "era of limits." There are some experts who are predicting that the 1980s should more realistically be viewed as an "era of decline," as stagflation (slow economic growth and double-digit inflation) is causing agencies to lay off employees, close facilities, cancel or cut back on programs, and stretch resources. Agencies are facing a new crisis, "fiscal stress," which according to Levine, is the:

gap between the needs and expectations of citizens and governmental employees for government services and benefits and the inability of the economy to generate enough economic growth to expand (or even sustain, in some places) tax supported programs without putting unacceptable demands on taxpayers' take home pay.[19]

Public executives, who have spent most of their professional careers operating in an era of growth, are finding themselves ill prepared to deal with this new phenomenon. Attrition, zero growth, cutbacks, freezes, priorities, and limits, have become common bywords for management strategies in the 1980s. Colleges and universities, facing an anticipated decline in enrollments and reduction in state and federal support, are experiencing problems of major proportions. Local government is confronted with similar problems as taxpayers' revolts, tax limitation measures, and cutbacks in federal funds are creating financial shortfalls. According to experts, these are not temporary problems but will confront municipalities for years to come.

Many local officials are responding to this situation with managerial tactics initiated with the expectation of muddling through what they feel is a short-term problem. Often the immediate reaction to the fiscal crisis is to seek additional revenues so that programs and services can be continued and employees can be retained. Alternative funding is sought, fees and charges increased, new fees and charges are introduced for programs that were previously free to the public, and mandates for better productivity are issued by legislative bodies. When additional revenues fail to meet the ever increasing costs of operating programs and services, other managerial tactics are employed. Hiring and wage freezes are mandated, across the board cuts are made, equipment replacements are deferred, and maintenance of facilities is neglected. These tactics create employee unrest, resistance, and frustration and only delay the inevitable equipment replacement and maintenance costs until future years.

Advocates of zero-base budgeting suggest that this

---

[18]John W. Christian, in a paper presented to the Fifth National Workshop on Computers in Recreation and Parks, Indiana University, Bloomington, 1981, p. 11.

[19]Charles H. Levine, *Managing Fiscal Stress,* Chatham House, Chatham, N.J., 1980, p. 4.

new approach to budgeting is a way of reallocating tight fiscal resources for the highest priority programs. By presenting alternatives as a part of each decision package, decision makers are supposed to be in a better position to cope with the resources available. Park and recreation professionals have the responsibility for presenting alternatives that will allow their agencies to operate in the most effective manner as they attempt to adjust to limited resources. The various approaches in developing alternatives are discussed in Chapter 5.

Administrators that are managing agencies faced with fiscal stress must recognize that cutback management often results in personnel problems. If employees are to be discharged, seniority or tenure often dictates a policy of "last in-first out." The greatest losers in this system are the young professionals, minorities, and women. The latter two are the ones that benefited most from affirmative action programs in recent years. A hiring freeze, often considered as a short-term solution and one of buying time, relies on natural attrition (resignations, retirements, and death) and meets less resistance among employees, for it does not directly affect them. It must be remembered that cutbacks of employees ultimately affect the scope of programs and services that can be rendered by the agency. Unless reduction of programs and services result, the quality of departmental activities will suffer.

Not all leisure service agencies are facing fiscal stress resulting in the need for cutting back agency's functions. However, professionals must be prepared to adopt appropriate strategies that will enable the agency to respond effectively to societal concerns and leisure needs. There is no standard prescription that can be given that will treat the problems resulting from declining financial resources. However, McTighe presents the following series of questions that administrators might ask themselves in formulating their strategies for dealing with fiscal stress and possible cutbacks.

I. *Examine Organization Mission*
   a. What are the organization "musts" or mandates?
   b. What are the present organizational nonmandated functions?
   c. What are the activities the organization does well?
   d. What are the activities the organization does poorly?
   e. What have been the recent trends that are relevant to the organization's mission?
   f. What are the time-honored functions of the organization that have not undergone close scrutiny in recent years?

II. *Examine Marginal Investments*
   a. What programs have high unit costs?
   b. What programs serve a relatively small or isolated clientele?
   c. What programs provide services that are available from other organizations, public or private?
   d. What programs have consistently fallen below their goals and expectations?
   e. What programs, if cut back, would have long-term pressures and greater future costs?

III. *Install Rational Choice Mechanisms*
   a. What management tools have been developed to assist managers and policymakers in making rational choices among competing demands?
   b. Does some form of PPBS exist?
   c. What program evaluation techniques have been used?
   d. Can zero-base budgeting aid in decisions?

IV. *Encourage Employee Participation*
   a. Have employees been asked to suggest candidates for reduction?
   b. Do incentives exist to encourage employee participation?
   c. Has management openly discussed resource problems with employee unions?
   d. Have employee unions indicated a concern to work with management in achieving economies?
   e. Have productivity programs with sufficient incentive been tried or explored?
   f. Once made, are personnel decisions quickly carried out?

V. *Retain Openness of the Organization*
   a. Has the manager communicated problems to clientele?
   b. Has the manager solicited assistance to clientele?
   c. Has the manager kept the political body informed?
   e. Has the manager kept the public informed?[20]

In summary, executives and boards faced with problems resulting from fiscal stress, should carefully analyze their central objectives, establish priorities, concentrate on what they can do best, and make sure that an agency is operating efficiently and effectively in offering quality programs and services. Using this overall strategy, leisure service agencies will continue to survive in this era of limits and decline.

THE CHALLENGE

In reviewing the contents of this book, the reader might well view financial management as a process of controlling, accounting, and managing the finan-

[20]John J. McTighe, "Management Strategies to Deal with Shrinking Resources," *Public Administrative Review,* January–February 1979, p. 88.

cial resources of an organization. In this context, programs and services are developed, budgets approved, accounting records and controls established, and financial reports issued to the public and legislative officials. Emphasis is placed on efficient management and maximizing the financial resources of the agency.

Management strategies in financing parks and recreation could also be looked at in a different light. With the impact of societal concerns, the problems confronting urban America, the increasing needs for providing programs and services, and the inability of local agencies to finance these services, financial management takes on additional dimensions. No longer can programs and services be provided without careful analysis of their values and effectiveness in solving community problems. With some of the newer concepts of budgeting and increased technology available, management has assumed a role of analyzing problems, establishing priorities, developing alternative courses of action, and making better judgements for the decision makers. Legislative bodies are demanding information that will facilitate decision making and enhance the planning process. Electronic data processing has greatly increased management's capacity for more comprehensive analysis of ongoing operations. It is inevitable that the managers of the future will require greater professionalism and competence than ever before.

Professional leadership is fundamental to a creative management approach to leisure service organizations. The outstanding leaders in the park and recreation profession whom I have had the pleasure of knowing have been persons who establish goals and direction for their agencies, are masters in the art of delegation, create a favorable climate for their staff, recognize employees for their creativity and innovations, and allow their employees freedom of judgment in making calculated risk decisions. These leaders are proactors rather than reactors. They stimulate their employees to face the exciting challenges of change rather than to accept the dullness of being in a rut. They understand employees' fear of change and the unknown that often produces conditions of instability and uncertainty and find ways to improve their employees' ability to change themselves and to accept change.

Managers of the future will be facing a more complex, more professional, more challenging, and certainly a more exciting job in their mission of providing meaningful leisure programs for their communities. Creative management, as discussed in Chapter 1, will enable administrators to be effective leaders in the 1980s and beyond.

Summary

A text on finance and budgeting would not be complete without some discussion of auditing, risk management, computers, and a relatively recent concern, managing fiscal stress.

Although auditing and insurance (risk management) have been an integral part of management for some time, these two fiscal concerns have taken on new meaning in recent years. Audits probing the financial status and procedures of organizations have been conducted for years. Primarily as a result of federal intergovernmental grant programs, performance audits have been initiated to address such internal concerns as efficiency and effectiveness of agency operation and whether programs are meeting goals and objectives. Risk management, an outgrowth and expansion of insurance management, is rapidly becoming recognized as an accepted discipline with a mandate to develop solutions to risk problems and to protect agency resources from accidental loss. Emphasis is placed on analyzing significant exposures to loss and taking steps to prevent financial loss from liability suits and accidents. As a result of rapidly rising costs of insurance, local governments have established their own self-insurance programs where they assume all or a portion of the risks involved.

Computerization of park and recreation functions has grown in recent years, enabling organizations to operate many of their management functions more quickly, accurately, and efficiently. Computers are being substituted for many of the manual approaches of standard business operations such as accounting, budgeting, purchasing, payrolls, inventory, and mailing and word-processing functions. Several agencies have established complete management information systems; however, most agencies use only one or two computer applications for park and recreation purposes. Some of the more common applications currently in use include: reservations, registrations, athletic league management, cost tracking/cost analysis, land-use planning graphics, recreation needs assessment studies, and street tree inventory and management systems.

Some experts are predicting that management strategies in the 1980s will be influenced by a new crisis confronting urban America—fiscal stress. Administrators must be prepared to adopt appropriate management strategies that will enable the agency to respond effectively to societal concerns and leisure needs in an era of declining financial resources.

It is apparent that the creative management of an agency in the 1980s will require greater professionalism and competence than ever before. Managers will be facing more complex, more challenging, and more exciting opportunities in providing leisure service programs for their communities.

Selected References

Auditing

Local Government Auditing, Council on Municipal Performance, New York, 1979, 86 pp.

Standards for Audit of Governmental Organizations, Programs, Activities, and Functions, U.S. General Accounting Office, Washington, D.C., 1972, 54 pp.

Risk Management

"Risk Management in Local Government," *Governmental Finance,* Vol. 6, No. 2, May 1977. (Entire May issue pertains to risk management in local government.)

van der Smissen, Betty, *Legal Liability of Cities and Schools for Injuries in Recreation and Parks, 1975 Supplement,* Anderson, Cincinnati, 1975, 209 pp.

Computers

"Computers in Local Government," *Governmental Finance,* Vol. 6, No. 3, August 1977. (Entire August issue pertains to computers in local government.)

Harrell, Rhett, *Developing a Financial Management Information System for Local Governments: The Key Issues,* Municipal Finance Officers Association, Washington, D.C. 1980, 42 pp.

Sharpless, Daniel, and Doyle E. Allen, *The Minicomputer in Parks and Recreation,* Leisure Research Institute, Indiana University, Bloomington, 1980, 79 pp.

Fiscal Stress

Levine, Charles H., *Managing Fiscal Stress,* Chatham House, Chatham, N.J., 1980, 344 pp.

Appendix D

Budgets—Format and Contents

PARKS AND RECREATION

1982 SUMMARY BUDGET

PROGRAM	1980 ACTUAL	1981 BUDGET	1981 REVISED	1982 BUDGET
Vegetation Control	$ 221,877	$ 191,662	$ 210,838	$ 201,010
General Recreation	450,432	569,964	582,008	898,218
Park Maintenance	910,796	901,495	906,499	941,252
Youth Development	105,730	110,339	122,423	99,892
Senior Citizen Activities	146,574	146,959	151,624	153,587
Special Populations	47,659	52,315	52,660	56,666
Heritage and Cultural Activities	30,884	38,972	41,238	40,574
Parks and Recreation Administration	188,700	176,758	191,579	186,556
Building Maintenance	1,231,535	1,123,391	1,165,793	1,198,585
Parkland Acquisition	446,995	1,150,000	1,600,000	380,000
Park Planning	91,405	52,000	61,456	75,788
Park Development	622,887	273,000	1,467,125	1,629,321
TOTAL	$ 4,495,474	$ 4,786,855	$ 6,553,243	$ 5,861,449

CATEGORY	1980 ACTUAL	1981 BUDGET	1981 REVISED	1982 BUDGET
PERSONAL SERVICES	$ 1,594,970	$ 1,681,300	$ 1,741,955	$ 1,916,120
OPERATING & MAINTENANCE SUPPLIES	206,082	223,224	213,781	183,867
CHARGES & SERVICES	1,508,356	1,424,878	1,672,257	1,596,238
CAPITAL OUTLAY	1,186,066	1,457,453	2,925,250	2,165,224
TOTAL	$ 4,495,474	$ 4,786,855	$ 6,553,243	$ 5,861,449

FUNDS	1980 ACTUAL	1981 BUDGET	1981 REVISED	1982 BUDGET
GENERAL	$ 3,323,126	$ 3,286,530	$ 3,354,745	$ 3,392,108
GENERAL REVENUE SHARING	---	325,000	323,456	---
CONSERVATION TRUST	81,781	---	---	---
CAPITAL IMPROVEMENT FUND	102,194	---	890,125	1,745,709
LEASE/PURCHASE	---	---	45,312	314,009
GRANTS	541,378	25,325	339,605	29,623
JEFFCO OPEN SPACE	446,995	1,150,000	1,600,000	380,000
TOTAL	$ 4,495,474	$ 4,786,855	$ 6,553,243	$ 5,861,449

Figure D.1 Budget summary, parks and recreation, Lakewood, Colorado.

DEPARTMENT OF PARKS AND
RECREATION
City of _____
Program: Swimming Pool
Description: To operate the Mills Pool from May 20 to
September 4 for aquatic activities: open swimming,
swim lessons, swim team, lifesaving classes, and
expanded programs for the handicapped and
senior citizens.

Object of Expenditures	Current Budget	Proposed Budget
Personal services	$17,000	$18,500
Supplies	5,400	6,000
Other services and charges	7,000	7,500
Capital outlays	2,000	2,200
Total	$31,400	$34,200

Figure D.2 Program budget for a swimming pool.

LEISURE

HUMAN RESOURCES

PROGRAM	SPECIAL POPULATIONS

PROGRAM DESCRIPTION	To provide recreation and enrichment programs for the mentally and physically handicapped citizens of Lakewood.

PERFORMANCE OBJECTIVES

1. Provide programs for handicapped persons at a minimal cost.
2. Maintain 100% of the programs with at least 85% enrollment.

INDICATORS OF PERFORMANCE

MEASUREMENT	OBJECTIVE	1980 ACTUAL	1981 PROJECTED	1981 REVISED	1982 PROJECTED
DEMAND					
Estimated Registrations: Youth Programs	1	3,000	1,723	1,723	2,581
Adult Programs	1	4,300	2,520	2,520	4,100
Approximate Population of Handicapped in Lakewood	1	17,700	13,300	17,700	17,700
WORKLOAD					
Actual Registrations: Youth	1	2,695	1,723	1,800	2,581
Adult	1	5,900	2,520	2,600	4,100
Youth Classes and Activities Planned/Offered	1	66/76	33/33	44/42	40/40
Adult Classes and Activities Planned/Offered	1	67/63	25/25	38/34	35/35
PRODUCTIVITY					
Average Cost per Person Served	1	$ 5.54	$ 11.20	$ 11.96	$ 8.48
EFFECTIVENESS					
Donations	1	50	500	72	80
Total Revenue	1	$ 2,742	$ 2,402	$ 8,863	$ 13,414
Percent Actual Registration of Estimated Registration	1,2	117%	100%	100%	100%
Percent Classes/Activities with 85-95% Enrollment	2	26%	40%	43%	53%
Percent Classes/Activities with 100% Enrollment	2	74%	60%	57%	37%

ANALYSIS

Activity levels in this program are expected to increase significantly in 1982. This is partially due to an expansion of the summer day camp activities from ½ day to a full day. Also, the special population swimming activities can be expanded due to the addition of an indoor pool at Green Mountain. Funding will increase slightly in 1982.

RESOURCES

	1980 ACTUAL	1981 BUDGET	1981 REVISED	1982 BUDGET
CATEGORY: PERSONNEL	$ 45,262	$ 49,152	$ 49,967	$ 51,740
OPERATING/MAINTENANCE SUPPLIES	1,707	2,111	1,796	2,177
CHARGES & SERVICES	690	1,052	897	2,749
CAPITAL OUTLAY	---	---	---	---
TOTAL	$ 47,659	$ 52,315	$ 52,660	$ 56,666
FUNDS: GENERAL	$ 47,659	$ 52,315	$ 52,660	$ 56,666
TOTAL	$ 47,659	$ 52,315	$ 52,660	$ 56,666

Figure D.3 Program performance budget, Lakewood, Colorado.

PARK RESERVE DISTRICT 1981 | **Program** Outdoor Recreation Services

Sub-Program Picnicking (8030) | **Location** Coon Rapids Dam (18)

Description

The District operates and maintains three picnic areas at Coon Rapids Dam Regional Park. A picnic shelter on the Brooklyn Park side is available for group and family outings. 200 picnic sites, with grills, water facilities and horseshoe playing areas allow for maximum picnic user occassions. Newly established turf and shrubs and installation of an underground irrigation system assure maintenance of clean and attractive picnic areas.

1980 will see development of two upstream picnic sites for boaters and hikers and an additional picnic area near the river on the Brooklyn Park side. Small satellite picnic sites will be installed at various points along the Coon Rapids and Brooklyn Park trails.

Receptionists provide clerical and information services. Gate attendants provide parking fee collection, public relations, and distribution of information. Night-watchmen are on duty April through October for security.

Objectives

1. To provide picnicking opportunities that are safe, clean, enjoyable, and attractive to users.
   A. Maintain picnic area and facilities in compliance with District standards.
   B. To assure safe picnicking opportunities.
   C. To assure a high level of user satisfaction.

2. To serve 18,000 picnicker occasions.
   A. To conduct two special events for picnickers.

3. To increase user satisfaction.
   A. To develop trailside picnic sites.
   B. To install outdoor latrines on island.

4. To assure that the work program for picnicking is effective.

Summation

List of Activities	1979 Actual	1980 Budget	1981 Request
Leadership Support Services	N/A	3,780	$ 639
Maintenance	N/A	26,491	25,761
Public Entry	N/A	4,292	4,601
Guarding/Patrol	N/A	2,797	100
Rental/Sales Service	N/A	-	-
Totals	N/A	37,340	$ 31,101

Sub-Program Evaluation

Measurement

Use/Output

	Objective	1979 Est.	1979 Actual	1980 Est.	1981 Est.
Number of picnickers	2	30,000	11,857	30,000	18,000
Construction of new facilities/sites	2,3	1	3	1	0
Conduct special events	2,3	0	2	1	2

Effectiveness/Efficiency

	Objective	1979 Est.	1979 Actual	1980 Est.	1981 Est.
Percent of satisfied users	1,3	60	70	75	80
Number of accidents reported per 1000 users	1	1	.5	1	.5

Explanation

Actual picnicking user occasions in 1979 were substantially off the estimate made in 1978. This is due primarily to the on-going development of the picnic area on the Brooklyn Park side, the infancy of the park itself, and the natural error in making a prediction of this nature. Use in 1980 may also be limited in light of the extensive site work (irrigation system, plantings) in picnic areas.

User occasions and satisfaction in 1981 will be promoted dramatically through the landscaping project, installation of latrines on the island, and expansion of opportunities - developemnt of trailside picnic areas and special events.

Total sub-program cost is expected to increase only marginally in 1981.

Figure D.4 Program Budget Picnicking), Hennepin County Park Reserve District, Minnesota.

PR	01	SWIMMING POOL SEASON		2/3	B	4.4	36,500	5	
PROG.	FUND GROUP	DECISION PACKAGE NAME		LEVEL	B/S	POS.	NET COST	DEPARTMENT RANK	MGR. RATING

DIVISION	DIVISION RANK	ACTIVITY
Recreation	7/20	Sports and Aquatics

DESCRIPTION

The current swimming pool season is 13 weeks. This decision unit (2 of 3) would restore the pool season to 13 weeks from a reduced level of 12 weeks.

PROGRAM IMPACT BENEFITS OF FUNDING AND CONSEQUENCES OF NOT FUNDING

BENEFITS OF FUNDING: The pools would be open through Labor Day, September 4, rather than closing August 26 and permit 17,000 swimmers to participate.

CONSEQUENCES OF NOT FUNDING: The pools would be closed when very warm temperatures prevail when most students have not returned to school.

COST DATA

PERSONAL SERVICES	36,000
CONTRACTUAL SERVICES	2,800
COMMODITIES	1,200
CAPITAL OUTLAY	
GROSS COST	40,000
EXPENDITURE CREDITS	
REVENUE CREDITS	3,500
NET COST	36,500
RECURRING ANNUAL COST	36,500

POSITION DATA

FULL-TIME	PART-TIME (FTE)
4.0	0.4
HIRING DATE	

CITY OF PHOENIX, ARIZONA
MANAGEMENT AND BUDGET DEPARTMENT

ZERO BASE BUDGET DECISION PACKAGE
1982-83 FISCAL YEAR

44-2D REV 12-81

Figure D.5 Decision package (1 of 3) for swimming pool budget, City of Phoenix, Arizona.

DEPARTMENT OF PARKS AND RECREATION
Swimming Pool
(Mills)

		Current Budget	Proposed Budget
1.	Personnel services		
	11 Manager	$ 3,000	$ 3,600
	Guards	5,900	6,200
	Instructors	3,000	3,900
	Attendants	1,750	900
	Custodian	2,350	2,800
	12 Employee benefits	1,000	1,300
		$17,000	$18,500
2.	Supplies		
	21 Office supplies	25	50
	22 Operating supplies (chlorine and other chemicals)	2,500	2,600
	23 Repair and maintenance supplies	2,500	2,700
	24 Other supplies	375	650
		$ 5,400	$ 6,000
3.	Other Supplies and Charges		
	32 Communication and transportation	500	550
	33 Printing and advertising	250	350
	34 Insurance	1,000	1,000
	35 Utility services	3,200	3,300
	36 Repair and maintenance	2,050	2,300
		$ 7,000	$ 7,500
4.	Capital outlay		
	44 Machinery and equipment	2,000	2,200
		$31,400	$34,200

Figure D.6   Operating cost supplement, Mills Pool.

RESOURCE ALLOCATION REQUIREMENTS

		1980 ACTUAL	1981 BUDGET	1981 REVISED	1982 BUDGET
DEPARTMENT PARKS AND RECREATION					
PROGRAM SPECIAL POPULATIONS		$ 47,659	$ 52,315	$ 52,660	$ 56,666

PERSONNEL

POSITIONS	NO. OF POSITIONS				EXPENDITURES			
	1980 ACTUAL	1981 BUDGET	1981 REVISED	1982 BUDGET	1980 ACTUAL	1981 BUDGET	1981 REVISED	1982 BUDGET
Recreation Leader	.20	.20	.20	---	$ 2,508	$ 2,924	$ 3,092	$ ---
Instructors, Coaches & Aides(P)	11940hrs	13626hrs	12140hrs	13679hrs	40,180	44,318	45,526	51,298
RETIREMENT					1,526	288	315	---
INSURANCE					1,048	1,622	1,034	442
OVERTIME					---	---	---	---
TOTAL	.20	.20	.20	---	$ 45,262	$ 49,152	$ 49,967	$ 51,740

SUPPLIES

CODE	DESCRIPTION OF EXPENDITURE	1980 ACTUAL	1981 BUDGET	1981 REVISED	1982 BUDGET
220	Operating Supplies	$ 1,707	$ 2,111	$ 1,796	$ 2,177
	TOTAL	$ 1,707	$ 2,111	$ 1,796	$ 2,177

CHARGES & SERVICES

CODE	DESCRIPTION OF EXPENDITURE	1980 ACTUAL	1981 BUDGET	1981 REVISED	1982 BUDGET
310	Professional Services	$ 566	$ 338	$ 338	$ 1,449
330	Transportation	33	30	59	---
340	Advertising and Printing	---	250	100	---
370	Repair and Maintenance Service	16	---	---	---
380	Rentals	75	400	400	1,300
390	Other Charges and Services	---	34	---	---
	TOTAL	$ 690	$ 1,052	$ 897	$ 2,749

CAPITAL OUTLAY

CODE	DESCRIPTION OF EXPENDITURE	1980 ACTUAL	1981 BUDGET	1981 REVISED	1982 BUDGET
	TOTAL				

Figure D.7 Resource allocation requirement for budget, special populations, Lakewood, Colorado.

Budget by Line·Item

Sub·Program Picnicking (8030) **Location** Coon Rapids Dam (18)

		Activities					
		Leadership Support (176) Services	Maintenance (201)	Public Entry (486)	Gaurding/ Patrol (466)	Rental/ Sales (436) Services	
Code	**Description**						
Personal Services							
8002	Salaries & Wages - Reg.		8,636				
8095	Fringe Benefits		2,556				
8004	Salaries & Wages - Temp.		4,235	3,965			
8098	Vacancy Factor		(221)				
80							
80							
80							
80							
80	**Totals**	$	$ 15,204	$ 3,965	$	$	$
Commodities							
8108	Tools		50				
8110	General Supplies	300	500	100	100		
8132	Housekeeping & Cleaning		200				
8162	Aggregate Materials		100				
8168	Landscape Materials		500				
8170	Building & Equipment						
81							
81							
81							
81	**Totals**	$ 300	$ 1,350	$ 100	$ 100	$	$
Services							
8221	Janitorial & Waste		1,000				
8229	Maint. & Repairs - Equip		250				
8232	Maint. & Repairs - Other		50	20			
8239	Printing	89	6,207	266			
8250	Rental - Equipment	250	100	250			
8266	Communication		1,500				
8270	Electricity						
82							
82							
82							
82	**Totals**	$ 339	$ 9,107	$ 536	$	$	$
Other							
88							
88							
88				100			
88							
88	**Totals**	$ -	$ -	$ -	$ -	$	$
Capital							
8625	Grills		100		100		
86							
86							
86							
86	**Totals**	$ 100	$ 100	$	$	$	$
	Grand Totals	$ 639	$ 25,761	$ 4,601	$	$	$

Schedule of Positions

Class Title (Salary Range)	Hours Required					1981 Salary Req.
	1979 Actual	1980 Appr.	1980 Adj.	1981 Req.		$
Permanent						
Park Maintenance WII (8.12)	N/A	468	468	624		5,067
Park Maintenance WIII (8.58)	N/A	520	520	416		3,569
Sub-Totals	N/A	988	988	1,040		$ 8,636
Seasonal						$
Gate Attendant	N/A	832	832	832		3,187
Receptionist	N/A	208	208	208		778
Maintenance	N/A	832	832	832		4,235
Assistant Manager Operations	N/A	416	416	-		-
Sub-Totals	N/A	2,548	2,548	1,872		$ 8,200
Personnel Summary						
01·Officials,Administrators						
02·Professionals						
03 & 05·Tech.,Para·Prof.						
04·Protective Service						
06·Office,Clerical						
07 & 08·Skilled Craft,Maint.	N/A	.475	.475	.5		8,636
Totals	N/A	.475	.475	.5		8,636

Revenue Projections

Description	1979 Act	1980 Est	1981 Monthly Estimates												Est. 1981 Total
	$	$	Jan	Feb	Mar	Apr	May	Jun	Jul	Aug	Sep	Oct	Nov	Dec	$
Daily Passes	1669	4,950	-	-	-	120	555	770	770	400	370	90	-	-	3075
Totals	$1669	$4,950	-	-	-	120	555	770	770	400	370	90	-	-	$3075

Figure D.8 Supplementary detail (picnicking), Hennepin County Park Reserve District, Minnesota.

PARKS AND RECREATION

1982 **AUTHORIZED POSITION SUMMARY**

POSITION TITLE	1980 No.	ACTUAL SALARIES	1981 No.	BUDGET SALARIES	1981 No.	REVISED SALARIES	1982 No.	BUDGET SALARIES
Director of Parks and Recreation	1.00	$ 40,150	1.00	$ 40,150	1.00	$ 45,015	1.00	$ 45,000
Asst. Director Parks and Recreation	1.00	30,000	1.00	30,000	1.00	33,911	1.00	33,900
Parks Manager	1.00	33,689	1.00	28,000	1.00	28,000	1.00	26,500
Youth Services Manager	1.00	22,750	1.00	21,500	1.00	26,889	1.00	26,880
Forester	1.00	22,125	1.00	20,750	1.00	25,858	1.00	25,850
Assistant Parks Manager	1.00	21,578	1.00	21,400	1.00	---	---	---
Parks Supervisor	---	---	---	---	---	---	1.00	20,000
Contract Coordinator	---	---	---	---	1.00	12,681	1.00	17,500
Recreation Supervisor II	1.00	19,588	1.00	21,750	1.00	25,210	1.00	25,200
Planner III	1.00	---	1.00	24,785	1.00	22,925	1.00	23,125
Recreation Supervisor I	3.00	54,496	3.00	54,258	3.00	56,908	3.00	54,070
Executive Secretary	1.00	15,500	1.00	14,257	1.00	16,954	1.00	15,126
Maintenance Crew Leader	4.00	75,501	4.00	73,632	4.00	82,464	4.00	80,856
Custodial Crew Leader	1.00	14,943	1.00	14,208	1.00	15,927	1.00	15,392
Special Services Technician II	3.00	47,512	3.00	50,688	3.00	54,551	2.00	35,637
Planning Technician	1.00	15,611	1.00	15,168	---	5,187	---	---
Recreation Leader	4.00	51,961	4.00	58,474	4.00	57,087	5.00	74,464
Special Services Technician I	1.00	13,728	1.00	13,860	1.00	15,076	2.00	29,536
Secretary	2.00	21,619	2.00	22,714	2.00	24,443	2.00	23,038
Clerk III	1.00	9,552	1.00	9,829	1.00	9,829	1.00	10,953
Clerk II	2.00	17,747	2.00	17,444	2.00	20,988	2.00	19,788
Skilled Crafts Specialist	4.00	65,765	3.00	52,258	4.00	79,778	4.00	76,549
Maintenance Specialist II	7.00	100,957	7.00	101,813	6.00	94,246	7.00	111,848
Maintenance Specialist I	7.00	64,335	7.00	91,314	6.00	62,346	5.00	71,938
Maintenance Worker II	3.00	54,981	3.00	34,624	5.00	39,877	5.00	63,719
Maintenance Worker I	10.00	104,701	8.00	82,945	8.00	94,267	8.00	92,352
Planner I	---	20,570	---	---	1.00	10,275	1.00	16,750
Clerk III(P)	---	7,540	---	13,205	---	1,129	---	1,129
Clerk II(P)	---	2,896	---	3,380	---	3,900	---	4,200
Laborer(P) (I,II,III,IV,V)	---	156,876	---	153,907	---	199,543	---	214,467
Bus Driver(P)	---	23,356	---	23,564	---	25,474	---	24,576
Instructors, Coaches and Aides(P)	---	287,400	---	363,241	---	351,058	---	441,875
SUBTOTAL	62.00	1,417,427	59.00	1,473,118	61.00	1,541,796	62.00	1,722,218
RETIREMENT	---	101,503	---	90,228	---	97,990	---	101,870
INSURANCE	---	68,239	---	101,854	---	86,459	---	78,932
OVERTIME	---	7,801	---	16,100	---	15,710	---	13,100
TOTAL	62.00	$1,594,970	59.00	$1,681,300	61.00	$1,741,955	62.00	$1,916,120

Figure D.9 Personnel summary, Department of Parks and Recreation, Lakewood, Colorado.

PARKS AND RECREATION

1982 OPERATING & MAINTENANCE SUPPLIES

ITEM		1980 ACTUAL	1981 BUDGET	1981 REVISED	1982 BUDGET
211	Publications	$ 1,177	$ 2,464	$ 2,302	$ 1,422
212	Office Supplies	6,555	8,225	7,176	7,425
213	Mapping and Drafting	142	490	490	---
221	Agricultural	37,419	39,160	39,160	29,710
222	Chemical and Labratory	3,310	2,845	2,845	2,845
223	Medical and Pharmacy	184	470	284	440
224	Cleaning	24,641	22,600	22,600	22,600
226	Fuel, Oil, Lubricants	10	229	229	154
227	Photo Supplies	859	821	785	725
228	Recreational	28,636	33,156	30,457	42,755
229	Wearing Apparel	3,397	5,051	1,474	500
231	Building Materials	59,176	63,111	58,611	38,825
232	Minor Equipment	28,480	23,931	23,939	22,021
233	Motor Vehicle Repair	---	---	119	---
234	Plumbing and Electricity	4,693	6,000	8,713	6,000
236	Structural Steel	4,719	5,500	5,385	3,500
239	Miscellaneous Repair/Maintenance	2,684	9,171	9,212	4,945
TOTAL		$ 206,082	$ 223,224	$ 213,781	$ 183,867

Figure D.10   Object summary, adapted from 1982 parks and recreation budget, Lakewood, Colorado.

PARKS AND RECREATION

1982 CHARGES & SERVICES

ITEM		1980 ACTUAL	1981 BUDGET	1981 REVISED	1982 BUDGET
311	Cleaning	$ 5	$ ---	$ ---	$ ---
313	Consulting	1,228	1,080	2,030	1,440
317	Photo Processing	1,450	2,005	1,735	1,100
318	General Legal	4,146	2,720	7,750	2,000
319	Other Professional	216,943	160,124	367,119	205,347
321	Telephone/Telegraph	25,748	27,450	27,496	30,195
322	Postage	33	---	---	---
325	Alarm Systems	11,587	11,664	11,664	11,664
331	Travel Expense	4,824	4,288	3,882	5,300
332	Training Expense	2,112	2,928	3,413	4,030
333	Motor Pool Charges	230,804	221,152	257,038	258,325
336	Towing Fees	200	---	---	---
338	Personal Auto Expense	8,425	9,967	10,298	8,885
341	Advertising	1,803	3,282	1,934	2,200
342	Printing	35,980	46,650	43,362	26,650
346	Graphics	847	---	---	---
361	Gas	42,596	53,491	56,957	60,943
362	Electricity	182,782	218,385	218,385	251,142
364	Water	88,603	119,685	119,685	135,489
365	Sanitation	22,251	20,950	20,950	20,950
373	Office Equipment Repair	141	1,170	1,011	870
374	Plant Equipment Repair	189	1,200	1,447	500
375	Mobile Radio Repair	11,641	10,368	10,368	---
382	Buildings	583,598	483,250	483,190	550,138
383	Machinery and Equipment	12,409	14,564	14,173	11,590
384	Vehicular Equipment	3,034	3,150	3,301	3,550
393	Transfer to Other Funds	8,493	---	---	---
396	Membership Expenses	1,965	3,054	2,800	3,130
398	Meal Expense	194	300	300	300
399	Miscellaneous Expenses	4,325	2,001	1,969	500
TOTAL		$ 1,508,356	$ 1,424,878	$ 1,672,257	$ 1,596,238

Figure D.10 (continued)

PARKS AND RECREATION
1982 CAPITAL OUTLAY

ITEM		1980 ACTUAL	1981 BUDGET	1981 REVISED	1982 BUDGET
421	Buildings/Fixed Equipment	$ 16,787	$ 66,800	$ 59,991	$ ---
439	Other Improvements	552	---	---	---
441	Office Furniture and Equipment	2,745	1,080	1,058	---
442	Motor Vehicles	5,358	---	---	---
443	Radio and Communications Equipment	1,862	---	---	---
444	Plant Equipment	22,306	9,664	6,070	---
445	Recreation Equipment	7,415	3,170	22,571	17,986
446	Engineer and Construction Equipment	6,987	---	---	---
447	Shop Equipment	2,016	2,221	2,229	945
449	Other Equipment	52,717	24,518	5,968	5,268
451	Consulting Services	388	200,000	---	4,976
452	Supplies	---	---	---	7,759
453	Other Charges	---	---	---	39,030
461	Professional Services	31,238	---	---	---
463	Other Charges	---	---	300,000	300,000
464	Land	447,995	1,150,000	1,600,000	380,000
471	Construction	487,759	---	706,200	1,232,600
472	Supplies	15,670	---	17,584	---
473	Other Charges	---	---	5,267	---
475	Agricultural	12,919	---	---	---
481	Other Overhead	71,352	---	198,312	176,660
TOTAL		$ 1,186,066	$ 1,457,453	$ 2,925,250	$ 2,165,224

Figure D.10 (continued)

Appendix E

Chart of Cost Accounts for Park and Recreation Agency

CHART OF COST ACCOUNTS
for
Park and Recreation Agency

Specific Example—Swimming Pools

50—Parks and Recreation
  51—Division of Parks   (General function)
    .20—Swimming Pools
        201—Bryan Park Pool   (Specific function)
        202—North West
        203—Mills Pool
        204—South Pool
        205—Olcott Pool
            01—Open swimming
            02—Swimming lessons
            03—Life-saving lessons   (Activity)
            04—Swim team
            05—Water carnival
            06—Handicapped program
            07—Water polo
            08—Group use—rental
                401—Adminstration
                402—Coaching—swim team   (Work)
                403—Instruction—swimming lessons
                404—Instruction—life-saving lessons
                405—Instruction—handicapped program
                406—Coaching—water polo
                407—Supervision—open swimming
                408—Maintenance—building—locker rooms
                409—Maintenance—pool
                410—Maintenance—parking lot
                411—Maintenance—grounds
                   1 Personal Services
                     11—Salaries and wages
                     12—Employee benefits
                     13—Other personal services

(continued)

CHART OF COST ACCOUNTS (continued)

2 Supplies
  21—Office supplies
  22—Operating supplies
  23—Repair and maintenance supplies
  24—Other supplies
3 Other Services and Charges
  31—Professional services
  32—Communication and transportation
  33—Printing and advertising
  34—Insurance
  35—Utility services   (Object)
  36—Repairs and maintenance
  37—Rentals
  38—Debt service
  39—Other services and charges
4 Capital Outlays
  41—Land
  42—Buildings
  43—Improvements other than buildings
  44—Machinery and equipment
  45—Other capital outlays

Figure E.1   Chart of cost accounts for swimming pools.

Appendix F

Financial Reports

PARKS AND RECREATION
Enterprise, U.S.A.
Financial Report Summary
Actual and Budgeted Expenditures and Encumbrances
For Month Ending June 30, 19xx and Year Ending Dec. 31, 19xx

Function and Object	Appro-priation	This Month			Total to Date				Encum-brances	Un-encum-bered Balance
		Estimated	Actual	Under or (Over)	Estimated	Actual	Under or (Over)	Unex-pended Balance		
Parks and Recreation Administration	$85,000	$7,000	$7,150	$(150)	$41,000	$40,700	$300	$44,300	$400	$43,900
Division of Parks										
Administration	40,000	3,200	3,100	100	19,000	17,500	1,500	22,500	1,000	21,500
Parks	115,000	10,000	10,500	(500)	34,000	32,700	1,300	82,300	1,7	80,600
Beaches	12,000	3,500	3,275	225	4,000	3,925	75	8,075	56	8,019
Botanical garden	22,000	1,000	1,125	(125)	9,750	9,860	(110)	12,140	625	11,515
Golf courses	42,000	6,250	6,010	240	18,500	17,100	1,400	24,900	600	24,300
Nursery	16,000	1,500	1,650	(150)	7,500	7,600	(100)	8,400	200	8,200
Marinas	7,500	1,200	1,150	50	3,000	2,500	500	5,000	600	4,400
Outdoor skating rink	4,600	0	0	—	1,600	1,700	(100)	2,900	—	2,900
Parkways	15,200	1,500	1,425	75	8,400	8,000	400	7,200	—	7,200
Swimming pools	34,000	8,400	8,100	300	10,000	8,750	1,250	25,250	1,400	23,850
Division of Recreation										
Administration	42,000	3,600	3,350	250	22,000	21,500	500	20,500	—	20,500
Athletics	24,500	4,575	4,600	(25)	11,000	10,300	700	14,200	800	13,400
Aquatics	2,500	800	700	100	1,000	800	200	1,700	—	1,700
Community centers	35,000	2,500	2,800	(300)	18,000	16,500	1,500	18,500	1,280	17,220
Community events	5,000	0	0	0	1,600	1,400	200	3,600	—	3,600
Fine arts	6,500	600	650	(50)	3,000	3,160	(160)	3,340	—	3,340
Outdoor recreation	5,000	750	700	50	2,250	2,100	150	2,900	—	2,900
Senior citizens	22,000	1,170	1,400	(230)	10,000	9,600	400	12,400	600	11,800
Handicapped	26,000	2,000	1,800	200	12,000	11,400	600	14,600	250	14,350
Supervisory playground	25,000	3,500	3,600	(100)	3,500	3,600	(100)	21,400	600	20,800
Total	$586,800	$63,045	$63,085	$(40)	$241,100	$230,695	$10,405	$356,105	$10,111	$345,994
Personnel services	410,760	44,000	44,500	(500)	168,770	169,700	(930)	241,060	0	241,060
Supplies	75,000	6,545	6,285	260	25,000	23,600	1,400	51,400	1,611	49,789
Other supplies and charges	86,040	9,500	9,300	200	41,330	31,395	9,935	54,645	8,500	46,145
Capital outlays	15,000	3,000	3,000	0	6,000	6,000	0	9,000	0	9,000
Total	$586,800	$63,045	$63,085	$(40)	$241,100	$230,695	$10,405	$356,105	$10,111	$345,994

Figure F.1 Summary monthly financial report of actual and budget expenditures and encumbrances.

PARKS AND RECREATION
Enterprise, U.S.A.
Financial Report Summary
Actual and Estimated Receipts
For Month Ending June 30, 19xx and Year Ending December 31, 19xx

Source	Total Estimated Year	This Month			Total to Date			Balance to be Collected
		Estimated	Actual	Over or (Under)	Estimated	Actual	Over or (Under)	
Parks								
Beaches	$6,000	$2,500	$2,000	$(500)	$3,000	$2,800	$(200)	$3,200
Botanical gardens	2,500	300	250	(50)	1,200	1,100	(100)	1,400
Golf courses	45,000	5,000	5,300	300	20,000	21,000	1,000	24,000
Marinas	14,000	3,000	2,800	(200)	5,000	5,200	200	8,800
Swimming pools	31,000	8,550	8,555	5	16,550	16,670	120	14,330
Total	98,500	19,350	18,905	(445)	45,750	46,770	1,020	51,730
Recreation								
Athletics	16,000	2,000	2,150	150	6,000	6,100	100	9,900
Community centers	24,000	500	475	(25)	10,000	9,750	(250)	14,250
Fine arts	2,000	300	325	25	900	950	50	1,050
Outdoor recreation	8,500	2,200	2,100	(100)	3,400	3,200	(200)	5,300
Senior citizens	30,000	2,500	2,700	200	14,500	15,100	600	14,900
Handicapped	6,500	1,000	1,050	50	3,000	3,125	125	3,375
Supervised playground	12,000	2,500	2,250	(250)	2,500	2,250	(250)	9,750
Total	$99,000	$11,000	$11,050	$50	$40,300	$40,475	$175	$58,525

Figure F.2   Summary monthly financial report of actual and estimated receipts.

THE MARYLAND-NATIONAL CAPITAL PARK AND PLANNING COMMISSION

Combining Balance Sheet
All Enterprise Funds
June 30, 1980

Montgomery County

ASSETS	Ice Rinks	Golf Courses	Regional Park Facilities	Tennis Bubble	Brookside Plant Shop	Totals June 30, 1980	Totals June 30, 1979 (Note B)
Current Assets:							
Equity in Pooled Cash and Investments	$ (63,741)	$ (177,834)	$ (72,720)	$ 163,089	$14,390	$ (136,816)	$ 3,160
Other Cash	---	1,550	1,500	200	---	3,250	3,100
Accounts Receivable	---	2,387	---	---	---	2,387	3,503
Inventories, at Cost	6,872	81,047	11,877	1,257	---	101,053	99,918
Total Current Assets	(56,869)	(92,850)	(59,343)	164,546	14,390	(30,126)	109,681
Fixed Assets, at Cost:							
Land	13,400	630,000	---	---	---	643,400	643,400
Buildings	548,456	185,502	633,303	1,002	---	1,368,263	1,362,252
Improvements Other Than Buildings	178,320	10,565	6,517	255,201	6,712	457,315	351,252
Machinery and Equipment	94,622	348,861	310,383	18,512	---	772,378	695,152
	834,798	1,174,928	950,203	274,715	6,712	3,241,356	3,052,056
Less-Accumulated Depreciation	(423,799)	(332,117)	(279,432)	(119,109)	---	(1,154,457)	(1,006,474)
Net Fixed Assets	410,999	842,811	670,771	155,606	6,712	2,086,899	2,045,582
Total Assets	$ 354,130	$ 749,961	$ 611,428	$ 320,152	$21,102	$ 2,056,773	$ 2,155,263
LIABILITIES AND FUND EQUITY							
Current Liabilities:							
Current Portion of Notes Payable	$ ---	$ ---	$ 1,333	$ 29,027	$ ---	$ 30,360	$ ---
Accounts Payable	1,838	9,888	11,680	1,512	---	24,918	24,690
Accrued Salaries and Benefits	1,922	24,274	12,628	1,276	---	40,100	36,734
Other Accrued Liabilities	---	417	1,126	---	---	1,543	1,547
Revenue Collected in Advance	6,045	---	---	40,031	---	46,076	43,507
Total Current Liabilities	9,805	34,579	26,767	71,846	---	142,997	106,478
Notes Payable - Net of Current Portion	---	---	5,695	58,331	---	64,026	---
Total Liabilities	9,805	34,579	32,462	130,177	---	207,023	106,478
Fund Equity:							
Contributed Capital	583,775	838,601	592,821	129,831	---	2,145,028	2,144,318
Retained Earnings (Deficit)	(239,450)	(123,219)	(13,855)	60,144	21,102	(295,278)	(95,533)
Total Fund Equity	344,325	715,382	578,966	189,975	21,102	1,849,750	2,048,785
Total Liabilities and Fund Equity	$ 354,130	$ 749,961	$ 611,428	$ 320,152	$21,102	$ 2,056,773	$ 2,155,263

Figure F.3 Balance sheet, Enterprise Fund, Maryland National Capital Park and Planning Commision.

PARKS AND RECREATION
Enterprise, U.S.A.

Financial Report
(Summary)

Actual and Budgeted Expenditures and Encumbrances
For Fiscal Year, January 1, 19xx to December 31, 19xx

Function	Appropriation	Actual	Balance	Encumbrances	Unencumbered Balance
Parks and Recreation					
Administration	$85,000	$84,870	$130	—	$130
Division of Parks					
Administration	40,000	39,600	400	—	400
Parks	115,000	114,500	500	750	(250)
Beaches	12,000	11,950	50	—	50

PARKS AND RECREATION
Enterprise, U.S.A.

Financial Report
(Summary)

Actual and Estimated Receipts
For Fiscal Year, January 1, 19xx to December 31, 19xx

Function	Estimated	Actual	Over or (Under)
Parks			
Beaches	$6,000	$5,800	$(200)
Botanic gardens	2,500	2,400	(100)
Golf courses	45,000	46,500	1500
Marinas	14,000	14,650	650

Figure F.4 Summary annual financial reports of expenditures and receipts.

Index

Index